Tourisı

Tourism and Travel in Ireland

CERT

The State Tourism Training Agency

Gill & Macmillan

Published by
Gill & Macmillan Ltd
Goldenbridge
Dublin 8
with associated companies throughout the world
© CERT — The State Tourism Training Agency 1993
0 7171 2065 1
Print origination by
Seton Music Graphics Ltd, Bantry, Co. Cork
Printed by ColourBooks Ltd, Dublin

A catalogue record is available for this book
from the British Library.

Contents

Foreword

Tourism is one of the world's fastest growing industries. In Ireland it ranks as one of the country's most important sources of employment and revenue at present contributing up to 9% of GNP and with over 133,000 employees in permanent employment.

Tourism is a major influence on both our economy and national development, and there has been a corresponding upsurge and interest in tourism training provision. Tourism's popularity as a career choice is increasing; CERT and VECs in particular have responded by developing new post-Leaving Certificate courses. The lack of an Irish-produced textbook aimed at this level of student has prompted Gill & Macmillan to join forces with CERT to publish a textbook that examines the structure of the Irish tourism and travel industry and its key aspects.

This book will be relevant to students taking PLC and VPT-2 courses in tourism and those following the Tourism Awareness Programme which is co-ordinated by CERT. It will also be relevant to those following CERT programmes in Regional Technical Colleges such as Tourism Skills, Advanced Tourism Operations and the day-release course in Tourism and Customer Skills. The book will also be of interest to those studying tourism as part of hotel management, leisure and marketing programmes at third level.

The global concepts of tourism, its definition and historical development are treated in Chapter 1. The structure of tourism in Ireland is examined in Chapter 2 with reference to government departments and agencies along with private sector and voluntary organisations. The main Irish tourism products — Transport, Accommodation and Catering and Tourist Attractions are covered in Chapters 3, 4 and 5. Throughout the text Irish examples (including Northern Ireland) are cited and current statistics given.

Changing trends in tourism worldwide, such as awareness of the dangers of over-exposure to the sun and 'green' consciousness have led to the development of new tourism products in Ireland. These are examined in terms of environmental, heritage and leisure tourism in Chapters 6, 7 and 8. Tourism in relation to the economy and employment in Ireland is dealt with in Chapters 9 and 10. Information in Chapter 10 on training opportunities, education courses, and career paths in tourism should be particularly useful for young people contemplating careers in the industry. The nature of the Irish travel trade with an examination of the roles of the travel agent, tour operator and ground handling agent are explored in Chapters 11 and 12. The final chapter analyses the strategies involved in marketing tourism.

Learning objectives are identified at the beginning of each chapter with student questions and assignments given at the end. A number of case studies based on Irish tourism businesses and products have been developed to highlight certain concepts and to stimulate student analysis and discussion. A glossary of tourism-related terms and abbreviations is also included.

Every effort has been made to ensure accuracy prior to publication. However, tourism policy, structures and products are constantly changing and evolving. The Shannon stopover, the siting of interpretative centres and the role of Regional Tourism Organisations were some of the controversial issues of 1992. This ever-changing nature of tourism means that new policies and products can be quickly overtaken by even newer ones. This, while somewhat of a headache for publishers and editors, means that the study of tourism never becomes dull and static.

Linda McLoughlin
July 1993

Acknowledgments

CERT would like to thank the many people involved in the preparation of this book — its advisory and administrative staff, tourism teachers and industry consultants.

In particular CERT would like to acknowledge the role of David Pyle and Linda McLoughlin in researching, compiling and editing material. David Pyle is a Publishing Consultant with experience in tourism and management. Linda McLoughlin is a Curriculum Development Adviser responsible for the development, publication and marketing of CERT training manuals and textbooks.

Special thanks are due also for the valuable assistance and contributions made by the following teachers and consultants:

Joe Brunton
Michael Comyn
Lorraine Delaney
Sally Friel
Jachanthia Santry
Neil Steedman.

The publishers thank the following for the use of illustrations/photos: Bord Fáilte, pages 4, 27, 29, 32, 47, 65, 66, 67, 71, 82, 87, 93, 97, 99, 112, 115, 119, 126, 183; Shannon Development, 29; Ireland West Tourism, 30; Northern Ireland Tourist Board, 32, 34, 89; The National Trust, Northern Ireland, 36; Aer Rianta, 45; Aer Lingus, front cover, 177, 178, 219; CERT, front cover, 155, 158, 159, 160, 161, 165, 166, 169, 221; Bus Éireann, 50; Connacht Regional Airport, 56; Doyle Hotel Group, 62; Jurys Hotel Group, 63; Great Southern Hotels, 63; Town & Country Homes Association, 64; Irish Youth Hostel Association/An Óige, 64; Irish Cottage Holiday Homes, 65; Kildare Hotel and Country Club, 75; Aillwee Cave, Co. Clare, 81; Marble Arch Caves, Co. Fermanagh, 82; Office of Public Works, 30, 83, 111, 117; Newry & Mourne District Council Tourist Office, Newry, 85; Ulster History Park, Omagh, 85; Celtworld, 86; Terry Willers, 88; Irish Country Homes, 100, 101; Peatland World, Lullymore, 102; Ballyhoura Fáilte Society Ltd, 105; Lismore Heritage Town, Co. Waterford, 111; Geraldine Tralee, 114; Mayo 5000, 116; Shannon Heritage Ltd, 116; Carlingford Lough Heritage Trust, 121, 122; Rent A Bike, 129; Irish National Stud, 130; Mount Juliet Ltd, 133; Brittany Ferries, 181; Stena Sealink, 181; Irish Ferries, 182; Joe Walsh Tours, 195; Abbey Sun, 195; Ireland of the Welcomes, 219, and much useful reference materials.

1 Concept and Development of Tourism

Objectives

At the end of this chapter, the reader will be able to:

- define tourism, and be able to tell the difference between a visitor, a tourist and an excursionist

- discuss various ways in which the tourism business differs from many other businesses

- list and briefly discuss travel motivators

- discuss the social, cultural and environmental impact of mass tourism

- outline the history and growth of tourism generally

- identify milestones in the development of Irish tourism.

Tourism is a great modern industry that is not only becoming a top currency earner in the developed world, and promising incalculable wealth for the less advanced countries, but is also the driving force behind the development or improvement of the infrastructures of many countries, to the direct and indirect advantage of the inhabitants.

Yet tourism has acquired as many definitions as there are misconceptions. The World Tourism Organisation (WTO) and other interested bodies are working with great urgency to co-ordinate the diverse interests and define more clearly the various ingredients of the industry. This is necessary because not only does tourism need a new image in the long term, but it must be carefully and clearly defined so that the complex combination of people and services that underpins the tourism infrastructure of a country can be employed to the greatest effect.

The word *tourist* is wearing badly. It has unfortunately become associated in the public consciousness with mass travel, with coach loads of people being hustled from city to city and packed at night into inhospitable accommodation, where everything is paid for by voucher and where a departure from a set menu almost seems an international incident. This misconception persists among sections of the industry itself, leading to inferior standards of value and service.

Even the dictionary defines tourist class as 'a class of accommodation for steamship passengers, lower than cabin class'. This can now be extended to cover air travel and could well appear as 'a class of accommodation for airline passengers, lower than business class'.

It is, perhaps, the fault of the tourism industry itself that its importance is not universally understood. If one were to stop an average person in the street and ask for a list of the leading industries of the world, chances are that manufacturing, agriculture and computer technology would be suggested. It is unlikely that tourism would receive a mention.

Most people outside the industry are not aware of tourism's size and complexity nor of the vast amounts of money it generates. Despite its dramatic impact on the world economy, tourism is still a very diverse and fragmented industry, incorporating as it does travel agencies, transport, accommodation and food, shopping, visitor attractions, leisure facilities, entertainment and many other ingredients.

Tourism is a complex subject with a long history and immense potential. In that long history, it has been closely associated with the development of transport. It is increasingly being seen as a serious topic and some anthropologists are debating whether it should be studied as a theoretical subject on its own or incorporated as an element of some broader field such as the study of play, the process of acculturation or the transformation of the pre-industrial world. Academics have found new definitions for tourism such as 'the commercialisation of leisure', and 'commercialised hospitality.'

Tourism grew out of the natural desire of mankind to travel. At first this arose out of necessity: in the distant past before people settled down to cultivate land and domesticate animals, they were forced to range far and wide in search of food. Things were always better over the next hill; that instinct persists to the present day.

In ancient Greece, people travelled to see and participate in the Olympic Games. In Roman times the concept of travel or tourism was well developed among the nobility. But it was not until the coming of the railways in the early 19th century that it began to develop the popularity that we understand. Even then, it was the prerogative of the leisured classes — working people had neither the money nor the time to travel except to make day trips to seaside resorts.

At the beginning of this century a typical worker worked six days, at least 70 hours, a week. The weekend was not known as a period of free time and the first bank holidays were given to allow recuperation so that people could work all the better afterwards. Even up to 50 years ago many employers did not pay workers during their holiday period, which was often only one week. With little leisure and no holiday pay, they might manage a day trip to the seaside; otherwise they simply stayed at home. The reduction in the working week and growing affluence brought a gradual change; the concept of mass travel was about to surface. Developments in transport made it possible: in turn railways, steam ships, cars, aeroplanes and finally wide-bodied jet aircraft made cheaper transport more available, changing the pattern of travel and encouraging wider and stronger links between distant communities. Faster travel has facilitated the growth of long haul holidays to meet public demand for new travel and tourism experiences.

In the years following World War II, tourism developed worldwide. Figures from the WTO show that in 1950 there were 25 million international tourist arrivals (people from one country arriving in another). Twenty years later, by 1970, this number had grown more than seven times to 183 million, an increase of 158 million. This represents a growth rate of 10% compound a year. The rate of growth slowed in the early 1970s to 5% a year, still a healthy annual increase.

Tourism Defined

There are three fundamentals in the definition of tourism:

- movement from place of residence

- a particular length of stay

- a particular purpose.

Tourism is just one form of recreation along with sports activities, hobbies and pastimes which take up leisure-allocated time. It normally involves expenditure and a stay of at least 24 hours in a destination.

Travel is the common thread to most kinds of tourism. Travel is also linked to the discretionary time available to potential tourists: most of those who travel have blocks of free time during their annual holidays or at weekends and it is during these times that travel and tourism peaks. In general, younger and older people have most discretionary time and money. People between these two groups have less disposable income: they are paying off mortgages and raising families.

Generally the word tourist derives from the word tour, meaning a circular trip that starts at a specific place and eventually returns there, following a particular itinerary. A tourist is, however, more than a person on holiday to visit a distant place, see the sights, visit friends and relatives or do little other than relax, possibly participating in leisure and recreational activities. Besides those on holiday there are business people, conference delegates, and other travellers.

There are various definitions of a tourist; governments, tourism industry associations and other interested parties may use their own definitions to suit the data they require and the uses to which they put that data.

For international purposes, one of the most commonly used definitions of a tourist was developed by the 1963 United Nations Conference on Travel and Tourism held in Rome. It was then adopted in 1968 by the International Union of Official Travel Organisations (later to become the World Tourism Organisation).

Visitors

A visitor is defined as any person travelling to a country, other than that in which he or she normally resides, for any reason other than following an occupation remunerated from within the country visited. This definition was created for international travellers but can be adapted for tourists travelling within their own country (domestic tourists) by substituting the word region or area for country. Visitors can be further defined as tourists or excursionists.

Tourists

A tourist is any visitor staying more than 24 hours in a country and making an overnight stay for any of the following reasons:

- VFR — visiting friends and relatives

- Business

- Leisure, recreation, sport

- Culture, historic interest

- Study, conference, religion, health.

In other words, virtually anyone visiting a country or an area for more than a day and making an overnight stay is a tourist. However, a person who travels to another country or area to take up paid work would not fit into this definition of a tourist.

Excursionists

Visitors who stay for less than 24 hours are defined by the United Nations as excursionists or day visitors. The main difference between excursionists and tourists is the overnight stay. Travellers visiting a country on a cruise ship or the crew of an aircraft visiting a country fall into this excursionist category.

Tourist Destinations

A tourist destination is an area with natural attributes, features or attractions that appeals to non-local visitors, excursionists and tourists.

There are many factors affecting the choice of a tourist destination. That choice may be related to a series of factors referred to as motivators: the circumstances and influences that motivate the tourist to visit a tourist destination.

The Tourism Product

Among the factors that distinguish the tourism industry from other industries are :

1. **Intangibility**: in a manufacturing industry, the product is packaged and shipped through wholesalers to retailers to be bought by the consumer at local level. With tourism, the consumer or tourist has to be brought to the product before it can be consumed. It is a product that is sold sight unseen.

2. **Perishability**: the tourism product, such as rooms, seats and tickets to attractions, cannot be stored. An hotel must try to fill all rooms each night; to fail to do so means that there is lost revenue that cannot be made up at a later date.

3. **Complexity**: the tourism product is made up of a series of products, including services, travel, accommodation, and restaurants. Successful sale of these combined products requires a high level of co-operation between the suppliers and an interdependence in their marketing.

4. **Interdependence**: the product is often located a long way from the consumer. This requires an infrastructure of transport, travel agents and tour wholesalers.

5. **Finite supply**: it is difficult to increase the supply of a tourism product if there is a sudden increase in popularity. The supply is fixed: hotels take time to adapt and add new rooms; airlines need time to add aircraft to their fleets.

Travel Motivators

Today, marketing is used in a more sophisticated way than it was 20 years ago as can be seen in the application of the study of consumer behaviour to tourism. The industry now understands the need to determine visitor needs and wants, the use of market segmentation, and the specialised application of marketing communications techniques.

Economic and Social Class: tourists from different economic and social classes will have different motivations when choosing tourist destinations. One group may be driven by the desire to improve their knowledge, broaden their minds or impress their friends. Another group may be more influenced by opportunities to get food and drink at low prices, to achieve impressive suntans or to explore the night life.

Social class, or socio-economic grouping, is based on occupation, where a person lives, and income and wealth; it is a tool developed to rank consumers. The higher the class, the higher the prestige. Various generalisations are made when using socio-economic grouping to identify tourism consumers. Upper-class consumers typically do not engage in conspicuous consumption: they are conservative in their purchasing and tastes, and they represent a market for high value, unique products. Lower-upper class engage in conspicuous consumption: they are motivated by status and ego satisfaction in their purchasing. Upper-middle class are quality-conscious, generally attempting to imitate the upper-class group but also willing to experiment with new products or ideas. Lower-middle class consumers focus on value: they are traditional in choice of destination and services used whilst on holiday. Lower-class consumers use credit extensively and buy on impulse. These considerations can be matched to the buying behaviour of the tourist in the market place.

Demographic characteristics: include age, gender, income, race, occupation, family structure and social class. For instance, a holiday destination which is targeting upper-income 18–30-year-olds is segmenting the market by demographic characteristics (in this case age and income).

Nationality and Culture: there exists amongst some travellers a desire to trace their ethnic roots. This has been a motivating factor for many years in the attraction of visitors to Ireland from the United States of America. The definition of tourists by nationality is still the main method employed in the collection of data for use by the tourism industry. Another social influence on the behaviour of the tourism consumer is culture. Culture comprises symbols, knowledge, attitudes and beliefs held by a group of people that are passed from one generation to the next. These cultural traits can lead to a series of expectations in relation to the visited country and its people. The cultural expectations of the tourist may require that the tourism product be amended or indeed deliberately left unchanged to satisfy visitor expectations.

Sport: sport and sport-related activities are the basis for many activity-based holidays. Spectators are willing to travel long distances in support of their favourite teams or sports stars. The advent of mass transport and charter travel has opened this field as a key area for tourism development.

Shopping: differences between countries in taxes and prices and association with quality and specialisation in products such as cut glass, linen and speciality foods has seen the development of the shopping excursionist or tourist.

Health: health spas were among the early reasons for tourism in Europe. While spas have been overtaken as primary destinations, health is still a motivator for activity-based holidays, seaside-based holidays and, though perhaps no longer considered healthy, sun-based holidays.

Visiting Friends and Relatives: one of the travel motivators most important to Ireland is that of visiting friends and relatives (VFR). Here the route travelled and the mode of transport used is of more concern than the services provided at the destination.

Whatever the motivation of the tourist, one must be aware of the elements of each purchase decision. *Consumer behaviour* is the way people act, or react, to the situations and influences involved in their buying decisions, for example, in the choice of tourist destinations. The study of consumer behaviour shows that the visitor chooses a destination or tourism product as a result of a perception that the service or product will satisfy a felt need. That need can be real or imaginary. Customer satisfaction is achieved when that customer's expectation is met or exceeded by the product or service.

Ireland's Tourism Markets

Ireland's main source markets are Britain, North America, Germany and France. The main motive for visiting Ireland is holidaymaking; however the VFR and business visitor segments are key contributors to overall tourism demand.

North America is Ireland's most important source in terms of the revenue. According to Martin Dully, former Executive Chairman of Bord Fáilte (*The Irish Times*, 10 August, 1990), it takes about IR£20,000 of tourism spending to create one job in Ireland. That equates to about 48 North American, 68 Continental, or 118 British visitors producing one job.

British tourists come to Ireland, in the main, to visit friends and relatives, and for holidaymaking.

Twenty-five per cent of all visitors from the United States are on a package holiday. They tend to be an older and more up-market group. They are generally attracted to Ireland because of emotional or ancestral ties, the welcoming people, the tranquil scenery and the relatively unspoilt countryside.

Most German and French tourists travel independently and tend to be an up-market group. In general, they are holidaymakers attracted to Ireland because of the scenery, the pace of life and special interests such as fishing and golf.

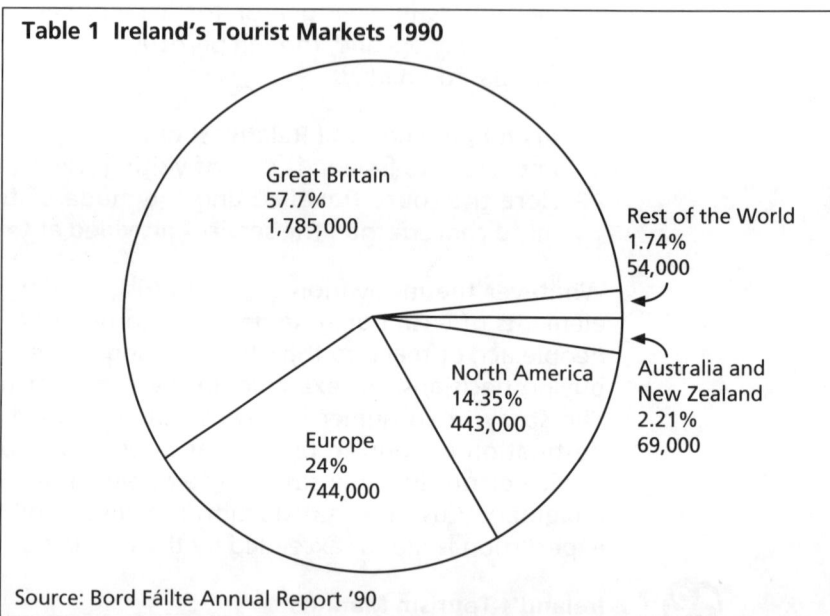

Table 1 Ireland's Tourist Markets 1990

Great Britain
57.7%
1,785,000

Rest of the World
1.74%
54,000

North America
14.35%
443,000

Australia and
New Zealand
2.21%
69,000

Europe
24%
744,000

Source: Bord Fáilte Annual Report '90

Economic Impact of Tourism

Tourism has a considerable impact on Ireland's economy.

Residents of the Republic of Ireland took over 5.7 million holidays and short breaks in 1991 worth about IR£875m. This represented an increase of over 60% in number and 20% in value on 1987. It is of interest that within these figures there was a reduction of 17% in the number of holidays taken abroad over the same period, worth IR£455m; holidays at home in Ireland doubled in number and value over the same period (see Table 3).

Table 2 Breakdown of Continental European Visitor Market, 1990	
France	198,000
Germany	178,000
Netherlands	72,000
Italy	73,000
Spain	54,000
Switzerland	41,000
Belgium/Luxembourg	37,000
Denmark	16,000
Norway/Sweden	26,000
Rest of Europe	49,000
	744,000

Source: Bord Fáilte Annual Report '90

Foreign and domestic tourism expenditure of IR£1,551.7m in 1990 represented 6.8% of Ireland's GNP. This figure relates only to the direct effects of tourism spending and does not include the indirect or ripple effects of further spending in the economy through the *multiplier effect*.

Table 3 Holidaytaking by Irish Residents

No (000s) Expenditure (IR£m)	1988	1989	1990	1991	1991/90 +/-%
Total Holidays	3, 565	3,807	4,627	5,782	25.0
	730.2	728.23	789.5	875.7	10.9
Home Long Holidays	1,118	1,294	1,692	2,009	18.7
(4+ nights)	124.4	150.1	204.6	246.4	20.4
Home Short Holidays	1,244	1,351	1,901	2,772	45.8
(1–3 nights)	92.3	96.3	137.2	174.7	27.3
Holidays Abroad	1,203	1,162	1,034	1,001	-3.2
	513.5	481.8	447.7	454.6	1.5
Other Domestic Trips	1,799	2,415	1,469	1,378	-6.2
(Duty Trips)	94.4	84.5	70.9	83.7	18.1

Source: Irish Travel Survey, Bord Fáilte (Tourism Facts)

A significant proportion of foreign tourism spending in Ireland goes to the Exchequer through VAT and other taxation. In 1990 the Exchequer received an estimated IR£306m from foreign tourism, and a further IR£121m from domestic tourism, a total of IR£427m.

Out-of-state tourism revenue accounted for 7.1% of all exports of goods and services in 1990. This compared with 6.2% in 1989.

Tourism also makes an important contribution to employment. By its nature tourism is a highly labour-intensive industry as it relies so much on personal service. Furthermore, much of the employment supported by tourism is in areas which are otherwise economically under-developed.

In recent years tourism has helped sustain the growth of employment in Ireland. As with tourism expenditure, employment figures for tourism in Ireland reflect the numbers of people directly involved in tourist-related activities. However, each person employed generates income which is spent on goods and services mainly within the country. Thus, through a multiplier effect, each new person employed in tourism helps to create employment elsewhere in the country.

While tourism grew steadily worldwide during the 1980s, despite war and recession, more spectacular growth may lie ahead. Apart from the expansion promised by the end of the Cold War, most experts agree that the developed world is on the verge of the greatest leisure revolution in history. There are two main reasons for this:

(i) people have more leisure time; mechanisation, as well as enlargement of the labour force through social change, has brought a shorter working week and the virtual disappearance of full employment in major industrial countries.

(ii) people live longer, a trend that has been apparent since early this century.

These developments offer the prospect of a huge expansion in the leisure industry beyond what we know and understand today as the tourism industry.

The need for an understanding of how the tourism industry operates has become apparent. To appreciate its impact and enormous potential, all aspects of tourism must be studied. Issues range from those which affect everyone, such as the environmental and cultural impact of mass tourism, and the breakdown of barriers between peoples, to the training and qualification of those who may work in or near the industry.

Government and Tourism

International tourism would not exist without prior high-level government involvement. Diplomatic relations and commercial arrangements known as treaties of amity, commerce and navigation must be set in place. These treaties guarantee the protection of the traveller between the countries involved.

For many countries, international tourism is important as a source of foreign revenue. Terrorism, weather, changing currency rates and other factors can affect this flow of revenue. A government will find itself under pressure from tourism suppliers to ensure good order, and to provide ever better infrastructure and conditions to increase tourism revenue.

The role and function of government and its departments is discussed in Chapter 2.

Social, Cultural and Environmental Effects

The effects of substantial growth in tourism are felt far beyond the tourist industry itself. In a report on the impact of tourism on the environment, the OECD said: 'A high quality environment is essential for tourism. On the other hand, the quality of the environment is threatened by tourism development itself which is promoted . . . because of its economic importance.' To put it another way, tourism can destroy tourism.

Surveys of potential visitors show that Ireland's scenery remains the country's principal attraction as a tourist destination. The environment is still perceived as being clean, restful and unspoilt. Without it, Ireland would have little to offer.

Unfortunately the environment is under attack. Land and buildings are left derelict: unsightly developments, litter and water pollution occur. Tourism can contribute to the deterioration of the environment where the desire to promote employment overcomes objections to tourist-related projects on environmental grounds. Minor tourism interests can contribute to the problem with proliferation of directional signs. If environmental standards are permitted to decline, the much-needed economic and employment benefits of tourism will be in danger.

The impact of tourism on cultural and social life is gradual, subtle and complex. By its nature, tourism provides opportunities for increased social contact. It can bring people together and foster intercultural understanding. However mass tourism may have the opposite effect. Little insight may be available into the lives of the local people, and traditional cultures can be trivialised by the demands of tourists; instead local culture may itself become staged and packaged, while the local people absorb aspects of the visitors' culture.

Increased tourist numbers can affect the stability of local life: on goods and services (such as transport, water supplies and everyday necessaries) prices may rise, or their usual supply and range change, leading to tension between local people and visitors. In some rural areas mass tourism can provide a window into an affluent world and encourage migration to cities.

The negative effects of smaller tourist numbers can be even more pronounced in less developed destinations where the presence of apparently rich people alongside the local poor can lead to disillusionment, discontent and even crime. Carefully handled, however, there can be a valuable positive side to the influence of tourism: heightened awareness of natural resources and cultural heritage can foster and finance the restoration and preservation of that heritage. Revival of traditional events, social and cultural festivals, restoration of ancient and historic monuments and the spur to make town and country tidy can benefit a local community. It benefits, too, from the provision of recreational and sports facilities, amenities, entertainment and places to visit.

Development of Tourism

Tourism has been identified as one of the few potential growth sectors in mature economies and it is estimated that by the end of this century it will be the world's largest industry. Tourism is one of Ireland's oldest established industries and a major source of employment and external revenue.

Early Tourism

Mass tourism is a modern phenomenon. But travel, hospitality, and changes of location for recreational and educational purposes are as old as recorded history. Tourist graffiti — the ancient equivalent of 'Kilroy was here' — were found on Djoser's pyramid at Gizeh, in Egypt, dating from 1244 BC.

Such was its growth in classical civilisations that tourism developed some of the more unsavoury aspects we know today, such as grubby inns and tawdry souvenirs — and, as today, tourism had its detractors. The celebrated Roman philosopher and statesman Seneca (4 BC–65 AD), who was tutor to the young Nero, was trenchant in his mocking of travel mania in one of his celebrated essays.

The ancient Romans developed a network of roads connecting Rome with the various outposts of the Empire, primarily for military and administrative purposes but, of course, providing the ordinary citizen with a means to travel. Taverns were built in towns and villages on the main routes to provide accommodation for travellers and stabling for their horses. St Paul was met by some of his friends from Rome at a well-known tavern: 'The Christians there had news for us and came out to meet us as far as . . . Tres Tabernae . . .' (Acts 28:15). The taverns were noisy and cheap and used mainly by humble travellers. Bread and wine cost about 0.2p; food for a mule set the traveller back about twice as much. Many wealthy Romans left the capital in summer to holiday on the coast. On their journeys they were more likely to stay with friends, or even sleep in carriages built for comfort rather than speed. Caesar and Cicero, like many well-to-do youths of the day, made the equivalent of the Grand Tour of Greece and Asia Minor. Travel by sea was uncomfortable: there were no passenger ships so travel was always by merchant ship. And travel by land could be dangerous: travellers could die or disappear into slavery after encounters with brigands and robbers.

From Monasteries to Health Spas

In later centuries, monasteries offered hospitality to travellers and pilgrims and indeed some built special dormitories for this purpose. Manor houses gave free accommodation to travellers and many later became commercial inns. During that period in Europe, and up to the middle of the 18th century, travel was most often for pilgrimages or for business or official purposes.

Yet people were beginning to travel for other reasons, at first for educational purposes and later to satisfy new curiosity about the way people of other countries lived. In 1776, Samuel Johnson wrote: 'A man who has not been to Italy is always conscious of an inferiority for his having not seen what is expected a man should see. The grand object of travelling is to see the shores of the Mediterranean . . . All our religion, art, laws, that is almost all that sets us above the savages, came from these shores.'

In this one sentence Johnson encapsulates the idea of the Grand Tour — the journey through the great cities of Europe like Rome, Florence and Paris, by which wealthy young people might become civilised by exposure to European art, architecture and manners. In other words, foreign travel was seen as a part of an aristocrat's education. Before long, the concept of the Grand Tour was to go beyond this narrow market.

The 18th century also saw the growth of the health spa in Europe. People travelled to drink and bathe in natural mineral waters; towns such as Bath, Leamington Spa and Lisdoonvarna became popular resorts for the wealthy when tourist facilities such as hotel accommodation and entertainment were made available in addition to the health waters. This was the beginning of tourism as we know it today.

However, tourism was still the privilege of the wealthy. The vast majority of Europe's population did not travel beyond their own villages or market towns. The idea of work with leisure did not exist for most people, but things were changing.

The Industrial Age

That change was brought about in dramatic fashion by the impact of the industrial revolution between 1750 and 1850 not only in Great Britain but in Ireland, because of its proximity to Britain, and in the other countries of Europe which had to compete with sudden economic expansion. In this period, Britain's population increased from

5.5 million to 25 million. The rise in population was accompanied by a drift from rural areas to the newly emerging industrial towns. In turn, urban households with new purchasing power were to become the principal market for new modes of transport as they developed. This trend was to be followed all over Europe.

First came the canals. In Ireland the first trunk canal, the Grand, opened its first section to passengers in 1780, from Dublin to Sallins. Only four years later the first hotel opened at Sallins; others were built at Robertstown, Tullamore, Portobello (Dublin) and Shannon Harbour — the last being completed in 1806. Together they cost IR£30,000 to build and maintain up to 1812, but they were not a financial success.

The canal company's passage boats were comfortable but slow; sailings from Dublin to Athy, 42 miles, started at 5 a.m. and completed their journey at 6 p.m. They carried 45 passengers in the state cabin and 35 in the common cabin. Cooking was done in the stern of the boat in two large pots on a small stove.

The fly boats (the same term as *bateaux mouches*), introduced in 1834, were lighter and faster, though still horse-drawn. They had no cooking facilities but served cold meat and limited liquor.

By the beginning of the 1800s the main cities and towns of Ireland were linked with Dublin by the Royal Mail coaches which carried mail and passengers. Fares were expensive.

Charles Bianconi

The face of popular transport was changed, however, due to an Italian immigrant, Charles Bianconi, who recognised the need for a cheap and speedy passenger service. He began operations in 1815 with a coach service between Clonmel and Cahir and was soon carrying mail and passengers between towns not serviced by the main post office coaches. Bianconi later invented the famous long cars which could carry 16 to 20 passengers, drawn by four horses. Within 25 years, his network of coach services served most of Munster, Leinster and Connacht.

Bianconi cars were cheap, fast and efficient. Fares were based on one and a half pence a mile (about 0.5p today); average speeds of up to eight miles an hour were reached and he catered for all classes of society.

Writing about their travels in 1840, Mr and Mrs Hall described Bianconi's public cars: 'They resemble the common outside jaunting car, but are calculated to hold twelve, fourteen or sixteen persons. They are well horsed, have cautious and experienced drivers, are generally driven with three horses . . . they are open cars but a huge apron of leather affords considerable protection against rain and they may be described in all respects as very comfortable and convenient vehicles.'

Bianconi's service reached its peak in the 1840s when upwards of 3,500 miles were covered daily by over 100 of his cars. Coaching inns and hotels were built to cater for his customers. The service was gradually eclipsed in the 1850s and 1860s by the railway network which began to spread across the country.

The Railways

As in other countries, the railways had a tremendous impact on Irish life. Travel on the roads and canals had been slow and expensive. Trains on the other hand were fast and cheap and they transformed ordinary people's ideas about travel.

Until this time, travel had been viewed as a burden, something to be done only when it was absolutely necessary. By providing a quick, comfortable and inexpensive means of transport, trains encouraged ordinary people to travel on business and pleasure. They encouraged migration to cities and provided manufacturers with a fast and cheap way to transport goods. As in Britain, they helped the development of seaside resorts and it is important to note that the growth of the Lakes of Killarney as a tourist resort, years before some other parts of the country, was closely connected with the completion of the railway line from Dublin to Killarney in 1853.

The present Great Southern Hotel in Killarney which opened in 1854 was the first railway hotel in Ireland. Other hotels built by various railway companies included those at Galway, Kenmare, Parknasilla, Bundoran, Warrenpoint and Rostrevor. This movement was a pioneering form of tourism marketing.

Thomas Cook

The day excursion to the seaside became popular and the seaside resort with holiday hotels, as we know them today, came into being. At around the same time, that other vital ingredient in tourism, the travel agent, came to prominence. In 1818 a Mr Emery of Charing Cross in London organised 14-day coach tours of Switzerland at a cost of 20 guineas.

In 1841 Thomas Cook began to organise his excursions and in 1852, he started operations into Ireland. He had been quick to realise the potential of this country, and is quoted in *Thomas Cook — 150 Years of Popular Tourism* by Piers Brendon (Secker & Warburg, 1991) as declaring he would be 'not a little delighted if some future observer should be led to say that Ireland has become familiarised to the people of England by the Hand Books and other instrumentalities of one Cook of Leicester'. Cook intoduced his short excursions and longer tours to Ireland writing enthusiastically: 'From Derby to Dublin and back for 13 shillings [65p today] is an astounding announcement; and the artisan and mechanic classes may now regale their spirits with the pleasurable libations of travel.' The following year he took thousands of people to the Dublin Exhibition, part of an effort to stimulate industry and to revive the Irish economy after the Famine. Cook was optimistic about its effects: 'The good time coming is the theme of every heart.' He particularly rejoiced about the development of the railway, writing in 1854: 'the means of transit have reached a perfection never before attained'.

But he also found it necessary to warn his clients about the impositions of 'Irish car drivers . . . as jovial a set of Jehus as ever took whip in hand'. Subsequently Cook conducted a number of parties to Ireland. In 1856, for example, he filled two special trains with about 1,500 people. However, in due course the rivalry of the railway companies frustrated his efforts, though his firm was later to wax lyrical about the beauties of the Emerald Isle and to introduce many visitors, particularly Americans, to the Lakes of Killarney and the mountains of Donegal.

Although Ireland was slowly awakening to the potential of tourism, and the publishing industry began to print guide books, handbooks and maps, progress was slow. It was 1895 before the first package tour from the United States arrived in Killarney and Glengarriff.

Twentieth Century Tourism

Two significant changes to affect travelling habits in the 20th century were the introduction and the rapid rise in private ownership of the motor car and the growth of air travel.

In Ireland, the first official tourist office was opened in the 1920s, but another thirty years were to pass before growth, as we know it today, manifested itself.

The contribution made by Aer Lingus, the national airline, to the development of Irish tourism must be emphasised. After its inauguration in 1936, the development of Aer Lingus was slowed by World War II, but in the years following it expanded rapidly as passenger and cargo traffic continued to rise. New routes were inaugurated between Ireland and most of the capitals of continental Europe.

The transatlantic route had been opened by the flying boat air service from Foynes in Co. Limerick during the 1940s. Its position on the extreme west of Europe gave Ireland a key role in the early transatlantic flights and made the development of an international airport on the Shannon almost inevitable.

Two regular transatlantic routes from Dublin to New York and Boston through Shannon were inaugurated in 1958. In subsequent years further transatlantic routes were opened up. Today, Ireland has a second Irish-owned airline, Ryanair. Further expansion in air traffic has seen the development of regional airports.

The contribution made by sea carriers to Irish tourism is significant. Today, ships still provide a valuable service in the transport of freight and heavy cargoes.

Ferry services between Ireland and Britain and between Ireland and the Continent give people the option of bringing their cars with them on holiday. This development has been very successful, with an increasing number of Irish people opting to motor through continental Europe and an increasing number of people from the Continent who select a similar holiday in Ireland. At present, there are 14 ferry routes in and out of Ireland being serviced by Brittany Ferries, Cork/Swansea Ferries (seasonal), Hoverspeed Great Britain, Irish Continental Group (incorporating Irish Ferries and B & I), Isle of Man Packet, P & O European Ferries and Stena Sealink. Some of these also serve as the landbridge, which involves travelling through Great Britain to the North Sea and English Channel ferries to the Continent. The Channel (Euro) Tunnel will also serve the landbridge route.

The Rise of Mass Tourism

The post-war explosion of the industry into mass tourism was influenced by:

- increased prosperity

- more leisure time

- higher standards of education and greater curiosity about other cultures

- the introduction of paid annual leave for employees

- lower air fares and more comfortable and faster travel

- the introduction of packaged holidays with group travel, block booking of hotels and chartered planes

- tourism marketing and improved standards of service, accommodation and tourist facilities

- changed attitudes to leisure and tourism. More people regard a holiday as a necessity, rather than a luxury.

Numbers of world holidaymakers have increased threefold since 1960 and the world-wide market is expected to grow by an annual 7% to 1996. Since 1986, there has been a significant increase in Irish tourism and in 1989, the growth rate was 15%, or twice the world average.

Potential for Irish Tourism

The potential for Irish tourism to sustain this rapid expansion exists if it secures an increased share of the expected growth in tourism expenditure which is likely to be associated with the creation of an integrated European market.

The Irish Government's Programme for National Recovery (1987) set as objectives an increase in tourism revenue by IR£500m through the doubling of overseas visitor numbers over a five-year period and the creation of 25,000 new jobs.

Ireland's Operational Programme for Tourism (1989–93) is a multi-funded programme concerned with developing and marketing Ireland's tourist amenities so as to achieve the government's five-year targets.

The programme will involve total expenditure of nearly IR£300m, consisting of IR£147m of European Community support, IR£33m from the Irish Exchequer and IR£120m from the private sector. Investment under the programme will be directed particularly towards product development, including training, support and marketing. It will reflect the policies of the European Commission, which call for better stag-gering of holidays, the creation of alternative tourist destinations, the promotion of new forms of tourism such as rural, social and cultural tourism and the protection of the environment.

If the potential of Irish tourism is realised it will become one of the sectors contributing most to economic growth and development.

Student Questions and Assignments

1. Define the term tourism and differentiate between a visitor, a tourist and an excursionist.

2. 'Tourism cannot be stored, it is a perishable product.' Discuss.

3. In early times, people travelled to spas for health reasons. Give examples of travel today for health reasons.

4. How has tourism been influenced by social change and employment practices?

5. It is suggested that in the future people will take more frequent and shorter breaks. How will this affect the tourism industry?

6. List and describe three travel motivators and identify several appropriate tourism products for each.

7. Suggest ways and give examples of how tourism can promote intercultural understanding.

8. Research the lives and achievements of some of the early pioneers of transport and communications such as Charles Bianconi, John McAdam, William Dargan, the Wright brothers and Henry Ford.

9. Trace the development of a tourist destination in your region. Identify the changes and influences over the years and evaluate the potential for future growth.

10. Refer to the most up-to-date government policy on tourism. Define its targets and evaluate its effectiveness.

2 *Structure of Tourism in Ireland*

Objectives

At the end of this chapter the reader will be able to:

- identify and explain the role of the main public sector bodies involved with the development and promotion of Irish tourism both north and south of the border

- list private sector and voluntary organisations that represent the tourism industry in Ireland.

This chapter identifies the main organisations responsible for the promotion and development of Irish tourism in the Republic of Ireland and Northern Ireland. The bodies responsible can be divided into two main groups: the first are largely public sector and include government funded or government appointed organisations (see Fig. 1). These operate at national level and are involved with the tourism industry in economic or employment-providing activities or in developing the tourism product. The second, or private sector group includes associations or organisations which represent the tourism industry. While these groups do not have legislative power, each in its own right reflects the viewpoint of an economic base with a sizeable workforce and as such is considered to be an effective lobby group. The associations, representing their particular sectors can focus on issues relevant to their members which in turn helps to upgrade the whole industry and promote tourism both at home and abroad.

Both of these main groups work closely together; in more recent years greater links have been forged between organisations in the Republic with similar bodies in Northern Ireland.

Fig. 1 Main Public and Private Sector Bodies Responsible for Tourism

Public Sector Bodies

Republic of Ireland	Northern Ireland
• Bord Fáilte	• Northern Ireland Tourist Board
• CERT	• District and Borough Council Tourist Information Offices
• CIE and its subsidiaries — Iarnród Éireann — Bus Éireann — Bus Átha Cliath	• Tourism and Hospitality Council
• OPW	• Northern Ireland Railways
• Shannon Development and Regional Tourism Organisations and Enterprise Partnership Boards	• Ulsterbus
• Aer Lingus	• Department of the Environment (NI)
• Aer Rianta	

Private Sector Bodies

Republic of Ireland	Northern Ireland
• An Taisce	• The National Trust
• IHF	• Northern Ireland Hotel & Catering Assoc.
• ITIC	• Ulster Tourist Development Assoc. Ltd

In the first direct government intervention in tourism, the Minister for Industry and Commerce set up the Irish Tourist Association in 1925. Since then the role of successive governments has largely been in policy formulation, with more detailed and specific responsibilities for tourism divided among state and semi-state bodies. As the economic importance of the industry grew, so too did a number of government initiatives by means of policy and financing schemes.

Fig. 2 Structure of Tourism in the Republic of Ireland

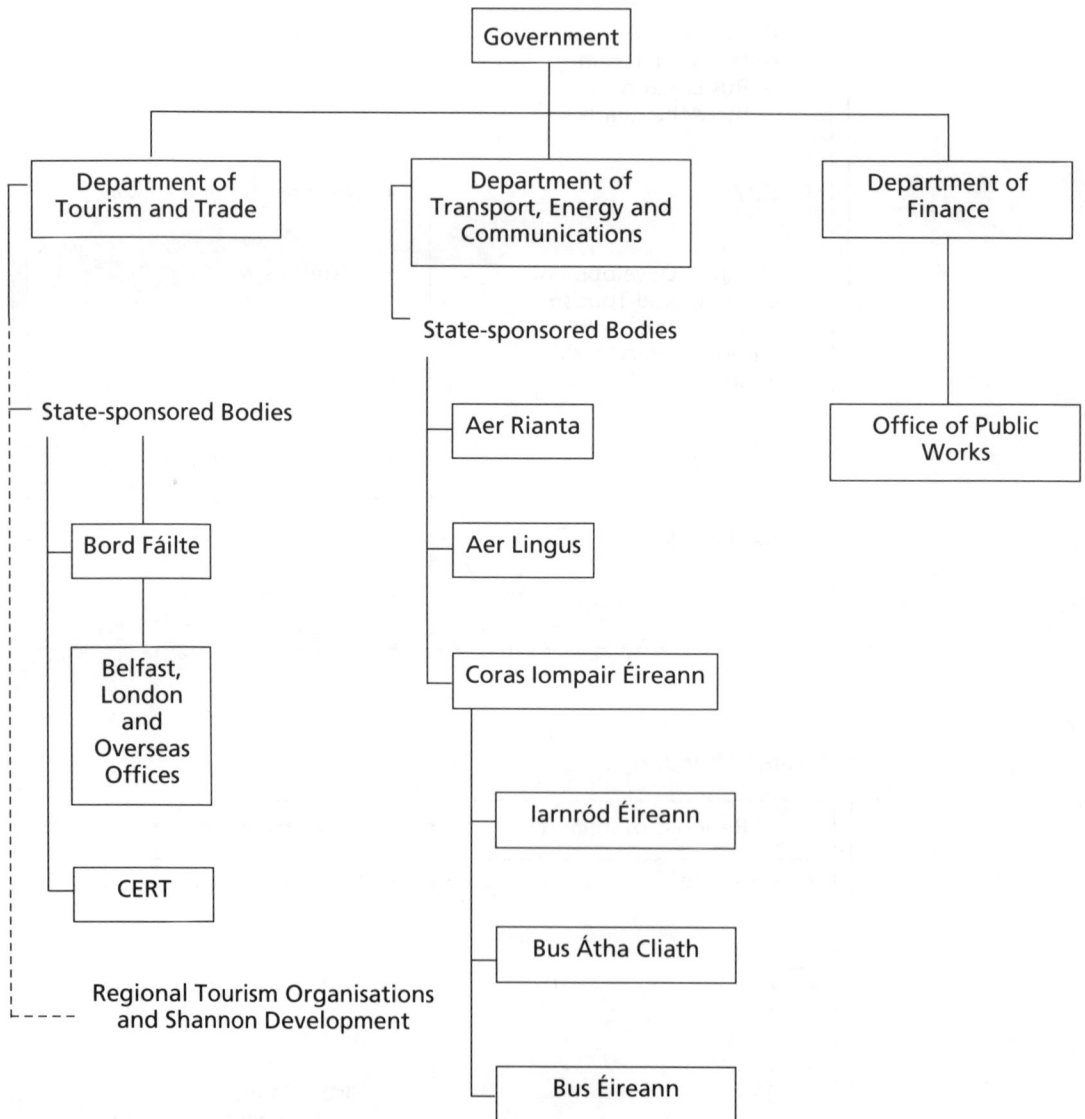

```
                          ┌──────────────┐
                          │  Government  │
                          └──────────────┘

┌──────────────────┐  ┌──────────────────┐  ┌──────────────────┐
│  Department of   │  │  Department of   │  │  Department of   │
│ Tourism and Trade│  │ Transport, Energy│  │     Finance      │
│                  │  │ and Communications│  │                  │
└──────────────────┘  └──────────────────┘  └──────────────────┘

                        State-sponsored Bodies

  State-sponsored Bodies    ┌──────────────┐      ┌──────────────┐
                            │  Aer Rianta  │      │Office of Public│
                            └──────────────┘      │    Works     │
                                                  └──────────────┘
    ┌──────────────┐        ┌──────────────┐
    │ Bord Fáilte  │        │  Aer Lingus  │
    └──────────────┘        └──────────────┘

    ┌──────────────┐        ┌──────────────────────┐
    │   Belfast,   │        │ Coras Iompair Éireann │
    │   London     │        └──────────────────────┘
    │     and      │
    │  Overseas    │             ┌──────────────┐
    │   Offices    │             │ Iarnród Éireann│
    └──────────────┘             └──────────────┘

    ┌──────────────┐             ┌──────────────┐
    │    CERT      │             │ Bus Átha Cliath│
    └──────────────┘             └──────────────┘

  Regional Tourism Organisations  ┌──────────────┐
    and Shannon Development        │  Bus Éireann │
                                   └──────────────┘
```

Government Departments

Department of Tourism and Trade

In 1993 the Department of Tourism was merged with the Department of Trade to form the Department of Tourism and Trade. Since 1977 tourism has been given greater emphasis by being included in a department's title.

The Department of Tourism and Trade is responsible for the formulation of national policies connected with tourism and trade matters. The state-sponsored bodies and executive offices under the aegis of the Department are charged with the implementation of these policies. These state-sponsored bodies include Bord Fáilte and CERT.

Also in 1993, the Department of Energy was merged with the Department of Transport and Communications to form the Department of Transport, Energy and Communications. This Department is responsible for formulating national policies connected with aviation, rail and road transport, the supply and use of energy and exploration and postal, telecommunication and broadcasting matters. The state-sponsored bodies and executive offices under the aegis of the Department include:

- Coras Iompair Éireann and its three subsidiaries: Iarnród Éireann, Bus Átha Cliath, Bus Éireann — road and rail transport

- Aer Lingus — domestic and international air transport

- Aer Rianta — airport management

A combination of EC and government funding in tourism projects has greatly contributed to the development of the industry. The European Regional Development Fund or ERDF and the European Social Fund have for example committed a total of IR£147m while the government has pledged a further investment of IR£33m with IR£102m of private sector funds. This financing was vital to the objectives of the National Development Plan 1989–93 which set the targets for the industry of an additional 25,000 jobs, doubling the number of foreign visitors and increasing annual revenue to IR£500m within this period. See Figure 2 for an overview of the structure of the Irish tourism industry.

The Department of Economic Development (NI)

In Northern Ireland the government department responsible for tourism (see Fig. 3) is the Department of Economic Development (DED) which was formed in 1982 by the amalgamation of the former Departments of Commerce and Manpower Services. The Department administers Northern Ireland tourism legislation — the main provisions of which are contained in two statutes — the Development of Tourist

Traffic Act (NI) 1948 and the Development of Tourist Traffic (NI) Order 1972, and has responsibility for the management of funds allocated annually by Parliament for tourism.

The Department operates the two principal schemes of grant assistance to the Northern Ireland tourist industry, the Tourism Accommodation Grants Scheme and the Tourist Amenity Grants Scheme.

It works closely with the Northern Ireland Tourist Board (NITB) and is responsible for funding the Board's operations. Appointments to the Board are made by the Minister with responsibility for the DED and each year the Board is required to furnish the Department with a report of its activities and its accounts.

The Department seeks, in consultation with the Board, to formulate and keep under review broad policy guidelines for the development of tourism in Northern Ireland. It also has the task of keeping abreast of relevant changes in policy in Great Britain and directives on tourism by the European Community.

Fig. 3 Structure of Tourism in Northern Ireland

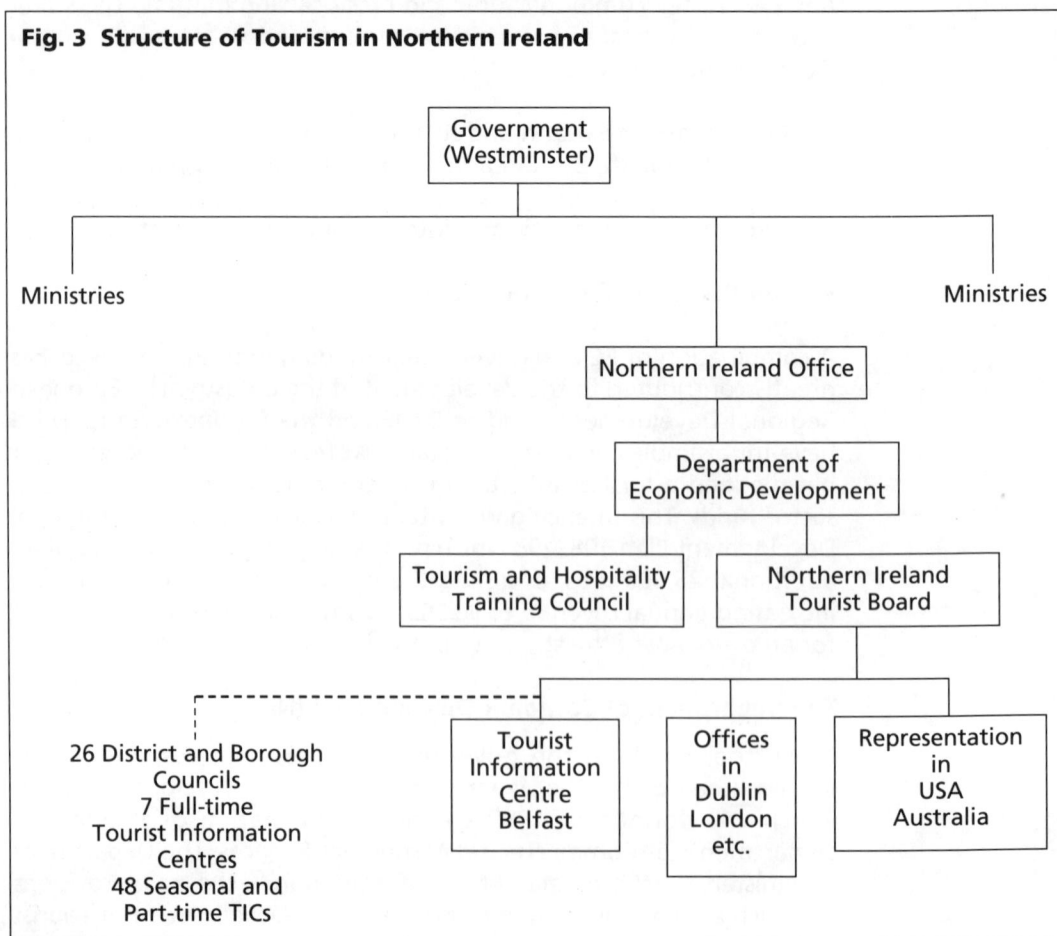

A. Public Sector Bodies — Republic of Ireland

(i) Bord Fáilte

Bord Fáilte Éireann was established in 1955 as a result of the amalgamation of two tourism bodies: Fógra Fáilte, which had responsibility for information and publicity, and An Bord Fáilte, which assumed all other duties. The organisation is a semi-state agency responsible to the Department of Tourism and Trade. While its funding comes primarily from government sources, the EC and the tourist industry provide the balance.

Bord Fáilte is the main tourism development and marketing agency in the country. Under the Tourism Traffic Act of 1939 the organisation has responsibility for implementing government policy including the classification and grading of hotels and guesthouses (covered in more detail in Chapter 4), and carrying out a number of other activities.

Bord Fáilte
Irish Tourist Board

Promoting Ireland as a Tourist Destination

As illustrated by the Bord Fáilte Budget Allocation 1990, 76.8% of the organisation's overall budget is spent on marketing. Table 1 reflects the emphasis by Bord Fáilte on marketing Ireland at home and abroad. Media campaigns include television and radio and the print media, which are used at international, national and regional levels.

The organisation publishes a range of 21 colour brochures annually, portraying the choice of products and services available in several languages. These publications vary from very specific ones such as Golfing in Ireland to more general publications such as the Discover Ireland brochure. Bord Fáilte also participates in several promotional events throughout the year. Holiday and leisure fairs worldwide often have Bord Fáilte representation. These fairs may be consumer-oriented, which the public are welcome to attend like the annual holiday fair held in Dublin, or exclusive to the trade, at which Bord Fáilte and Irish tourism representatives meet with travel wholesalers to organise and negotiate attractive packages for tours, conferences and other visits.

While a successful advertising campaign, such as the 1991 media campaign using the well-known TV chef Keith Floyd, is well worth the money spent, most organisations, Bord Fáilte included, prefer free publicity! Many journalists and others have been brought to Ireland by Bord Fáilte to experience the country for themselves and their subsequent features in the media have been invaluable. Tourism suppliers such as hotels and restaurants often give services at a reduced rate or even free of charge to create a favourable impression.

Table 1 Bord Fáilte Budget Allocation, 1990 (%)	
Total Budget was £21.013m	
	%
Marketing	76.80
Development	4.12
Administration	7.94
Regional Tourism Organisations	7.43
Superannuation	3.71
	100.00
Source : Bord Fáilte Annual Report '91	

Developing the Irish Tourism Product

The Irish tourism product has traditionally emphasised Irish scenery, the friendliness of the people and Irish culture. Bord Fáilte has sought to make this product even more competitive by taking the traditional emphasis and aiming it at specific target tourism markets. Thus it promotes a range of leisure activities in a clean environment, and Ireland's cultural heritage. Another target market is the number of Irish people worldwide of Irish descent, and one campaign led to the Irish Homecoming Festival in September 1992. This development of the Irish tourism product has come about as a result of careful planning by Bord Fáilte including the financing of amenities and tourism infrastructure as well as annual media campaigns discussed earlier.

A combination of public incentives and EC government and private investment has resulted in a massive injection of finance into the industry in the late 80s and early 90s. The government's tax incentives through the Business Expansion Scheme and grants provided by the International Fund for Ireland enabled many projects to be initiated, with Bord Fáilte playing a major role in the approval and distribution of finance.

Parallel with the development of tourism has been the need to conserve the environment and the image of the country as a 'non-resort' region and maintain the image of a green, spacious country. Every effort has been made by Bord Fáilte and the relevant planning bodies to achieve this, and the invaluable work of conservation bodies such as An Taisce in highlighting the need for caution in planning and development in relation to the environment must be noted.

Table 2 Regional Distribution of Tourism Revenue 1991 (£m)

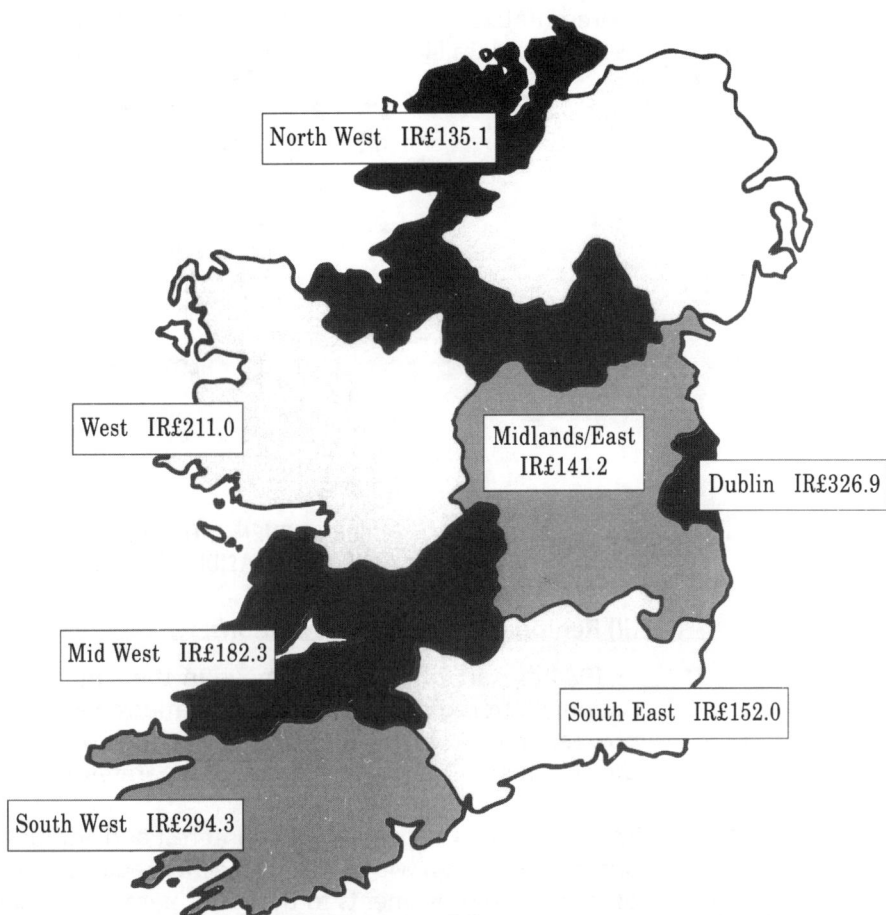

North West   IR£135.1

West   IR£211.0

Midlands/East
IR£141.2

Dublin   IR£326.9

Mid West   IR£182.3

South East   IR£152.0

South West   IR£294.3

The continuation and growth in popularity of the Bord Fáilte Tidy Towns competition reflects its role at local community level. The effort involved in competing improves the environment, and the prestige gained by winning confers countrywide recognition which can then be used as a marketing tool for the regions.

Gulliver

A joint venture between the Northern Ireland Tourist Board and Bord Fáilte has revolutionised the information and reservation system for the tourism industry in the 32 counties. Funded by both tourist boards and the International Fund for Ireland, the system is known as Gulliver. It provides up to date information on a wide range of services, ranging from accommodation and transport to events and activities. Visitors can get answers to specific questions quickly and efficiently without having to consult brochures or guides, and instant reservations can be made for a range of services.

Gulliver is available at most tourist information offices, some hotels and guesthouses, and will eventually be available at Bord Fáilte offices and representative centres overseas, on computer reservation systems such as Sabre and Gallileo and at key access points countrywide.

GULLIVER

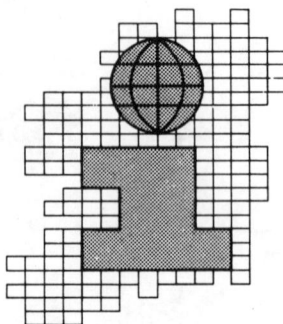

IRISH TOURISM INFORMATION
AND RESERVATIONS SYSTEM

(ii) Regional Tourism Organisations

In 1964 as part of an overall move in the country towards regional-isation, eight regional tourism organisations were set up. This number, now reduced to seven with the amalgamation of two, includes Shannon Development which will be discussed separately later in this chapter.

Their function is to generate local interest and enthusiasm for the development of tourism within their respective regions, through the provision of services, improvements to the tourism infrastructure and so on — all within the overall national tourism policy as regulated by Bord Fáilte.

The regions were initially chosen on the basis of their compatibility and a further restructuring commencing in 1989 redefined the RTOs to correspond with EC regional planning areas. Each regional organisation was set up as a public company limited by guarantee with its board made up of local authority members, local industry representatives and members of the public. Funding has been mainly provided by Bord Fáilte with the remainder made up by local authorities, commercial activities and subscription fees.

Each RTO works closely with Bord Fáilte, while providing regionally what the main organisation provides at a national level. Together they have established a network of tourist information offices throughout the Republic which have visitor information and accommodation booking services. In 1990 there were 27 year-round offices and 58 seasonal offices handling a total of 2.5 million callers. The RTOs also produce local maps and brochures.

LETTERKENNY
Dunglow
Donegal
Bundoran
SLIGO
Ballina
Achill
MONAGHAN
Carrick-on CAVAN DUNDALK
Boyle -Shannon
Castlebar
WESTPORT KNOCK AIRPORT
Knock Village Longford Newgrange Drogheda
Roscommon Skerries
Clifden Tuam Athlone DUBLIN AIRPORT
Galway Airport MULLINGAR
GALWAY DUBLIN
Salthill Aughrim DUN LAOGHAIRE
Aran Islands Thoor Ballylee Clonmacnois Newbridge Bray
(Kilronan)
Cliffs of Moher Birr
ENNIS Portlaoise WICKLOW
Nenagh Carlow
SHANNON AIRPORT Killaloe Arklow
Kilkee Bunratty KILKENNY Gorey
Kilrush LIMERICK Enniscorthy
Adare Cashel
Listowel Tipperary Town New Ross
TRALEE Cahir Clonmel
Dingle Carrick-on-Suir WEXFORD TOWN
Kerry Airport WATERFORD ROSSLARE
KILLARNEY Tramore TERMINAL
Lismore Dungarvan Rosslare
Kenmare Ardmore Harbour
Glengariff Cork Youghal ■ Offices open year-round
Bantry Kinsale Airport Cork Ferryport ● Seasonal offices
Clonakilty (Ringaskiddy)
SKIBBEREEN CORK

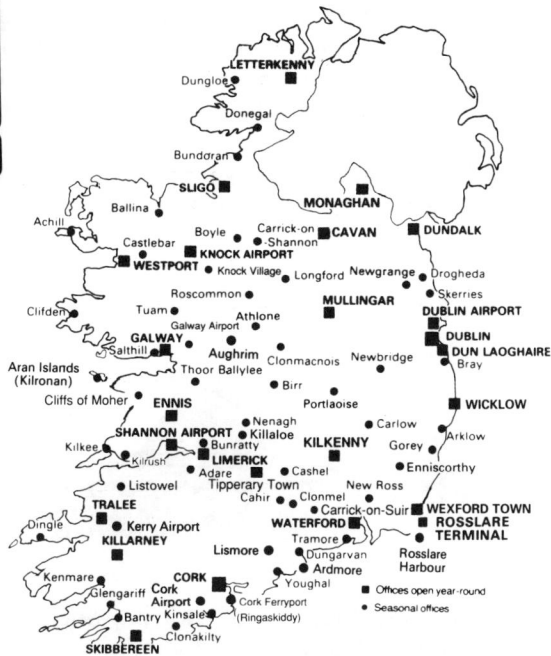

The importance of tourism to the regions in terms of employment cannot be over-emphasised. Although the disparity between the distribution of tourism revenue may be great (see Table 2), the industry is vital to the economy of each region. For example, in the North West, West, and South West regions, tourism accounts for one in every ten jobs.

(iii) Shannon Development

The Shannon Free Airport Development Company, or Shannon Development as it is now known, was established to ensure the future of Shannon Airport, which was losing business as transatlantic jets did not need to stop there for refuelling.

SHANNON
DEVELOPMENT

Since it was established in 1959, the company has been innovative in developing both the airport and the Shannon region in a number of ways. The world's first duty-free airport shop was established there and the first Airport Free Zone which quickly attracted overseas industry to operate in its customs-free environment.

Tourist attractions such as the Rent-an-Irish-Cottage scheme were developed, as were mediaeval banquets and other attractions, to promote the region as a tourist destination and encourage visitors. The compulsory stop-over at Shannon for transatlantic flights to and from Ireland, introduced in 1947, was a major boost to the region. In 1968 the government extended the industrial development responsibility of Shannon Development to include the mid-West region (Clare, Limerick and N. Tipperary) and in 1988 tourism development was added to its portfolio. Its region includes: Counties Clare, Limerick, N. Tipperary, West and South West Offaly and N. Kerry.

IRELAND WEST TOURISM

The development of industry and tourism together has resulted in successful projects in towns and rural communities. King John's Castle in Limerick City and the Ballyhoura Fáilte Tourism Co-operative are two such ventures.

Shannon airport and the Shannon Gateway Policy have helped the development of tourism in the region. The Shannon stop-over has been the subject of much debate.

(iv) Office of Public Works

Founded in 1831 to carry out public works such as the construction of roads, bridges and provide employment, the Office of Public Works, now has a broad role in providing and maintaining property for government, and some of the supplies used by government departments.

The OPW has three important responsibilities relevant to tourism.

Newgrange, Co. Meath

National Monuments and Historic Properties

Originally this responsibility was confined to ecclesiastical monuments throughout the country. Of the estimated 120,000 monuments and archaeological sites in Ireland, the OPW has guardianship of 600. The remainder are protected under the National Monuments Acts of 1930 and 1987. The OPW has carefully restored many of the monuments and buildings in its care and provides visitor access to many of them. While the number of tourists visiting these sites may be low, well-known sites can attract thousands of visitors (for example Kilkenny Castle had 142,000 in 1991).

Waterways Service

The OPW is also responsible for the most extensive waterways system in the country. Since 1831 it has been committed to the development of the River Shannon; in 1986 under the Canals Act both the Grand and Royal Canals were transferred to the OPW from CIE — and this marked both the growing emphasis of the waterways as tourist and visitor amenities, and the end of the transport era which was their initial purpose. The Erne-Shannon link canal at Ballyconnell will join the Fermanagh Lakelands to the Shannon. The importance of the re-opening of the canal to the tourism industry has yet to be seen. However, the 1,400 or so boats currently on the Shannon, together with those on the Northern waters, should stimulate interest and development in the area.

National Parks and Wildlife Service

During the 1860s the OPW was given responsibility for the Phoenix Park in Dublin, and it now manages a range of parks and gardens throughout the country, varying in size from the very large to the quite small. There are three National Parks: Killarney, Co. Kerry, Glenveagh, Co. Donegal and Connemara in Co. Galway. Two other parks in the Burren, Co. Clare and in Co. Wicklow are being developed.

The essential purpose of the national parks as defined by the OPW is to conserve natural plant and animal communities, scenic landscapes which are both extensive and of national importance and under conditions compatible with that objective to enable people to visit and appreciate them.

To help visitors in their appreciation of the parks, the OPW created a number of interpretative centres on site. These centres interpret the area by showing a video of the region and landscape, with a brief description and history of the area and its formation. In recent years the OPW has been strongly criticised for its siting of two such centres in the new national parks, in Counties Clare and Wicklow. Earlier centres were built where an infrastructure already existed, but these latest proposed sites would be constructed in the heart of wild and beautiful countryside. Conservationists argue that such centres, if needed, should be built in local towns or villages where less environmental damage would be done; the OPW says that for such centres to be of value they must be on site so that visitors can experience at first hand the attractions and beauty being interpreted. The controversies over Mullaghmore and Luggala are recent examples of this.

(v) CERT

CERT is a state-sponsored agency which was set up in 1963 with responsibility for education, recruitment and training in the tourism industry. Its objective is to 'ensure high operational standards in the industry through a professionally trained workforce and business support service'. The company is an agency of the Department of Tourism and Trade and acts as an advisory body to the government on manpower and training needs for the industry, while providing some of the training services necessary to meet its objective. The role of CERT will be discussed in greater detail in Chapter 10.

B. Public Sector Bodies — Northern Ireland

Northern Ireland Tourist Board

The Northern Ireland Tourist Board (NITB) was set up under the Development of Tourist Traffic Act, (NIO 1948) with the primary objective of promoting 'the development of tourist traffic in Northern Ireland and encourage persons who reside elsewhere to visit Northern Ireland'.

There are some common elements between the NITB and Bord Fáilte including their tourism products, and their roles. Both bodies are largely funded by their respective governments.

It is official policy between the governments of the Republic of Ireland and the United Kingdom that Ireland should be promoted abroad as a single tourist destination. So in media campaigns abroad the names of both the NITB and Bord Fáilte appear, as do Carrickfergus Castle and King John's Castle in Limerick, the Giant's Causeway and Ladies' View in Killarney. The Homecoming Festival campaign was run by the NITB with Bord Fáilte and many of the visitors saw both parts of Ireland.

irish homecoming festival

While all the elements and strengths of a tourist product are evident in the North — beautiful scenery, friendly people, attractions and activities, the greatest obstacle facing the development of the tourism industry has been the image portrayed worldwide of a war-torn region.

Visitor numbers dropped rapidly during the first two years of 'the troubles'. Since then, with one or two setbacks, they have climbed back. 1990 was Northern Ireland's best tourist year ever with 1.15

Table 3 Visitors to Northern Ireland 1970–90

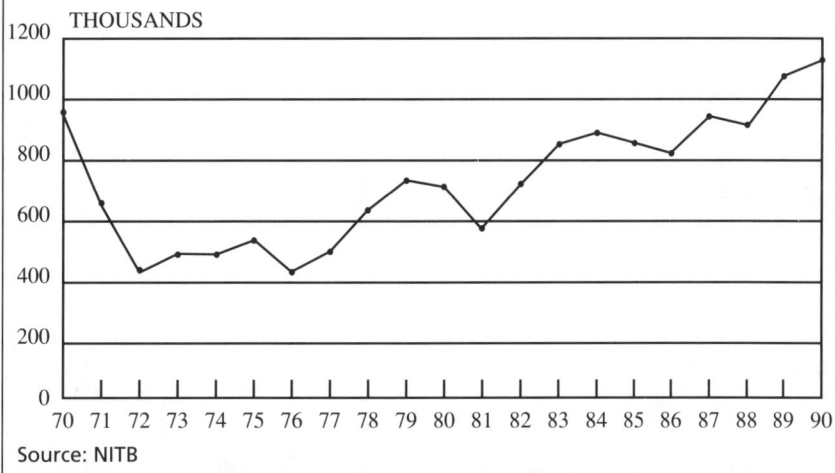

Source: NITB

million visitors who spent stg£153m (see Tables 3 and 4) plus another nearly 1 million home holidaymakers making a total spend of over stg£210m. About 9,000 people were employed.

Table 4 Revenue Distribution by Main Markets 1990 (NI)

Base - £153 million

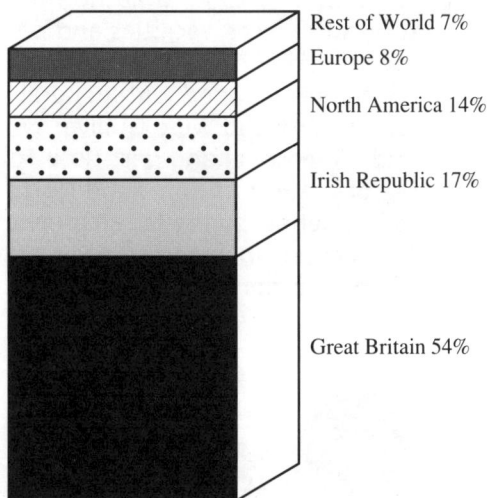

Rest of World 7%
Europe 8%
North America 14%
Irish Republic 17%
Great Britain 54%

Source: NITB

As in the Republic, the majority of visitors to the North are visiting friends and relatives (VFR); with sightseeing and curiosity being the next major influences for visiting the region (see Table 5).

Table 5 Reasons for Visit to Northern Ireland 1990

Market Area	All Holiday Visitors 65,500	Great Britain 43,700	Europe 9,000	North America 7,900	Rest of World 4,900
Base	100%	100%	100%	100%	100%
*less than 1%					
Main influence to visit Northern Ireland 1990					
Visiting friends/relatives	51	64	18	29	33
Sightseeing	9	5	20	8	24
Recommended	4	2	4	7	11
Curiosity	9	5	18	12	17
Part of tour	8	3	25	12	5
Return visit	6	7	6	2	3
Advertising	*	*	—	—	—
Ancestoral	4	*	—	26	7
Fishing/Golf/ other activity	*	1	2	—	—
Other reason	9	12	7	4	—

Source: NITB

Under the 1972 Local Government (NI) Act, the allocation of tourism responsibility to local authorities throughout the North means that tourism services, facilities and promotion are provided at local level. Twenty-six local authorities operate Tourist Information Centres which are provided with general support by the NITB and are linked with the Ireland-wide Gulliver system. In all there are seven full-time and 48 seasonal and part-time Tourist Information Centres operated by local authorities around Northern Ireland; one full-time centre is run in Belfast by the NITB. Tourist Information Offices (NITB) are also located in Dublin and London and in shared facilities with the British Tourist Authority overseas.

Northern Ireland
Tourist Board

C. Private Sector Bodies — Republic of Ireland and Northern Ireland

These organisations, as mentioned in the introduction to this chapter, do not have legislative power but as representatives of the tourism industry throughout the country, they have a considerable lobby which has been very effective on a number of issues.

Many government-appointed bodies have representatives on these private sector organisations and the feedback, promotion of ideas and research carried out by them has greatly influenced government policy on tourism throughout the years.

(i) ITIC

The Irish Tourist Industry Confederation, ITIC was set up in 1984 as a replacement for the National Tourism Council. It is a national body with no regional sub-structure and represents 21 member companies and organisations from all sectors of the industry. The Confederation brings together all diverse commercial tourism interests and stimulates co-operation between them to maximise tourism growth. ITIC has been innovative in carrying out research and publishing reports on behalf of the industry on topics such as the environment and its importance for the industry, taxation and the EC and the development of the industry.

(ii) Ulster Tourist Development Association Ltd

The Northern equivalent of ITIC is the Ulster Tourist Development Association Ltd. Founded in 1924 and based in Ballymoney the association originally had the responsibility of publicising Northern Ireland and providing tourist information.

With the founding of the Northern Ireland Tourist Board in 1948, a formal agreement was worked out which made the UTDA an independent voluntary organisation which was to work in harmony with the Board. In 1972 this agreement was dissolved and the grant system which supported the body discontinued. After a few years of uncertainty the association was revived and is now instrumental in promoting tourism in Northern Ireland. The body supports an annual award ceremony to, among others, the best guesthouse, farmhouse and tourist facility, while also continuing to be an effective lobby body on behalf of the industry.

(iii) The National Trust

The National Trust is an independent charity founded in 1895. It is the most active conservation charity in the United Kingdom. The trust was established to protect places of historic interest or natural beauty from development and make them available to the public. It has grown to become the third largest landowner in Britain with more than 560,000 acres and over 520 miles of coastline, more than 200 historic houses and over 100 gardens. The National Trust is independent of the government and relies on donations and subscriptions for funds.

In Northern Ireland, the Trust owns more than 13,000 acres and 29 properties; this is one of its fastest growing regions, with a membership of 20,000.

The National Trust has played a major role in the development of tourism in the North. Hundreds of thousands of visitors, both domestic and overseas, visit its properties which include 17th-century houses such as Springhill, the well-known Crown Bar in Belfast, a restored Victorian public house, the famous basalt formation at the Giant's Causeway and the Carrick-a-Rede rope bridge.

(iv) An Taisce

While the National Trust operates in Northern Ireland, An Taisce is the equivalent body in the Republic. It is concerned with conserving Irish heritage and in highlighting any development which might infringe on that objective. As an independent voluntary body, which has no state support, the body relies on donations and subscriptions to survive, and currently has a membership of over 7,000 members in 31 local associations throughout the Republic.

An Taisce is widely recognised as being a most influential conservation body. It has contributed significantly towards issues of conservation since it was founded in 1948, and has promoted changes in legislation. It also maintains properties for the purpose of research and for the public.

(v) IHF

The Irish Hotel Federation (IHF) was founded in 1937 to represent the hotel and guesthouse industry while providing a range of services including economic and legal advice to their membership which includes 70% of all registered hotels and guesthouses.

Its Board is made up of industry representatives — some of whom also act as IHF representatives on other bodies in the industry. In recent years the IHF has extended its activities to market and publish the highly successful hotel and guesthouse guide for Ireland 'Be Our Guest'.

D. Other Representative Bodies

Irish Farm Holidays in the Republic and the *NI Farm and Country Holiday Association* both represent their specific sectors and have been instrumental in publicising farm holidays at home and abroad, with their respective guides.

The *Town and Country Homes Association* set up in 1972 and its Northern counterpart the *NI Town and Seaside House Association* have been equally successful. These private sector organisations have succeeded in promoting their members as a group while also allowing the establishments to retain their individuality.

Other private sector representative bodies include:

— *Fáilte Tuaithe*: represents some operators of farmhouses

— *Restaurant Association of Ireland*: the representative body for gourmet, visitor, family and fast-food restaurants

— *Irish Caravan Council*: representing caravan parks

— *Irish Cottage and Holiday Homes Association*: represents operators of cottages and holiday homes

— *Irish Budget Hostels*: independent hostels group representing budget-price hostels.

International Fund for Ireland

The International Fund For Ireland was established in 1986 by the British and Irish governments with the objectives of promoting economic and social advance particularly in the areas most affected by the instability of recent years. It is financed by international contributions from the United States, Canada, New Zealand and the European Community.

The IFI has been very supportive of the tourist boards both North and South — especially in projects which market or promote the island as one tourist destination. A total of IR£435,000 was committed to the Irish Homecoming Festival in 1992, for example.

The IFI contributed generously to the Gulliver project, and has introduced tourism grant schemes which have assisted the development of the accommodation industry and tourist amenities such as the Tyrone Crystal factory visitor centre.

Finance has also been pledged to the Erne-Shannon (Ballyconnell) link canal (IR£3.7m) — a project chosen for its cross-border location and the potential for other economic development in the region.

Student Questions and Assignments

1. Given that, as far as the rest of the world is concerned, 'Ireland' is perceived as a single holiday destination, discuss the implications of this for both the Northern Ireland Tourist Board and Bord Fáilte Éireann and identify areas of product development and marketing where the two bodies could work more closely together.

2. Gulliver represents an innovative change by the two tourist boards. Identify the information and booking procedures used before Gulliver and what differences the new technology will make to the tourism industry.

3. Discuss the importance of conservation bodies in Ireland. In your answer consider two sensitive issues, whether national or international, which highlight the importance of conservation.

4. 'The continuing promotion of Ireland as an historical and environmentally conscious country may attract tourists to the detriment of industrial development.' Discuss.

5. Discuss the role of private sector organisations in promoting and developing the Irish tourism industry and research in some detail the role, aims and structure of one such organisation.

6. Choose one of the public sector tourism organisations discussed in this chapter and develop a strategic plan to further its aims assuming unlimited funding was available to this organisation.

7. Describe the organisation of tourism at regional level and identify the services and support provided within your region. Evaluate the respective merits of regional and national tourism development strategies.

8. Examine the specific influence and impact of public and private sector tourism organisations in your locality. Which organisations are represented and what do they achieve at local level?

3

Tourism Product 1: Transport

Objectives

At the end of this chapter the reader will be able to:

- identify transport as a key component of the tourism product

- list the main Irish access and internal transport networks and services

- demonstrate an awareness of means of transport as tourist attractions

- outline travel regulations pertaining to incoming and out-bound tourism in Ireland.

The Irish tourism product includes many features which may be taken together in three main groups:

— Transport

— Accommodation and Catering

— Attractions and Services.

This chapter will deal with the first of these — Transport, including access and internal transport. The following two chapters will discuss Accommodation and Catering and Attractions and Services.

With the opening of the Eurotunnel between Britain and France Ireland will become the only member state of the EC physically separated from the Continent. Isolation means that access to the country is limited to sea and air, and speed and cost become important issues.

While the access and internal transport systems of any country are not exclusive to the tourism industry, good networks to and within any country are vital to the survival and development of the industry. In some cases transport may be the purpose of a visit, for example, cruising. Modes of access transport chosen by overseas visitors are illustrated in Table 1.

A wide range and choice of transport must be available in order to cater for visitors: internal transport accounts for 13% of overseas tourism expenditure in Ireland (see Table 2).

Table 1 Modes of access transport for overseas visitors 1991

TOTAL VISITS	Total O'seas	Britain	Mainland Europe	North America	Other Areas
Base (000s)	3,015	1,710	841	356	124
Route of Entry	%	%	%	%	%
Britain Sea	33	42	19	20	29
Continental Sea	4	*	15	2	3
Total Sea	37	42	34	22	33
Britain Air	38	51	14	26	56
Continental Air	14	*	50	2	4
Transatlantic Air	6	*	*	46	2
Total Air	58	51	64	74	62
Via N. Ireland	5	7	2	4	5

Source: Bord Fáilte Annual Statistics '91

Table 2 Composition of overseas tourism expenditure in the Republic of Ireland by area of normal residence, 1989

(% of total)

	Accom-modation	Food/drink	Sightseeing/entertainment	Transport	Shopping	Other
Great Britain	16	35	10	12	14	13
Continental Europe	24	34	6	14	18	4
North America	21	22	5	15	28	9
Other areas	16	28	6	12	26	12
All markets	**19**	**31**	**8**	**13**	**19**	**10**

Source: Bord Fáilte

Air Transport

As has been discussed, one of the most important influences on the growth of tourism in the last generation has been the development of the mass movement of people by air. As the world became smaller and the cost of flying decreased, the tourist industry, particularly in countries along the Mediterranean, developed rapidly to cater for huge numbers, even millions, of visitors.

Air transport can be divided into two main classes: scheduled and chartered flights. Scheduled flights operate like other forms of time-tabled transport. Many countries have a national flag-carrier such as Aer Lingus, Lufthansa or British Airways, which fly to scheduled destinations regardless of their load factors.

Charter flights are generally booked by holiday companies. Tour operators charter planes from the airlines for the holiday periods of the summer months and Christmas when demand is greatest. Some charters operate on a flight-only basis offering a limited no-frills service, for example on particular dates to New York or, through London, to Australia. They rely on full passenger loads to make a profit. A charter flight can be cancelled at short notice, if there is insufficient demand, and pre-booked passengers are either transferred to another charter airline or the flight consolidated with another experiencing similar low loading. These flights are often cheap and provide seasonal direct links with destinations not served by scheduled airlines. For example, Ireland has no direct scheduled link with Canada but during holiday periods has several weekly charter flights there at low prices.

After slow beginnings the aviation industry in Ireland developed at a rapid rate, particularly following the foundation of the national airline, Aer Lingus, in 1936.

The aviation industry has of course developed worldwide; technological advancements in speed and capacity are enormous: Concorde can fly from London to New York in 3H hours and 747s carry up to 475 passengers.

Until the early 1980s, the airline industry was highly regulated throughout the world, making it difficult for new airline operators to enter the market. International agreements involving all major airlines restricted competition in areas such as fares and services. Bilateral agreements between governments allocated routes and frequencies, usually to national flag-carriers.

During the 1980s, in some countries including the US and the UK, there was a mood for liberalisation or deregulation of this closely regulated environment. Domestic operating licences became easier to obtain and fares were no longer maintained by government, so the public got more frequent flights, more flights at peak times and often at greatly reduced fares. In the US some airlines like Delta, managed to change carefully and survived; others could not adapt, grew too quickly or reduced excessively, and they failed. Major airlines like PanAm, TWA and Eastern went out of business.

International deregulation had its origins in the Chicago Convention on Civil Aviation in 1944. To encourage international air transport this meeting, attended by representatives of 80 governments, defined five freedoms of the air which may be summarised thus:

— flying across a country

— landing in a country other than to load or off-load (for example to refuel)

— off-loading passengers and freight from an aircraft of the country from which they came

— loading passengers and freight on an aircraft of the country to which they are going

— loading passengers and freight on an aircraft which is not from the country to which they are going, and off-loading passengers and freight from an aircraft not from the country from which they came.

The first four freedoms were adopted in bilateral agreements between governments all over the world, but the fifth posed difficulties.

Many factors contributed to the decision of the EC and the US Government to work towards the Fifth Freedom: these included public restiveness with what were seen as high fares being charged by flag-carriers, the political will to allow market forces to prevail, rather than regulation, and the apparent popularity of domestic deregulation in the United States. In 1988 the British and Irish governments agreed that Irish carriers flying to the Continent could pick up passengers in the UK. Thus international traffic is developing some of the features of the deregulation of domestic traffic.

In Ireland, following deregulation, private companies could now enter the market; the monopoly held by the national airline, Aer Lingus, ceased to exist. Ryanair entered the market in 1986 and as competition intensified for the busy Dublin to London route so too did British Midland and Virgin. Over-capacity led to low load factors and stiff fare competition; Virgin withdrew first, followed in 1991 by British Airways. On the other hand the new freedom to pick up passengers in other countries is being exercised by Aer Lingus.

The results of this deregulation were advantageous to the public who saw substantial reductions in air fares as carriers 'battled' for their market share; as a result the number of people flying the Dublin to London route soared from 1,482,000 in 1985 to 3,167,000 by 1989.

Airports

Dublin Airport was Ireland's first civil airport and opened at Collinstown in 1940. Now Dublin, Shannon, Cork and Belfast are international airports while Knock, Kerry, Sligo, Derry, Galway, Waterford and Donegal provide invaluable regional links. The international airports have all been affected by factors including worldwide recession, but the smaller airports have been particularly badly hit and their growth and development affected. After a period of good growth in the late 1980s, due to deregulation, the early 1990s have seen services cut substantially and losses incurred.

Table 3 Passenger Traffic Statistics (extract)

Passengers	1990	1987
OVERALL		
Transatlantic	662,978	584,100
Great Britain	4,178,276	2,675,906
Europe	1,490,185	1,090,573
Domestic	773,118	343,284
Transit	741,769	544,711
Total	7,846,326	5,238,574
DUBLIN		
Transatlantic	287,708	203,159
Great Britain	3,427,590	2,172,463
Europe	1,316,847	974,997
Domestic	459,410	171,339
Transit	17,928	29,074
Total	5,509,483	3,551,032
SHANNON		
Transatlantic	374,638	380,893
Great Britain	337,337	216,631
Europe	82,098	57,608
Domestic	139,739	84,558
Transit	694,953	506,516
Total	1,628,765	1,246,206
CORK		
Transatlantic	632	48
Great Britain	413,349	286,812
Europe	91,240	57,968
Domestic	173,969	87,387
Transit	28,888	9,121
Total	708,078	441,336

Source: Aer Rianta Annual Report '91

Shannon Airport was built in 1945 to cater for transatlantic traffic. Planes could carry only just enough fuel for the Atlantic crossing and Foynes built up a substantial business as a base for the first transatlantic airliners. The coming of land-based planes called for an airport and Shannon was a natural location. Soon, however, planes were able to carry more fuel so the function of Shannon as a refuelling centre diminished as it did at Gander in Newfoundland.

Direct flights from, say, New York to Dublin became possible, though Ireland was still a desirable stop for planes going on to the Continent. In 1940, the government decided that all transatlantic planes landing in Ireland must stop at Shannon.

For many years the Shannon region has enjoyed prosperity dependent on the airport. The world's first duty free airport shop made it popular with passengers and the first airport free zone brought industry. The flow of tourists led to the development of visitor attractions which remain to this day.

Aeroflot, the Soviet airline began refuelling in Shannon in 1980 en route to Cuba. This was the beginning of an excellent working relation-ship between Ireland and the former Soviet Union — evident in the number of business links since formed between the two. Later in 1988, a United States pre-clearance procedure was established enabling pas-sengers to avoid delays at immigration on arrival in the US. In 1990, Shannon handled 1,628,758 customers in a combination of UK, transatlantic, scheduled and charter flights.

As competition for air space intensifies, so congestion and pollution of the skies has increased. Heathrow Airport for example, is one of the most congested in the world. This has led to the extension of Gatwick, and the upgrading of Luton and Stansted airports, also in the London region.

Airports must compete for airline business. Pressure has grown for added runway space, storage and passenger facilities. It is claimed that airport noise and pollution is causing lasting damage to the environment and the development of airports, Dublin included, is being met with resistance from local communities.

Airports have changed considerably in recent years. As well as gift shops and duty free areas, most airports now have restaurants, banks, post offices and hairdressers. Many provide shower facilities and quiet seating areas with television and business facilities. The shopping areas at airports now offer a wide selection and variety of shops, many of which are familiar names.

Harrods in London, for example, opened its only sister shop in Pearson International airport in Toronto, Canada. As well as making airports more attractive to travellers, these facilities contribute significant revenue to the authorities.

AerRianta

Aer Rianta manages Shannon, Dublin and Cork airports. The company was founded under the Transport and Navigation Act of 1936 to develop aviation in Ireland. Since 1968, Aer Rianta broadened its business interests and has been particularly successful in duty free sales — IR£39.2m in 1989, and the company now has outlets in Moscow, St Petersburg and a number of other overseas locations. Airport business and passenger numbers have been increasing steadily. For example, Dublin airport had 16,769 aircraft movements in 1949; by 1979 this number had risen to 92,150. In 1990 5.5 million passengers used Dublin Airport; this may be compared to 710,000 in Cork in the same year, in itself a creditable performance.

Inland Transport

Canals

Canal construction in Ireland was financed entirely from government sources. An act authorising their construction was passed in 1715 and the first canal, the Newry Canal, was built between 1731 and 1742. Another scheme envisaged in the 1715 Act was a canal to link Dublin with the Shannon and the Barrow. Work on construction of the Grand Canal was begun in 1756 and it opened to goods traffic in 1779. In 1780 the first passenger boat began to ply between Sallins and Dublin twice a week. In fact the link with the Shannon was not properly completed until 1805. In 1810, 205,000 tons of goods were carried to and from Dublin.

When the Shannon Harbour opened, the fare for the journey on a horse-drawn passage boat from Dublin was 16s 3d (IR), about 81p for a state cabin and 9s 5½d(IR), about 47p in the common cabin. This may be compared with the weekly wage of the hotelkeeper at Robertstown (one of the company's hotels) of £1.2s.9d (IR) or IR£1.14.

Lighter fly boats were introduced in 1834 and the journey from Portobello to Tullamore (58 miles) took from 7 a.m. to only 4.05 p.m.

Charles Bianconi had been operating his horse-drawn open cars north and west from Clonmel when in 1836 he approached the Grand Canal Company to arrange services to meet boats at various points to serve Galway, Tuam and other parts at a standard fare of 1½d (IR), about ½p today, per mile. Competition, however, from the more flexible coaches and soon the faster and cheaper railways spelt the end of passenger boats around 1850, though commercial canal boats were only withdrawn by CIE in 1959.

Today, canals are recognised as valuable leisure resources. Boat trips and cruising are now available on some canals, and others are being restored or reconstructed. These are discussed later in this chapter.

Railways

Railways were slow to develop in Ireland. The first to be built ran from Dublin to Kingstown, now Dun Laoghaire. It was opened in 1834 with a gauge of 4 ft 8½ in, the standard track in Great Britain. By 1845 only 100 km of track were open to traffic in Ireland though over the next ten years this was extended to 500 km. As the railways developed, so too did the safety and comfort of travellers. By 1910, with 3,500 km of track managed by 30 different railway companies, Irish railways were at their peak.

A number of factors contributed to their decline. The growth in popularity of the motor car had a great impact as did the high costs of maintenance and modernisation of track and rolling stock — closures were inevitable. These were at first limited to the most uneconomic routes but later extended throughout the country. Smaller stations were closed and what had once been an extensive network was eventually reduced to one extending over some 2,000 km. (See fig. 1).

Responsibility for Irish railways lies with Iarnród Éireann, part of the holding company Coras Iompair Éireann (CIE) along with Dublin Bus and Bus Éireann, set up in its present form in 1987. The company operates freight trains, which carry anything from sugar beet to peat briquettes and which earned revenue of IR£21m in 1990, and passenger services on which revenue in the same year was almost IR£50m.

The rail network radiates from two major stations in Dublin: Heuston and Connolly. In Northern Ireland, Northern Ireland Railways are responsible for the railway and the only cross border link remaining is the Dublin to Belfast line. The three lines, to Dublin and Derry, Larne and Bangor are all concentrated on one station, Belfast Central.

Over the last decade, the effort to maintain an efficient railway service has gained support, though there is still concern about some lines. In Ireland as well as overseas, railways are becoming recognised as an environmentally friendly means of travel with low pollution and relatively efficient use of energy.

In France, for example, the SNCF has been developing a high speed rail network, Trains à Grand Vitesse (TGV), with purpose-built lines and trains capable of reaching speeds up to 270 km/h. The carriages have comfortable seating with phones and full business facilities available if required. These trains are now in direct competition with the airlines in terms of speed, comfort, service and cost. Germany, Italy, Sweden and Japan have also developed high speed rail links.

Fig. 1 Ireland's Rail Network

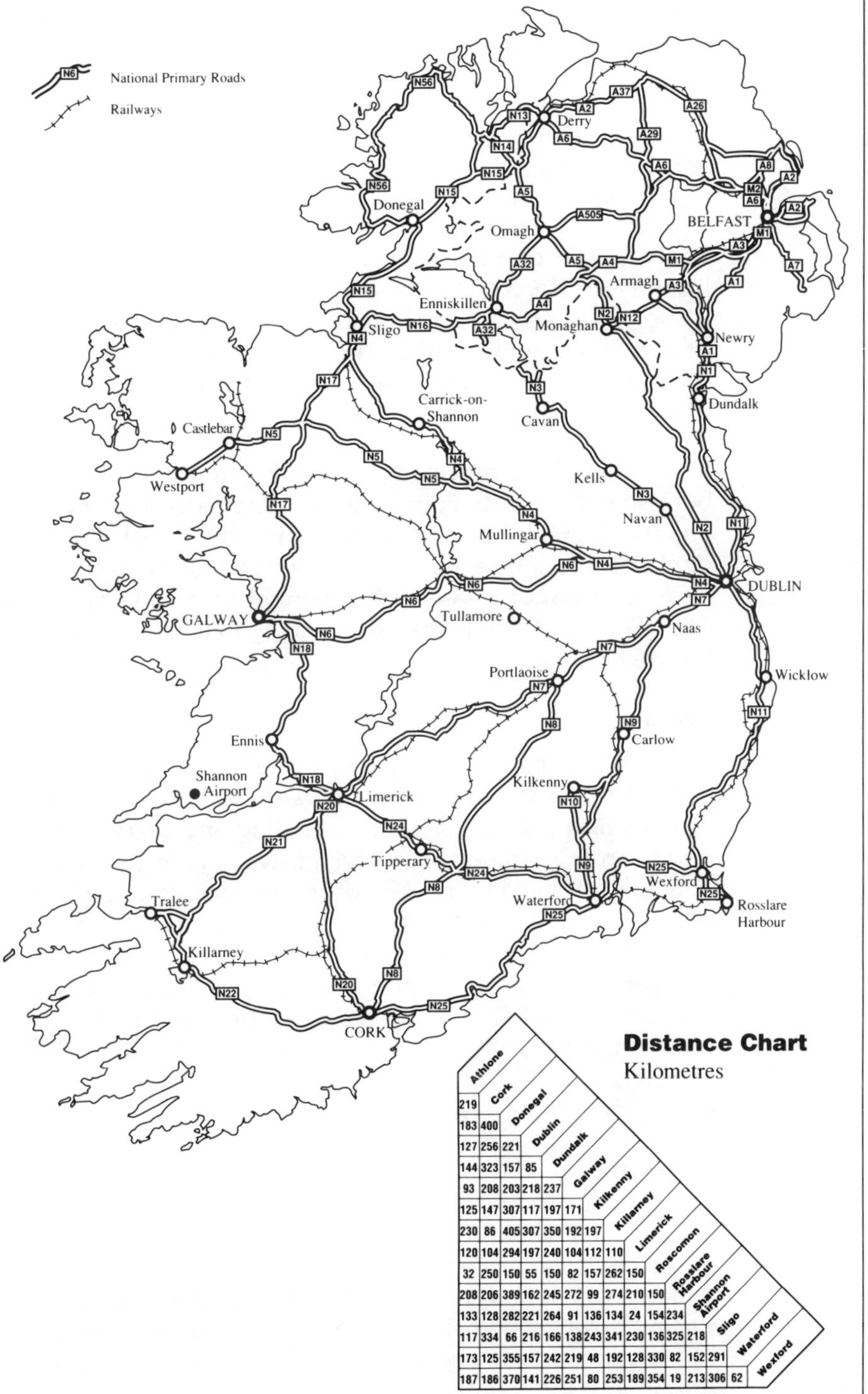

N6 — National Primary Roads

Railways

Distance Chart
Kilometres

Athlone	Cork	Donegal	Dublin	Dundalk	Galway	Kilkenny	Killarney	Limerick	Roscommon	Rosslare Harbour	Shannon Airport	Sligo	Waterford	Wexford
219	Cork													
183	400	Donegal												
127	256	221	Dublin											
144	323	157	85	Dundalk										
93	208	203	218	237	Galway									
125	147	307	117	197	171	Kilkenny								
230	86	405	307	350	192	197	Killarney							
120	104	294	197	240	104	112	110	Limerick						
32	250	150	55	150	82	157	262	150	Roscommon					
208	206	389	162	245	272	99	274	210	150	Rosslare Harbour				
133	128	282	221	264	91	136	134	24	154	234	Shannon Airport			
117	334	66	216	166	138	243	341	230	136	325	218	Sligo		
173	125	355	157	242	219	48	192	128	330	82	152	291	Waterford	
187	186	370	141	226	251	80	253	189	354	19	213	306	62	Wexford

The most recent development in Irish rail was the opening of DART (Dublin Area Rapid Transit) in Dublin in 1984. An electric train system covering 38 km from Howth to Bray, it is capable of carrying up to 80,000 passengers daily. Its success is evident from the doubling of commuter figures since its inauguration and the consequent reduction in road traffic congestion.

An upgrading of the line between Belfast and Dublin has been approved along with new high-speed rolling stock. Consideration is also being given to a light railway in Dublin which would use the route of the former Harcourt Street line.

Railways are popular with tourists not least because of the price incentives offered. Students, for example, travel at half price, while Rambler Tickets allow unlimited travel throughout the country for a period at a low fixed price. The international Eurorail card works on the same principle and is valid in up to about 25 countries; this type of holiday appeals to a growing number of tourists annually.

Steam trains have regained popularity — not only with rail enthusiasts but also with tourists. Railway centres and museums in Northern Ireland and the Republic have showrooms and exhibits with restored trains on display. Some centres have steam train excursions so visitors can experience this form of transport for themselves. Examples include: Shane's Castle in Co. Antrim, the Foyle Valley Railway Centre in Derry and Westrail in Tuam.

Roads

According to the last road survey (in 1977), there were 57,325 miles of public road in the Republic of Ireland: in 1992 there were 1,054,000 vehicles on these roads — not including any overseas traffic. In 1990 alone, an investment of IR£184.5m was made to improve the road network in Ireland for reasons of communication and the development of industry. However, the character of regional and minor roads , which weave through some of the most scenic countryside, are often the most popular with overseas visitors. The signposting of roads is a cause for concern. In certain areas available signs are inadequate. In some Gaeltacht areas with bilingual signs, place names in English have been removed, making it difficult for overseas visitors to find the way. In yet other places, signs have been vandalised.

Having the use of a car on holiday means freedom and flexibility to the traveller; for those unable to bring their own car, car hire is readily available in Ireland. There are an estimated 13,500 rental cars available in the peak season in the Republic. These are owned by large multi-national companies, such as Hertz, Avis, Budget and Europcar, and by smaller privately-owned companies. Larger operations are most often based at airports or city centres, while private companies are scattered throughout the country.

Many visitors purchase fly-drive packages which provide the flight and car rental for an all-inclusive price.

The principal problem facing the car hire business in Ireland is that of supply. At the end of a season, it can be difficult to sell used cars as there can be so many on the market at one time: therefore companies are reluctant to expand. When demand is greatest, the number of cars available may not be adequate; this is disappointing and may damage the reputation of car hire operators.

As well as renting a self-drive car it is possible to have a chauffeur-driven car. This is particularly useful to prospective industrialists visiting the country. Taxi services range from large companies in cities with a 24-hour service to a call-out service in rural communities.

Coach travel appeals to two broad markets: young people and senior citizens. Coach transport is a fast, cost-effective means of travel, and often appeals to the traveller on a budget. Bus Éireann, the national bus service, for example, offers an expressway service on over 75 routes (see map); in 1990 it carried 3 million passengers, many at weekends. Like Iarnród Éireann, Bus Éireann offers a Rambler Ticket for unlimited bus travel over a limited period at a low fixed price or a combination of rail and bus travel. These tickets are popular with domestic and overseas travellers.

Before the 1980s bus companies were restricted under the Road Transport Act of 1932. Under this legislation, private companies were denied operating licences if CIE operated a service along the route sought. This was to protect the state company which had an obligation to provide a network of services on uneconomic as well as popular routes.

The change in legislation means that travellers now have a wider variety of services with private operators providing buses and coaches throughout the country, alongside those operated by Bus Éireann.

Coach tours remain popular with a market in which senior citizens predominate. They provide a convenient door-to-door service; all baggage handling is taken care of and couriers are available to give assistance. A good number of Irish companies operate touring coaches. Some provide scheduled tours, from city and local ones lasting a few hours, to those of a week or more. Others charter coaches to overseas companies bringing groups to Ireland either as a single destination or as part of a British Isle or European tour. Coaches from other EC countries are also a familiar sight.

Tour guides are especially busy during the holiday seasons, and are mostly engaged full-time with visiting groups. Fluency in other languages is essential.

Fig. 2

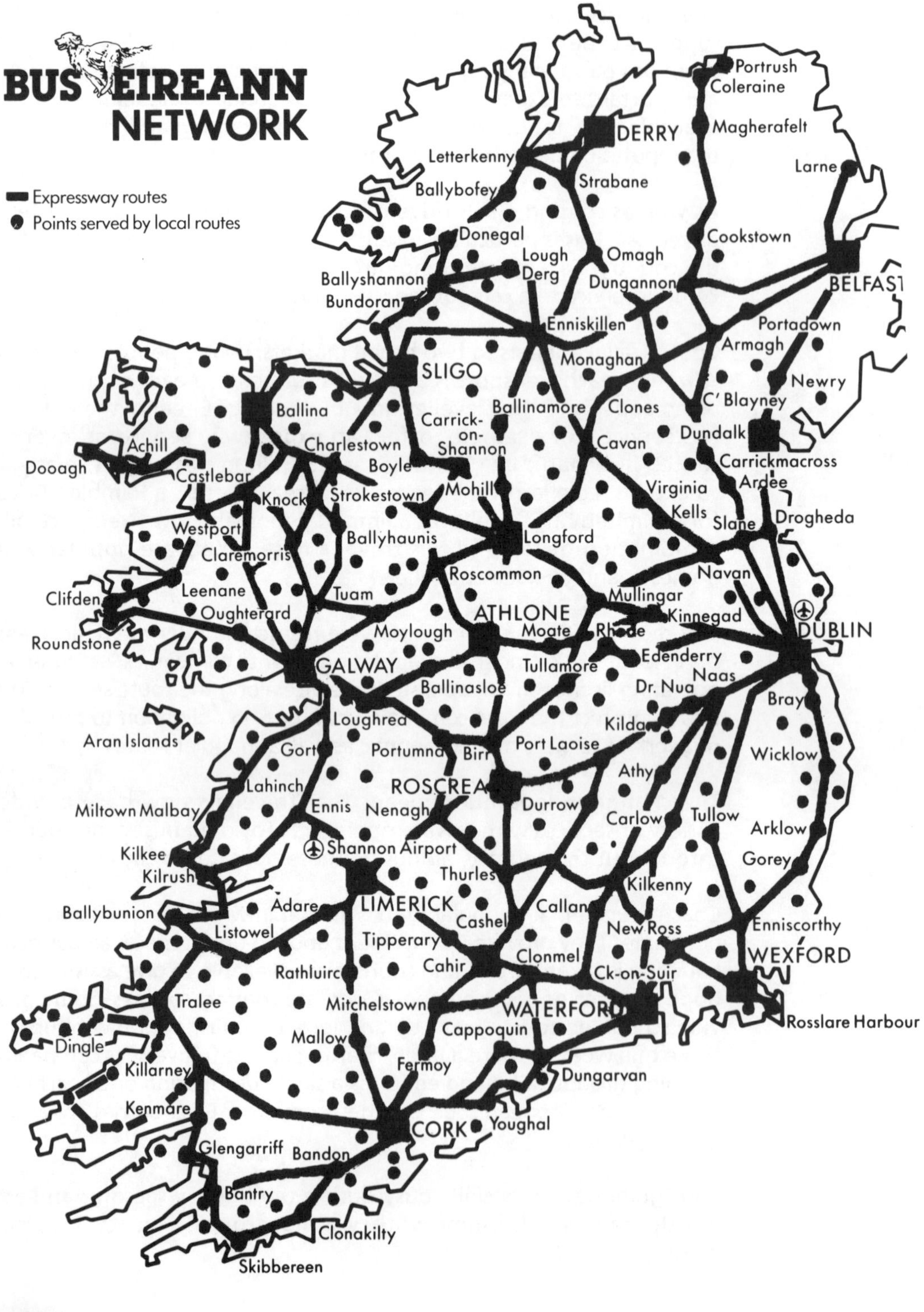

BUS EIREANN
NETWORK

■ Expressway routes
● Points served by local routes

Portrush
Coleraine
DERRY
Magherafelt
Larne
Letterkenny
Ballybofey
Strabane
Donegal
Omagh
Cookstown
Lough Derg
Dungannon
BELFAST
Ballyshannon
Bundoran
Enniskillen
Portadown
Armagh
Monaghan
Newry
SLIGO
Ballinamore
Clones
C' Blayney
Ballina
Carrick-on-Shannon
Cavan
Dundalk
Charlestown
Carrickmacross
Boyle
Ardee
Knock
Strokestown
Mohill
Virginia
Kells
Slane
Drogheda
Westport
Ballyhaunis
Longford
Claremorris
Roscommon
Navan
Clifden
Leenane
Tuam
Mullingar
Kinnegad
DUBLIN
Oughterard
ATHLONE
Moate
Rhode
Roundstone
Moylough
Edenderry
Naas
GALWAY
Tullamore
Dr. Nua
Bray
Aran Islands
Ballinasloe
Kildare
Loughrea
Wicklow
Gort
Portumna
Birr
Port Laoise
Lahinch
ROSCREA
Athy
Miltown Malbay
Ennis
Nenagh
Durrow
Carlow
Tullow
Arklow
Kilkee
Shannon Airport
Gorey
Kilrush
Thurles
Kilkenny
Ballybunion
Adare
LIMERICK
Callan
Enniscorthy
Listowel
Tipperary
Cashel
New Ross
WEXFORD
Rathluirc
Cahir
Clonmel
Ck-on-Suir
Tralee
Mitchelstown
WATERFORD
Rosslare Harbour
Dingle
Mallow
Cappoquin
Killarney
Fermoy
Dungarvan
Kenmare
Youghal
Glengarriff
Bandon
CORK
Bantry
Clonakilty
Skibbereen

Dooagh
Achill
Castlebar

50

Groups visiting Ireland escorted by their own guide often also employ Irish guides for their local knowledge and insight.

Table 4 Mileage of Public Roads, 1977	
Road Classification	Total
National Primary	1,633
National Secondary	1,631
Main (Trunk and Link) other than National	6,662
County	45,947
County Borough	843
Urban	609
	57,325

Sea Transport

As an island, Ireland has always been dependent on access by sea and this is a vital element in the development of the tourism industry.

In fact Ireland's history would have been very different had it not been for its natural approaches by water. The Celts and other early invaders arrived by boat. Christian missionaries travelled to Britain and Europe by sea and made extensive use of water transport around the coasts and along rivers and loughs. Later the Vikings made use of the same routes to attack settlements and maintain their outposts.

Following the discovery of America, Galway became one of the leading ports of Europe. Even today some of the facades of its warehouses survive. Cobh, then Queenstown, became an essential stop for trans-atlantic liners from early in the 19th century. Belfast had one of the largest ship-building industries in the world. Some famous transatlantic liners were built there, including the ill-fated *Titanic*.

Ferries

In the mid 1980s, when deregulation of the airline business resulted in substantially reduced fares, Irish ferry companies realised a change was necessary in their approach in order to remain competitive. This was achieved by introducing value holiday packages and making the packages already on offer more flexible. Short breaks, inclusive holi-days, more frequent sailings and attractive rates both in peak and off-peak season were introduced. The success of these changes is reflected in the growth in the number of cars using the B & I line: from 135,500 in 1986 to 171,000 in 1990.

Ferry companies offer a transport service combining all the amenities of a floating hotel with a range of services including accommodation, catering and entertainment.

The main ports in Ireland are Larne and Belfast in Northern Ireland and Dublin, Dun Laoghaire, Rosslare and Cork in the Republic. Services to and from these link several ports in Great Britain and France; the cross-channel routes are easily the busiest.

The large ferry boats, such as those operated by Irish Ferries or Stena Sealink, can accommodate up to 300 cars and 1,000 passengers on each sailing. The cross-channel journey takes 3–4 hours compared to one hour by plane; France is 17–21 hours away. A newly launched Seacat service from Belfast to Stranraer in 1992 reduced travel time to 90 minutes. This vessel can accommodate 450 passengers and 80 cars in each sailing and because of its speed it has more daily crossings than ferry services.

The impact of the Eurotunnel between England and France will undoubtedly affect all ferry services on the English Channel. The tunnel and the high speed trains using it will result in a 2H–3-hour journey between London and Paris. When it is in full operation it will have the capacity to move millions of people and their cars each year. The challenge facing the ferry companies is greater than ever before.

Smaller ferries also operate around Ireland providing invaluable links with the inhabited islands. A year-round service is provided, weather permitting, primarily for those living on the islands, although services may be increased during holiday periods to cope with demand. These island services include Rathlin, 6 miles off the coast of Antrim, Tory Island and Aran Mór off Co. Donegal and Inishbofin and the Aran Islands off Co. Galway.

Several ferries operate across estuaries around the coast of Ireland. They serve to shorten land journeys where it is not possible to construct bridges. The busiest of these are the Tarbert to Killimer ferry across the Shannon estuary and the Strangford to Portaferry service across Strangford Lough in Co. Down.

Inland Waterways

The inland waterways of Ireland include rivers, canals and loughs. Nowadays transport in itself may be the purpose of a holiday, short break or excursion and this is a market which is being successfully exploited.

A holiday cruise may conjure up a picture of tropical waters, open deck swimming pools and cocktails on board. In Ireland cruising is a self-drive affair, usually on a boat with from four to eight berths on the Shannon, Erne or Grand Canal systems. Although at the mercy of the Irish weather, it can be very pleasant indeed!

The growth in popularity of the inland waterways has resulted in further tourism developments. Hotels, restaurants, bed and breakfasts and marinas have been developed alongside them. Towns like Carrick on Shannon and Killaloe depend on income generated by the river and have developed accordingly. It is estimated that there are well over 500 cruisers and barges for hire on the Shannon, Erne and Grand Canal.

The canals of Ireland are currently the responsibility of the Office of Public Works as a result of the Canals Act 1986. Their task is to maintain the canals for the 'enjoyment and recreation of the public'. The completion of the Erne-Shannon link canal near Ballyconnell in 1993–4 at a cost of IR£30m will further extend and improve tourism links between North and South.

Excursions by boat have been a feature at many seaside resorts. Many years ago places like Bray, Co. Wicklow, had large open boats to carry groups of people across the bay or along the coast. In fact boat excursions are among the attractions that date back to the earliest days of mass holidays when small steam boats were used.

The introduction of tight safety regulations on boats and their crews caused most of these to cease until recent years. Boat excursions have re-appeared at inland towns like Athlone, Enniskillen and Killarney using modern continental-style water-buses, on rivers and canals often in modernised barges, and at sea, for example in Dublin Bay, using small ferries.

Travel Regulations

When going from one country to another the traveller must abide by various regulations. Most travel regulations have their origins in the efforts of national governments to improve public order and health within their borders, so they endeavour to prevent the travel of people deemed to be undesirable and to control the spread of certain health problems. However as similar standards of control are developing all over the world, so the need for national restrictions is reduced. This change is particularly noticeable in travel within the European Community.

Passports

Originally passports were issued by the authorities in one country to commend a traveller to the authorities of another. Now the passport is universally the most important identification document when travelling abroad. In those cases when it is not strictly necessary for entry to a country, it is still strongly recommended. For example in most countries within the EC, people are used to carrying identity papers; this is not so in Ireland and Britain, so the passport serves as identification papers for travellers.

Table 5 Ferry Routes and Carriers, 1992

Route		Carrier
• Rosslare to	Le Havre	Irish Ferries
	Cherbourg	Irish Ferries
	Pembroke	B & I (amalgam with Irish Ferries)
	Fishguard	Stena Sealink Line
• Cork to	Le Havre	Irish Ferries
	Roscoff	Brittany Ferries
	Swansea	Swansea/Cork Car Ferries
• Dublin to	Holyhead	B & I
	Douglas	Isle of Man Steam Packet Co.
• Dun Laoghaire to	Holyhead	Stena Sealink Line
• Larne to	Stranraer	Stena Sealink Line
	Cairnryan	P & O European Ferries
• Belfast to	Stranraer	(Seacat) Hoverspeed Gt Britain
	Douglas	Isle of Man Steam Packet Co.

Visas

While passports are issued by the authorities of a country to its citizens, visas are issued to citizens of other countries to visit the host country. A journey through a number of countries may therefore require a number of visas. Each visa permits one visit or a series of visits over a specified or unspecified period of time by a particular person. For example an Irish citizen is required to have a visa before entering the United States of America. Visa requirements may differ: a British citizen does not need a visa to enter the US. Visas are not required by EC citizens to travel within the EC.

Import Restrictions

Some countries ban the importation of certain goods and limit the value of other articles a traveller may carry. Most ban or restrict imports of firearms, ammunition and drugs; others, foods or plants. The breach of such regulations is usually a criminal offence.

Ireland's agricultural economy depends on being disease-free, therefore animal products and plants may not be imported by travellers without the required documentation. In addition any person who has visited a farm while outside Ireland is asked to contact officials of the Department of Agriculture on arrival.

Domestic pets, like dogs and cats, may be carried freely by those who travel between Britain and Ireland. In both countries diseases such as rabies are rare. However domestic animals may not be imported from the Continent or elsewhere abroad to either Ireland or Britain without their having gone through quarantine, which for dogs and cats is six months.

Duty Free Allowances

Most countries allow a tourist to carry a limited quantity of goods subject to certain conditions without being liable for duty and taxes on them. New regulations came into effect for those travelling within the EC from 1 January 1993 in relation to goods bought in other EC states: with the exception of cars and hydrocarbon oils, all goods bought for personal use and carried by travellers are not subject to duty, except that the traveller with large quantities of tobacco (for example 800 cigarettes) or drink (for example 10 litres of spirits) has to prove they are for personal use. Travellers within the EC will be able to buy duty-free goods until June 1999 subject to existing allowances (for example 200 cigarettes and 1 litre of spirits). Other limits apply to goods, tobacco and drink bought outside the EC.

VAT and Cashback

Value Added Tax applies to many goods and services bought in Ireland. Tourists may reclaim VAT paid on goods bought within two months of departure and carried out when leaving. At the time of purchase the tourist collects the shops' itemised receipts and submits these with the goods to the customs for verification when leaving.

Cashback is a system in which many retailers participate. Cashback vouchers are given to the customer and these may be redeemed at desks at Dublin and Shannon Airports. Travellers from other points have their vouchers stamped by customs, and mailed to the Cashback company for refund.

Exchange Controls

People travelling out of Ireland may be subject to control on the movement of capital, for example buying property abroad, or on the amount of currency they carry. These regulations change from time to time.

Many countries abroad exercise similar controls, and travellers found in possession of even small amounts of cash, albeit innocently, may find this treated very seriously by the authorities.

Innoculations

Whilst serious illnesses like cholera and smallpox are not usually found in Europe, they and many other diseases may be encountered overseas, particularly in tropical countries. For some destinations specified, innoculations against disease may be mandatory or recommended. The prospective tourist should enquire about these well in advance of travelling as some may involve elapsed time or several treatments before a journey.

■ **Case Study: Knock Airport (Connacht Regional Airport)**

On 30 May, 1986, Horan International Airport, or Knock Airport as it is more commonly known, was opened by the then Taoiseach, Mr C. J. Haughey. The development of the airport was due to the single-minded determination of Monsignor James Horan, parish priest of Knock, who hoped that the airport would promote Knock as a shrine as well as provide an airport for the people of the West of Ireland.

At a cost of over IR£13m, raised by private donations and from the government, the airport facilities have been further developed and now consist of a duty free shop, a full restaurant and a first floor observation lounge area.

The airport could not have opened at a better time: the 1980s were a boom period for air travel in Ireland. Despite the opening of other airports around the country, and despite its isolated location, Knock succeeded in attracting increasing visitor numbers throughout that period, growing from 54,000 passengers in 1987 to 170,000 in 1990.

Since the early 1990s, many of the regional airports around the country have suffered badly as a result of recession. Ryanair withdrew services from all regional airports in mid-1992 but has maintained services to and from Knock, Cork, Shannon and Dublin. In 1993 there was a daily service to Stansted from Knock and a bi-weekly service to Luton. In 1992 there were regular charter services to and from New York with American Transair and with Aer Lingus and Air France to European destinations for student and pilgrim traffic. Several local companies use the airport for their private planes.

1. For what reasons was Knock airport developed?

2. How has the airport developed since its opening?

3. What changes were taking place in air travel in Ireland at that time?

4. Study the location of Knock airport on a map;

   a) Consider the alternative means of transport in that area.

   b) What benefits and developments has the airport brought to the area?

5. If the airport at Knock ceased to exist, what would be the implications for the area in terms of tourism?

6. Design a tour package of the region and show how it should be marketed to attract increased business to the airport.

Student Questions and Assignments

1. Discuss the implications for Ireland of the opening of the Channel Tunnel.

2. Discuss the advantages and disadvantages of access to the country by sea and by air for tourists. Map the current access routes to and from Ireland and name the access carriers.

3. 'The need for airlinks between the mainland and the inhabited islands around it is vital for their survival.' Discuss.

4. Contact the ferry companies operating services between Ireland and Britain and compare the services offered — consider in your answers, speed, comfort, cost, flexibility and facilities.

5. What are the benefits derived and problems encountered in relation to the development of a high speed rail service?

6. Find out from your local CIE office the conditions of a Rambler Ticket and devise a marketing strategy, targeting a specific market, promoting the ticket.

7. What benefits did deregulation of the airlines bring to the tourism industry? Consider the importance of such a change to an island country.

8. Will the elimination of customs borders in 1993 benefit tourism in Ireland?

9. Design tour itineraries, using a different means of transport for each scenario;

   a) Twenty French school children, on a mid-term week's holiday to Ireland, aged 12–14 years, arriving by plane into Dublin and leaving via Belfast.

   b) A lone student traveller from Germany, visiting Ireland for a 3-day trip. Landing in Rosslare he plans to visit relations in Malin Head.

   c) An English family of two adults and four children (aged between 3 months and 8 years) visiting Ireland for a week.

   d) A honeymoon couple who have won an all expenses-paid luxurious trip to Ireland for 10–12 days. The couple are American and arrive in Shannon on 23 December.

   Consider cost, flexibility, client profile and the practicalities of the situation in your answers.

10. Why have transport terminals developed a range of services other than those directly related to transport?

4 Tourism Product 2: Accommodation and Catering

Objectives

At the end of this chapter the reader will be able to:

- recognise the range of tourist accommodation available in Ireland

- understand the classification and grading systems in operation in Ireland

- appreciate the distinction between serviced and non-serviced accommodation

- identify the catering facilities provided for tourists.

A tourist, whether travelling on business or pleasure, has two basic needs: accommodation and catering. Since they may affect over 50% of total expenditure (see Table 1) these two factors are significant. If a visitor has a bad experience concerning accommodation or catering, it will leave a negative impression of the whole stay, influence the decision to return and result in bad publicity when back home. Conversely, good experience bodes well for future business.

This chapter examines the scale and importance of the accommodation and catering sectors in the Republic of Ireland. As tourism grows, so too must these vital sectors. Products and services must be maintained to international standards so as to remain competitive.

Accommodation

Anyone making an overnight stay for any reason, will make that decision based on a number of factors, including location and cost. The decision made by a business traveller on an expense account will be different from that reached by a student on a summer holiday touring Europe with a Eurorail card. Each has individual tastes, needs, budgets and reasons for travelling. The accommodation industry must respond to this by offering a wide variety of establishments.

The accommodation industry has changed over the last ten years. With the introduction of new technology such as computerised reception

Table 1 Breakdown of Tourism Expenditure in the Republic of Ireland 1990

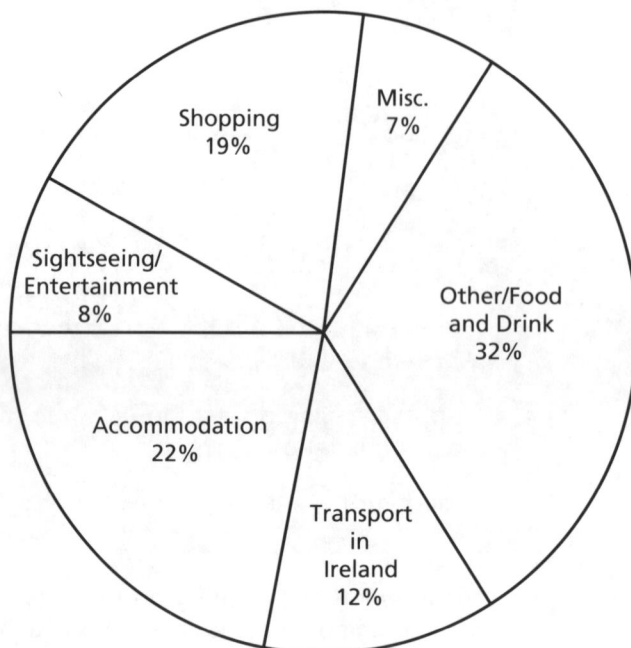

Shopping 19%

Misc. 7%

Sightseeing/ Entertainment 8%

Other/Food and Drink 32%

Accommodation 22%

Transport in Ireland 12%

Source: Bord Fáilte

desks, increased emphasis on staff training and higher standards, and increased expenditure on upgraded facilities, accommodation has gained new recognition of its importance and value in the tourist industry.

However, these changes cannot deal with the principal obstacle facing it: that of perishability. The accommodation product has a 'shelf-life' of exactly 24 hours. In a restaurant, for example, if a menu item is unsold, the food can be stored.

In accommodation, however, if the bed night is not sold, revenue is lost. Coupled with a relatively short season which actually means that many establishments must close for the winter months the accommodation industry has to continually market itself (see Table 2).

Attempts to lengthen the season have been successful to some extent: lower off-season rates, discounts and the promotion of weekend or activity breaks, such as 'golden getaways' for senior citizens—all of these incentives have added considerably to occupancy figures.

Serviced and Non-serviced Accommodation

Within the accommodation sector a distinction is made between serviced accommodation, where meals and housekeeping service are

Table 2 Timing of arrival (all overseas visitors %)									
	1982	1983	1984	1985	1986	1987	1988	1989	1990
Timing of Arrival									
Jan/Feb/March	16	15	14	15	16	14	14	14	14
April	7	6	8	8	6	8	7	7	7
May	8	9	8	8	9	9	9	9	9
June	11	11	12	13	11	11	12	12	12
July	18	19	18	17	17	15	16	17	16
August	16	16	16	15	14	15	14	13	14
September	10	10	9	9	10	10	9	10	10
Oct/Nov/Dec	13	13	15	15	16	17	19	18	16

Source: Bord Fáilte Statistics '91

provided, and non-serviced where they are not; the latter category is often referred to as self-catering. The distinction between the two categories may sometimes be blurred; for example Mosney Holiday Centre and certain youth hostels provide both.

Although Visiting Friends and Relatives (VFR) is the largest single category of people staying in Ireland, tourism trends and changes in the industry have greatly influenced the variety and range of accommo-dation services now available. Market demands have led to the development of different types of accommodation in response to the increasing numbers of visitors, their requirements and expectations (see Table 3).

The market for youth hostels, for example, used to be limited to the individual back-packer, but nowadays, youth hostels also attract families with children. The industry must be constantly aware of the demands of the market place and meet them.

The range and variety of serviced accommodation in Ireland has grown annually in response to the needs of the market. Government and EC funding has made available a number of financial incentives to assist establishments in upgrading their premises and facilities. Bedroom extensions, conference facilities and leisure areas are just some of the improvements made.

Hotels

Hotels may be divided principally into two categories: those operated by groups and those which are owner or family-run. International hotel chains such as Sheraton, Inter-Continental and Holiday Inn have been slow to enter the Irish market though the Forte hotel chain has a number of hotel properties in the Republic. In 1989 Hilton USA opened the

Table 3 Accommodation for Overseas Visitors

Accommodation Used %	Total O' seas	Britain	Mainland Europe	North America	Other Areas
Hotel	29	24	27	48	26
Guesthouse	6	4	5	8	15
Irish Home	17	8	25	32	24
Farmhouse	3	2	4	5	7
Rented	5	5	7	4	4
Caravan	2	2	3	—	1
Camping	3	1	9	1	1
Unlisted	7	5	8	13	11
Friends/Relatives	43	59	17	26	38
Youth Hostels	5	1	12	6	10

Source: Bord Fáilte Statistics '91

Conrad Hotel in Dublin and the Club Med leisure chain recently opened a hotel and leisure development in Waterville, Co. Kerry. As so very often happens, when one group enters the marketplace, rival groups then take an interest.

The main Irish-based hotel groups are Doyle Hotels, around Dublin, and Ryan Hotels, Jurys and Great Southern Hotels, which are country-wide. These groups alone account for over 4,000 bedrooms.

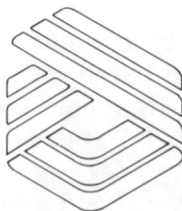

DOYLE HOTEL GROUP

The majority of hotels in Ireland are, however, family or owner-run. These properties range in size and type, each has something different to offer. This may in fact give some insight into why some international hotel chains marketing a standard product worldwide, have been slow to enter the Irish market. One of the main advantages hotel groups have over individual establishments is that of marketing as their combined budgets enable them to promote and market their properties extensively. To counteract this, some owner-run hotels have banded together under a common name and groups such as Manor House and Village Inn hotels allow member hotels to remain independent while enjoying the marketing benefits of a group.

Other guest accommodation marketing groups in Ireland include: Choice International Hotels Ireland; Best Western Hotels — Ireland; Platinum Ireland Hotels; among international marketing consortia to which some Irish properties are affiliated are: Small Luxury Hotels, Leading Hotels of the World and Relais et Chateaux.

JURYS
HOTEL GROUP
DUBLIN • CORK • LIMERICK • WATERFORD

While the luxury end of the market has flourished (see Table 4) demand also has remained constant for more basic accommodation, grades B and C. Luxury hotels such as the Kildare Hotel and Country Club or Sheen Falls Lodge, Co. Kerry have been built at the cost of millions of pounds. Less expensive hotels are also being developed, with several proposals for properties to be developed such as Forte Travelodge in Cork and the Jurys Inns in Galway and Dublin.

✿ Great Southern Hotel

Table 4 Number of Hotels by grade

	1985	1986	1987	1988	1989	1990	1991	1992
Grade A*	13	14	15	15	17	19	19	22
Grade A	107	106	105	109	113	116	120	123
Grade B*	141	145	144	144	153	158	162	178
Grade B	256	254	258	262	259	253	243	253
Grade C	116	124	128	135	117	106	107	110
Grade Pending	10	7	14	15	21	6	17	8
Total	643	650	664	680	680	658	668	694

Source: Bord Fáilte

Guesthouses and Bed and Breakfasts

The popularity of guesthouse, townhouse and farmhouse accommodation has also grown. This sector of serviced accommodation provides a quality product throughout the country. A lot of people like the intimacy of smaller establishments and the closer links that they may have with the local community. On a conservation point, many old

country houses have been carefully restored and renovated as guesthouses, whereas in the past many of them have been left derelict. The Town and Country Homes Association is a voluntary organisation which produces a handbook of listed members, about 1,200; the Association is very active in marketing on behalf of its members.

Hostels

Youth Hostelling (see Table 3), is particularly attractive to the European market. This is largely made up of individuals; youth hostels suit them perfectly. An Oige, the Irish Youth Hostel Association, was founded in 1931 with just two hostels and 215 members. By 1992, this number had increased to 40 hostels and 24,440 members.

An Oige is part of a worldwide network which numbers over 5,000 hostels. Groups, families and individuals are all catered for and An Oige has activity holidays on offer as well as simply providing accommodation. Buildings vary in size and type, from castles to cottages, while facilities are standard throughout. There are also a number of independent hostels around Ireland.

Self-catering

Non-serviced accommodation or self-catering is generally less expensive than serviced accommodation as overhead costs involved are lower. While cost is an important factor, the flexibility of self-catering is often equally attractive. Independence and the ability to come and go as they please appeals to many.

Self-catering accommodation ranges from the camp site, which offers basic facilities, to the Rent-an-Irish-Cottage scheme, which features a traditional Irish thatched cottage with all modern conveniences.

IRISH COTTAGE HOLIDAY HOMES

Rented accommodation has always been popular in Ireland, with both foreign and domestic visitors temporarily moving house and experiencing life in a different area. Coastal areas are particularly popular, especially to those who live in cities. Often, chalets or cottages to let are second homes which the owners rent for part, or all of the year, to supplement their income. Home exchange holidays through schemes such as Intervac are also becoming increasingly popular.

Time-share is usually associated with the United States and with European countries like Greece or Spain where one buys one or more weeks which will be available for holidays every year, with the price usually depending on the popularity of the time of year. Time-share is also now available in Ireland in a number of locations.

Classification and Grading

Most countries operate a hotel classification or grading scheme which categorises establishments by the facilities they provide. The value of such schemes is two-fold, in that they ensure specific standards within a certain grade or classification while also giving the customer a guide to facilities, price and so on. While other EC countries such as the UK or Denmark operate voluntary schemes, Ireland, under the control of Bord Fáilte, operates a compulsory scheme and it is based on national legislation (Tourism Traffic Act, 1939).

The existing scheme uses a grading system: hotels are graded under five categories A*, A, B*, B, and C; and guesthouses under three categories A, B and C. Each property must be registered with Bord Fáilte and an annual inspection assesses their facilities and quality. An example of Accommodation Guide entries appears opposite and a list of the symbols used appears below. A new system is planned which will adopt a five-star rating: 5*, 4*, 3*, 2* and 1*. This system will identify the presence of facilities rather than rank their quality as is the position at present. However, if the quality of the facilities is unacceptable, the establishment may not be graded at all. The new classifications will reflect only on the facilities provided and what makes a good or bad hotel will be left to the opinion of the visitor.

SYMBOLS

General Facilities

km	Distance from town
C	Price reduction for Children
R	Member of Regional Tourism Organisation
P	Car parking
	Central heating
	Elevator/Lift
	Facilities for pets
	Facilities for trained guide dogs
	Garden for visitors use
T	Can be booked through a travel agent
	Experience a working farm
	Conference facilities
	Family Friendly Hotel (facilities for children)

Bedroom Facilities

	Total number of rooms
	Number of rooms with bath/shower and toilet
	Direct dial from bedrooms
TV	TV in bedrooms

Meals and Drinks Facilities

	Licenced to sell all alcoholic drinks
	Licenced to sell wine only
àlc	A la carte meals provided

Sports Facilities

	Bicycles for hire
	Angling facilities
U	Horse riding/pony trekking facilities
	Games room
	Gym only
	Leisure complex
	Indoor swimming pool
	Outdoor swimming pool
	Sauna only
	Squash court
	Tennis court
S	Snooker (Full Size Table)
	9-hole golf Course
	18-hole golf Course

Credit Cards

VM	Visa/Barclay card accepted
AM	Access/Master card accepted
AE	American Express card accepted
DE	Diners card accepted

		Schull ⬤₉ 🎵									
H	B	**EAST END,** Main Street, Tel:(028)28101 15🛏 6🚻 AE VB 🚗 ⬅️ℙⓉⒸ	01/Jan-31/Dec	20.00	17.00	25.00	20.00	5.00f	12.00✕	45.00	
H	C	**COLLA HOUSE,** Tel:(028)28105/28497, Fax:28105 10🛏 8🚻 R 🚗 AM AE DE VB ☎ 🍴 🚗 ⬅️ℙⓉ🚗Ⓒ	01/Jan-31/Dec	16.00 18.50	15.00 17.50	20.00 25.00	18.00 22.00	6.00f	16.00✕	45.00 50.00	10
G	B*	**CORTHNA LODGE,** Tel:(028)28517, Fax:28517 1km 6🛏 6🚻 🚗 🚗 ❀ ⓎℙⓉⒸ	01/Mar-31/Dec	18.00 20.00		22.00 25.00					
C	I	**MRS. M. HEGARTY,** Cape View, Coorydorigan, Tel:(028)28446 3🛏 R ▤ ℙ	01/Jun-01/Sep		13.00				10.00✕		
C	I	**MRS. D. HOLT,** White Castle Cottage, Ardintenant, Tel:(028)28528 3km 3🛏 1🚻 R ▤ ℙ	01/Jan-31/Dec	15.00	13.00		16.00		12.00✕		
C	I	**MRS. MARIE MACFARLANE,** Hillside, Tel:(028)28248 3🛏 2🚻 R ▤ 🚗 ℙ	01/Apr-30/Sep	15.00	13.00		18.00				

In addition to Bord Fáilte's grading, there are many other private sector classification schemes. These schemes are voluntary and are undertaken by individuals or organisations. In most cases, the schemes are primarily marketing tools for the hoteliers and the classifying organisation. Organisations such as the Automobile Association (AA) and the Irish Country Houses and Restaurants produce annual guides, the AA Guide, and The Blue Book (see Table 5). These schemes may cover a wide variety of establishments or be limited to a specific market. For the hotelier or restaurant such publications represent a means of marketing, being promoted as a group, or targeting a specific market cost effectively. Some of the Accommodation and Catering Guides published by, or in co-operation with, Bord Fáilte include:

- Guest Accommodation

- Official Tourist Board guide to accommodation in hotels, guesthouses, homes in town and country and farmhouses and caravan and camping parks — published annually

- Caravan and Camping Guide

- Be Our Guest — An Irish Hotels Federation illustrated publication of hotels and guesthouses

- Self-Catering Guide

- Farmhouse Association Guide

- Dining in Ireland — premises range from serving haute cuisine to simple bar food

- Town and Country Homes Association Guide

- Special value Tourist Menu — listing of restaurants providing special value meals.

Table 5 Example of Private Sector Classification Scheme.

Automobile Association (AA).

* Hotels simply furnished, but clean and well kept; all bedrooms with hot and cold running water; adequate bath and lavatory facilities.

** Hotels offering a higher standard of accommodation; adequate bath and lavatory facilities on all main floors, and some private bathrooms and/or showers.

*** Well-appointed hotels, with a large number of bedrooms with private bathrooms/showers.

**** Exceptionally well-appointed hotels offering a very high standard of comfort and service with all bedrooms providing private bathrooms/showers.

***** Luxury hotels offering the highest international standards.

AA Hotels and Restaurants of Europe, 1990.

Catering for Tourists

Eating out is part of any holiday or business visit. While the accommodation industry almost exclusively serves markets outside the immediate area, the opposite can be true of the catering industry. Many catering establishments are year-round operations, serving the local population as well as visitors. More and more people are eating out. Changes in lifestyles, more disposable income and a greater variety of eating establishments have all contributed to this and variety ranges from expensive à la carte restaurants to take-away snacks.

Restaurants

The restaurant trade is subject to fashions and changes in taste. The emphasis some years ago on nouvelle cuisine has since changed to an emphasis on more healthy eating, with the public watching closely what is being presented. Recession and cutbacks can greatly affect this trade. Bord Fáilte produces annual Dining Out in Ireland guides and these indicate the cuisine on offer and an estimate of the price range for the à la carte and table d'hôte menus. In keeping with international practice the catering industry provides tourist menus. These are limited menus, generally offering a selection from the full menu at a competitive price. In a 1988 CERT study, there were 680 restaurants in the Republic

Eamon McKeon of the Great Southern Hotel group says its business from Italy looks set to increase by five or six per cent. The company made a deliberate policy of diversifying its market base some years ago so as to diminish what was correctly perceived to be an excessive reliance on American coach parties.

"If we'd still been dependent on the same market last year", claims Mr McKeon, "we'd have probably gone into a loss-making situation". He calculates that business from American coaches dropped some 35 per cent in 1991 and even though a revival is now due, that section of the hotel chain's turnover is just one-third of what it used to be.

Many hoteliers complain that continental Europeans are less likely to stay in the larger establishments and certainly Dublin's major hotels have suffered from a changing market. Most of them manage comfortably enough outside summer by providing accommodation for business visitors. But July and August have traditionally been the months when their rooms were given over to the tourist trade.

Unfortunately, the European traveller is not terribly interested in visiting Dublin because, as one continental operator bluntly explained, "we have better cities at home". Europeans prefer to head for the country and to stay in smaller hotels and guesthouses.

Mary McGee, chief executive of the Town and Country Homes Association, confirms the rise in business from Europe for her 1,300 members. Even economic troubles abroad have left this part of the market unaffected: "In a recession", says Ms McGee, "our accommodation is likely to do better than deluxe hotels".

She is "hoping for a reasonably good year", although like everyone else, she does not expect business to be as fantastic as in 1990, a year which has already acquired the status of a golden age.

In Galway, Mary McLoughlin has been running a bed and breakfast house for nearly 20 years and has therefore survived both the good years and the bad. "There are fewer Americans nowadays," she agrees, with the market "spread much more wide, with more continentals, right across the spectrum." The great strength of her business, she says, is talking to visitors. "People come to stay in your home because they want to chat about the country with you."

Hackneyed it may be, but the Irish people remains one of the country's best assets. "A very good selling point is the people here," says Bord Fáilte's German manager Gunther Klein. But he insists that the other advantage for European visitors is access to a wide variety of sporting facilities. So businesses involved in this side of the tourism industry have expanded steadily.

Carrick Crafts in Co Leitrim has been offering cruise boats on the Shannon for 20 years. The company has grown rapidly in the recent past, last year adding eight new luxury vessels to its fleet. According to manager, Liam Lalor, 70 per cent of the business comes from continental Europe, half of which is German. No wonder, therefore, that all manuals are available in a number of continental languages and the reception area contains as many notices in German as English. After a slow start to the season, booking picked up suddenly four weeks ago and now "I think it'll be as good as last year."

Fifty per cent of Carrick Craft's hirers are repeat business and Mr Lalor believes that "even if there is a recession, the last people affected will be the boating fraternity." The lesson here seems to be that if the product is popular, the tourist market can feel secure.

An article from *The Irish Times* on the effects of the economy on the accommodation industry today employing 10,570 people on full-time, casual or seasonal basis. The Restaurant Association of Ireland represents many of these restaurants, with a membership of 400 in 1992. Not only a lobby group, it also promotes the restaurant trade and organises campaigns to attract people to eat out. Private sector guides are also produced annually; and one of the best known is the Michelin Guide. *Guides Michelin* covers all of Europe and assesses restaurants under strict criteria. A rating in its publications is considered very prestigious and a welcome form of advertising. Only two restaurants in Ireland gained a 1* rating in 1992, the Roscoff restaurant in Belfast and Patrick Guilbaud's in Dublin.

The range and number of ethnic restaurants in Ireland has grown rapidly — Chinese, Indian, Greek, Japanese and so on. These restaurants are often owned, managed and staffed by families from these countries. In 1988, there were over 150 ethnic restaurants in Ireland; while the majority of these are located in major cities and towns, some have relocated to country areas.

Popular catering establishments have become very numerous in recent years. This category includes self-service cafés, fast-food outlets and so on, and represents the largest group of catering establishments — a total of 680 in 1988, employing 16,438.

Fast-food outlets such as multi-national companies like McDonalds or Burger King and national companies such as Abrakebabra and Supermac are expanding. These establishments are centrally located, with extended opening hours serving convenience food at reasonable prices. Many small family-run outlets operate throughout the country.

All catering establishments are governed by the Health, Safety and Welfare at Work Act, 1989. Caterers who fail to comply with the regulations may be fined or closed down.

Food Attractions

Mediaeval banquets and food festivals are two areas with particular

appeal for the tourist market. Banquets are held in the restored castles of Bunratty, Knappogue and Dunguaire, and musicians, singers and dancers entertain patrons throughout the evening. Banquets with traditional entertainment are also held elsewhere including the Brú Ború at Cashel, Tipperary. Annual food festivals such as the Kinsale Gourmet Festival, the Clarinbridge Oyster Festival and the World Barbecue Festival have gained worldwide recognition for Irish cuisine. These festivals concentrate on promoting the best of Irish produce and have flourished to become major events in the annual tourism calendar.

Some hotels have developed dinner/cabaret evenings usually featuring Irish music and entertainment; these include Jurys Irish Cabaret, Clontarf Castle, and Doyles Irish Cabaret in Dublin.

Pubs

In a 1990 survey of overseas business travellers Guinness and Baileys Irish Cream reached first and second place in awareness of an Irish product, even ahead of Waterford Crystal which came third. These products are as well known and famous worldwide as the thatched cottages and green fields of Ireland.

An estimated 14,500 premises are licensed to sell liquor in the country such as restaurants, pubs, clubs, off-licences and shops, all of which are governed by the Intoxicating Liquor Act ('88).

In villages and towns, the pub is central to the infrastructure of the local community, often also housing a shop or post office. In larger towns however, the pubs have become central to the overall tourism product offering food, drink, entertainment and in some cases, even accommodation.

The history of distilling in Ireland has also been promoted as a tourist attraction in itself. Bushmills in Co. Antrim, Guinness in Dublin and Midleton Breweries in Cork attract thousands of visitors annually. The history of the distilling process is explained, while the end-of-tour sampling of the finished product can extend the length of the visit considerably! Durty Nelly's pub in Bunratty, Co. Clare, is almost as famous as Bunratty castle and is considered a compulsory stop on many itineraries. In recent years there has been a substantial increase in the number of pubs serving food — ranging from snacks to full meals. Supervised children are welcome and this combined with the availability of food has resulted in a change of clientele now visiting pubs. Competitions such as the Caterplan National Bar Catering Competitions help to promote the concept of quality pub grub.

Visitors enjoy the informality of Irish pub life and the opportunity to mingle with local people. The Irish have a reputation for being gregarious and the type of casual acquaintance that may be struck up in pubs is an attractive facet of Irish life for visitors. Traditional entertainment whether planned or impromptu, is an appealing feature of pub life for tourists, as are old style ambience and open fires.

Hygiene, Health and Safety Regulations

The importance of hygiene, health and safety in the food industry cannot be ignored. Incidences of food poisoning or accidents through inadequate provision of fire safety equipment cause serious damage to the reputation of the whole tourist industry in Ireland. While there is legislation to protect the public, the obligation to meet the specified requirements lies with the industry; unfortunately it is not uncommon to find staff and management whose attitude to health and safety is unprofessional. However, increased awareness of the need for hygiene and safety among trained staff have resulted in changes, not only in meeting the requirements, but in terms of attitude.

Legislation such as the Safety, Health and Welfare at Work Act 1989 (Ireland) covers the national workforce and ensures the working environment for all staff is to a specific standard. The Food Hygiene Regulations 1950–71 (Ireland) relate primarily to proprietors in the food business and a breach of these regulations can result in a fine, a prison sentence or both. The first principle of the regulations lays down that 'no person shall sell or offer for sale for human consumption any article of food, food animal or food material which is diseased, contaminated, or otherwise unfit for human consumption.' Food workers are obliged to keep clean and to follow hygienic work practices. Premises may be checked by environmental health officers employed by the Health Boards who can recommend that a food premises' registration be cancelled.

The Fire Service Act, 1981 (Ireland) requires owners of premises to which the public has access to take all reasonable measures against the outbreak of fire.

The Hotel Proprietors Act, 1963 (Ireland), in the sections relating to health and safety says that 'the proprietor of the hotel is under duty to take reasonable care of the person of the guest and to ensure that for the purpose of the personal use by the guest, the premises are as safe as reasonable care and skill can make them'.

Hospitality and Customer Care

The development of Irish tourism has evolved over many years, and throughout this growth period one of the country's greatest assets has been the Irish people and their hospitable and welcoming nature. This has implications for the whole tourism industry and particularly for those in the accommodation and catering sectors who have close contact with visitors and holidaymakers.

Hospitality is essentially about service. There are two main types of service — material and personal. Material service relates to quality, quantity, price and timing of food, drink, physical comfort, information and working methods. This can range from an appetising lunch special to a well-appointed bedroom.

Material service is generally something concrete and visible which the customer can easily recognise. It is impossible to provide good personal service without the back-up of good material service. Yet the visitor is often unaware of material service no matter how high the standard. Comments are more likely to be made on a material service when it is below standard. 'What clean toilets!' is less likely to be heard than loud complaints if the toilets are dirty.

Because material service is easier to define and analyse, many companies give priority to this in their investment decisions and advertising. Yet research shows that it is the level of personal service that is most often the deciding factor in tourists' choice and where material service falls below par, it may well be forgiven if the tourist is treated with warmth and respect.

Good personal service is about creating a sense of well-being, a feeling that needs are being met, and business valued. It is difficult to define personal service as it cannot be weighed or measured, and its assessment is very subjective. Good service means different things to different people. The challenge for people in the tourism industry is to anticipate and meet the needs of tourists as far as possible; good service means giving customers a little more than they expect.

Often for customers the point of contact makes no impact, it is neutral, neither good nor bad. However, if they are ignored, treated rudely or cheated, they are left with feelings of anger and frustration and may never do business with that company again.

73

At other times the attention customers receive seems special. The service-giver is friendly, warm and attentive and is prepared to go to trouble for them. This leaves them with positive feelings of appreciation and pleasure which encourages them to do repeat business with the company in question and recommend it to others. Customer loyalty means good business.

There are many interpretations of the term service; it is difficult to define because it is such a subjective matter.

What makes it so subjective?

• Service in one country or culture can be viewed differently by people with different experience, education, age and background

• Service may be perceived differently by the same person at different times depending on immediate needs and mood

• Everybody has a different standard of quality

• How service is seen depends on people's expectations.

Customer relations is seen as a fundamental training subject for those dealing with people, not only in Ireland but throughout Europe. Some believe it should be available to everyone as a part of general education. Many countries, including Ireland, pride themselves on what in German is called *gemutlichkeit*: it is difficult to define precisely — something like a welcoming atmosphere. While this is a worthy objective, many people also have a feeling that contributing to good service in some way involves servility, something alien to the self-confidence and pride that individuals feel today.

In fact, providing good customer care consists of having high standards oneself and then treating other people in the same way; it is a good rule of life at work or at play. And good customer care can arise when not working in hospitality or when off duty. Individual visitors' impressions of a destination are not based solely on the service they pay for; the way they are treated by local people in general contributes to impressions. This becomes most apparent in the press and other media comment that reaches prospective visitors. However good the hotel and restaurant, however efficient the transport, it is often the public who provide the material for adverse publicity: for example people who insist on smoking in no-smoking areas, who litter the landscape, or make the environment noisy for others.

As there are so many interpretations of service, great efforts have been made by training, and educational bodies such as CERT, or in-house training schemes, to educate and make staff aware of the importance of this aspect of the overall product. New educational programmes have been developed to extend tourism awareness to the wider public so that everybody may contribute to the overall success of this major industry.

Case Study: The Kildare Hotel and Country Club

The Kildare Hotel and Country Club is a grade A* property located in Straffan, Co. Kildare, about 23 miles from Dublin. The property is set within 330 acres of countryside of mature woodland and lakes. The hotel is built around the original stately home, Barton House, and has been developed to create 'an hotel uniquely Irish and of the highest standard'; this ideal, coupled with an investment of IR£28m, earned the property the first AA 5 star hotel rating in Ireland.

The hotel has 45 bedrooms, 12 of which are suites. Each bedroom is decorated differently and every effort has been made to maintain the spaciousness and character of the old house while simultaneously providing up-to-date amenities. Each room has an audio-visual centre consisting of radio, television and video, mini-bar and individual personal safes. Room rates ranged from IR£190 per night to IR£800 for the Viceroy Suite in 1992.

There are five private dining rooms, with the cuisine on offer a combination of international with an Irish flavour. Two magnificent drawing rooms and an intimate cocktail bar are also beautifully furnished and in keeping with the period of the house.

The property has two private meeting/conference rooms which can accommodate 75 people. Video, slide-projection, recording and video conferencing are just some of the facilities and services on offer to visitors.

A pool complex adjacent to the hotel building has a bar, massage room, hairdressing and beauty salon, fully-equipped exercise room and saunas.

The 'K' Club is located 400 yards from the hotel. This maintains the privacy of the property while being close enough for hotel guests to avail of it. The 13,000 square foot clubhouse houses a bar and restaurant as well as a fully equipped office for those who require a business service.

The Arnold Palmer designed golf course which extends over 200 acres has already gained international recognition. The nearby sports complex houses tennis courts. The golf course is open to non-members and a daily sports pass is available for IR£110 which covers all facilities except the swimming pool. For use of the 18-hole golf course only, green fees are IR£70. Hotel guests may use the golf course for IR£50 per day; swimming, tennis, squash and croquet may also be enjoyed at no additional cost. In 1992, membership of the 'K' Club involved an initial payment of IR£10,000 and an annual subscription of IR£2,500. It includes all the facilities on offer at the 'K' Club and at the hotel.

Other on-site sporting facilities include fishing, both lake and river, and shooting. Equestrian facilities are on offer off-site.

1. 'Ireland was one of the few countries in the world that didn't have a rich man's playground.' How has the development of the Kildare Hotel and Country Club changed this? What other properties in Ireland cater for the luxury market?

2. Identify and analyse strengths, weaknesses, opportunities and threats in relation to the Kildare Hotel and Country Club.

3. What emphasis does this kind of establishment place on staff requirements? Consider in your answer, training, supervision, management, payment, service etc.

4. Design a luxury itinerary for a group of Continental Europeans, for a six-day period, arriving in Dublin and departing from Shannon.

Case Study: The Sligo Park Hotel

The Sligo Park Hotel is located in Sligo town, and is easily accessible by air, road and rail. The town lies on the North West coast of Ireland overlooking the Atlantic Ocean. The region of which the heart is Yeats Country, offers a varied landscape of sea, rivers, mountains and lakes.

The Sligo Park Hotel is a modern grade A* hotel set in seven acres off the main Sligo – Galway road. It has 90 bedrooms, each of which has bathroom, colour television, hairdryer and direct dial telephone. Executive rooms offer extra space and stylish furnishings to meet the needs of busy business people.

The Hazelwood restaurant offers a varied and interesting menu, specialising in local produce with a first rate service from highly qualified staff. Full Irish breakfast is available, with table d'hôte and à la carte menus available for lunch and dinner. The Rathanna bar, as well as being a place for locals and residents to meet and unwind, also has a range of snacks on offer. There is a resident pianist on Saturday and Sunday evenings.

Whether servicing a small conference or a large banquet, the staff of all departments will offer their skills and facilities to ensure a successful event for between 10 and 450 people. Access is available to a wide range of audio-visual equipment on request.

One of the most important features of the hotel is the leisure centre. Among the facilities available are the fully equipped gymnasium, swimming pool, whirlpool, plunge pool, children's pool, steam room, sauna, snooker, sunbed and two outdoor tennis courts — something to suit everyone's taste.

Three 18-hole golf courses are available nearby while pony-trekking, sailing, deep sea fishing, shooting and scenic tours of the area can easily be arranged. For the less energetic, there are miles of sandy beaches for walks or simply admiring the view!

1. Contact a tourist information office and enquire about accommodation available in Sligo town, ranging from youth hostels, bed and breakfasts, and camp sites to hotels. Compare and contrast the facilities available at each with the tariffs charged.

2. Design a luxury suite for the Sligo Park Hotel. Suggest several services which could be made available to guests, and also some bedroom and bathroom features to make the room more luxurious. For example, shoe shine service or bathrobes in the room.

3. Design a brochure for conference guests highlighting the features and attractions offered by the hotel which would especially appeal to business men and women.

4. Study Sligo on the map and draw up a 4-day touring holiday for a honeymoon couple, returning to the Sligo Park each evening, and market it accordingly.

5. Using key selling words to make the package as attractive as possible, design Christmas and New Year's holiday packages for the hotel.

Student Questions and Assignments

1. How has the accommodation industry changed in the last ten years? Discuss the implications of these changes from both the visitor and industry points of view.

2. What methods does the accommodation industry adopt to overcome the problems of perishability and seasonality? Give examples among city and country establishments.

3. Study Table 4 — Number of Hotels by Grade

   a) On a pie-chart, demonstrate the current percentages of all hotels in each grade.

   b) What hotels would fall under the category of 'grade pending'?

   c) Suggest reasons for the growth in the number of grade A hotels.

4. What are the principal differences between serviced and non-serviced accommodation? Compile a list of both types in your area.

5. Identify three other EC countries which operate a compulsory classification scheme and three which operate voluntary schemes. List some advantages and disadvantages in operating both types of scheme.

6. What are the principal changes from the former grading system in the new Bord Fáilte classification scheme? What problems are associated with the existing scheme?

7. Imagine the restaurants in your area came together to promote tourist dining out. Select about ten suitable establishments for the group and draw up a marketing plan for it.

8. Identify a food festival in your region and assess its benefit to the area with reference to employment, revenue and promotion of the area. How beneficial are food festivals to the Irish tourism industry?

9. Consider the importance of in-house procedures for the following situations:

   • a fire alarm

   • a suspicious parcel in the building

   • an accident in the hotel kitchen.

10. Using role plays, how should the following situations be handled?

   • a customer who claims that the meal is cold

   • a tourist who has checked into a twin room — but at 7 p.m. requests a change to a double room. The hotel is fully booked.

- a tourist who calls to a hotel seeking information about week-end packages — consider in your role-play how to sell the services of other departments within the establishment.

11. Assess and discuss a catering establishment in your local area under the following headings and say how these are inter-related:

- price

- product

- service.

5 Tourism Product 3: Attractions and Services

Objectives

At the end of this chapter the reader will be able to:

- know the range of major tourist attractions available to holidaymakers in Ireland

- classify tourist attractions under the headings of natural and man-made and link these to leisure, events and festivals, crafts, factory visits, theme parks and heritage centres

- recognise the contribution of attractions to overall visitor numbers and to holidaymakers' satisfaction levels.

No matter what the destination, the choice available and variety of tourist attractions, activities, entertainment and sightseeing plays a major part in the holiday. Each nationality is attracted to different pastimes and features among those that Ireland has to offer (see Table 1), so a wide range of attractions to cater for all markets has been developed.

Sightseeing and entertainment account for about 8% of the total holiday spend, so the visitor's expectations of a tourist attraction, value for money, entertainment content, cleanliness and accessibility can have implications for the whole holiday. Just as poor standards of accommodation can spoil a holiday and result in bad publicity, so too can badly managed tourist attractions: overcrowding, lack of cleanliness, poorly trained staff and high admission fees may all lead to a negative impression.

Day-trippers, too, often visit tourist attractions as part of a day out, and positive feedback from this market will encourage others. Tourist attractions, not only in Ireland, but worldwide, are marketed to attract as many visitors as possible. However a saturation point may eventually be reached; overcrowding results and numbers start to decline due to delays, lack of adequate parking and lengthy queues.

Tourist attractions can be classified into two groups, natural and man-made.

Table 1 Pastimes participated in by holidaymakers

	Country/Region		
	GB	US	Continental Europe
Historical/Cultural Places	37	79	70
Stately Homes/Gardens	9	34	24
Traditional Music	26	36	39
Banquets	2	21	2
Festivals	5	4	9

Source: Survey of Travellers (1985)

Natural Attractions

Natural attractions in Ireland range from caves such as those found in Mitchelstown, Co. Cork, Aillwee near Ballyvaughan, Co. Clare or Dunmore, Co. Kilkenny to wildlife parks and gardens throughout the country.

VISIT
AILLWEE
CAVE
-for a great day out

Ireland's climate is not conducive to some outdoor attractions — the idea of an open-air theme park doesn't compare with a similar idea for the Caribbean Islands! However that in itself is an attraction to many; Ireland's climate is moderate with no extremes of temperature and even its winter can be a draw to some.

The natural and green landscape of Ireland is world renowned, thus the climate becomes a feature, a unique selling point, given the distinct vegetation and variety in the landscape that attracts thousands to visit its National Parks annually, for example.

Man-made Attractions

Man-made attractions range from Kilkenny Castle built in 1172 and the Waterworld complex in Bundoran to the Tyrone Crystal Factory. There are many categories under this broad heading and some of these will be looked at in more detail in this chapter. Generally speaking, these attractions are weather-proof and aim to appeal to a broad market of all ages.

Attracting Tourist Numbers

Tourist attractions, natural and man-made, are very dependent on advertising to attract visitors in large numbers. If, for example, the Marble Arch Caves in Co. Fermanagh or Celtworld in Co. Waterford decided not to advertise, there would be no need for large-scale parking facilities, interpretative centres, tourist information centres, tea rooms and gift centres — the demand would not merit the investment. When attractions are advertised the converse is true: tourists are actively encouraged to visit them. Through admission charges, facilities such as car-parks and toilets are provided; tea shops, craft and gift centres encourage visitors to linger. Tourists visit well-equipped attractions in their thousands, (see Table 2); examples include Marble Arch Caves (55,000 in 1991) and Celtworld attracted 123,000 people in its first five months of operation.

Conservationists are becoming increasingly worried about the long-term effects of promoting natural areas of the countryside. The fear is that unique, natural features will be eroded due to the volume of visitors and may eventually be ruined. While some say that careful control and management can offset this danger, others argue that the natural feature should be left unexploited as nature created it.

Newgrange, Co. Meath, is the site of a magnificent 5,000-year-old passage grave containing the cremated remains of Stone-Age man. In 1991, a total of 131,352 people (see Table 2) visited the site. Its popularity is reflected in the waiting list for the annual winter solstice. On that date, the sun penetrates the strategically located gaps in the passage and lights up the heart of the grave. This event has a waiting list up to the year 2000! However, here too,the impact of the great numbers visiting is causing concern. The Office of Public Works must now find ways to limit damage while at the same time facilitating visitors. Similar problems have occurred at Stonehenge. The issue facing both man-made and natural attractions is that of development versus conservation and finding a balance between the two. Under strict guidelines and planning requirements and with the involvement of Bord Fáilte as a prescribed body, man-made attractions must complement the landscape.

Interpreting Ireland

EC legislation requires that an Environmental Impact Survey be carried out before EC funding, a vital source for all Irish tourism development, is granted. This was highlighted in relation to the siting of interpretative centres in National Parks. The OPW, which has responsibility for all National Parks in Ireland, has designated two new parks in Counties Wicklow and Clare. The new parks have been welcomed as a means of protecting the unique Burren landscape in Co. Clare and the greatest mountain mass in Co. Wicklow.

OPW

Oifig na nOibreacha Poiblí
The Office of Public Works

The siting of the interpretative centre at Mullaghmore, in the heart of the Burren, has however, upset conservationists who claimed that the fragile ecosystem would be damaged and said that the centre should have been sited elsewhere. The Office of Public Works' view was that the centre must be located as close to the Burren as possible. A number of environmental studies, including those at EC level, are proceeding.

Table 2 Top Visitor Attractions Republic of Ireland*		
	1990	1991
Dublin Zoo	442,064	440,000
Bunratty Castle and Folk Park	271,897	271,273
Royal Hospital Kilmainham	30,519	180,000
Fota Wildlife Park	158,618	169,200
Muckross House	163,949	166,755
Rock of Cashel	146,621	160,563
Lough Key Forest Park	150,000	150,000
Kilkenny Castle	127,043	141,847
Newgrange	132,005	131,352
Powerscourt Estate	140,065	120,265
Glenveagh National Park	102,000	102,161
National Heritage Park	90,766	100,000
Dublin Castle	44,683	92,000
Clonmacnois	74,155	90,119
J. F. Kennedy Park	80,900	86,700
Tallymon Forest Park	148,000	225,000
Belfast Zoo	209,000	189,000
Ulster Folk and Transport Museum	147,000	136,000
Ulster American Folk Park	114,000	129,000
Waterworld Portrush	122,000	115,000
Castlewellan Forest Park	65,000	100,000
Shane's Castle	32,000	100,000

Source: Bord Fáilte

*Attractions featured include only those charging admission and willing to participate in the survey. Some figures have been rounded off.

While the real impact of the interpretative centre locations will not be assessed for many years, the public debate evoked by the controversy highlights the issue of development versus conservation at national and even international level.

As fashions exist in any industry, so they do in tourist attractions. The traditional image of a museum is that of an exhibition behind glass, hushed voices and security guards; in recent years there has been a marked move towards active participation by visitors. Historical museums, such as steam railway museums, now offer short excursions on trains; outdoor Folk Parks such as those at Bunratty and the Ulster American Folk Park in Co. Tyrone, have staff dressed in period costume re-living life of that period. New museums include the Dublin Writers' Museum and Number 29, the Georgian House at Lower Fitzwilliam Street, Dublin, a house furnished in the style of a middle-class family of the period.

Art galleries, too, like the National Gallery of Ireland, have changed with the times. They now organise lectures, painting classes for children as well as special and visiting exhibitions over and above the permanent collection, to encourage people who have already visited to return.

Leisure Attractions

Ireland has magnificent natural resources and a growing reputation abroad as a sport-loving country and is successful at international level in football, cycling and boxing. Tourist Boards, both North and South, have actively pursued the development of leisure activities throughout the country. All water sports, as well as golf, horse-riding, gliding, shooting, walking and fishing are available in an unspoilt, uncrowded environment.

Theme Parks

Overseas, particularly in America and Britain, the number of theme parks has grown considerably. The market leader is easily Disney World in Florida, attracting over 12 million people annually. Theme parks usually cover a great area and a fixed admission charge covers all entertainment. In larger parks, facilities available include car-parks, hotels and a wide variety of restaurants. The thrill of the rides, roller-coasters, special effects and fantasy-like atmosphere appeals to children and grown-ups alike.

Great care is taken in choosing and marketing a theme park. The location must be accessible to a large target population. The opening of Euro Disney, near Paris in 1992 did not enjoy the automatic transfer of success from its associated parks in the US and attendance numbers were lower than expected, despite extensive advertising. Reasons suggested for the slow growth period include the recession. However, one point worth noting is that Mickey Mouse is not a household name in France. While there are no plans at present to develop a major theme park in Ireland, a similar concept was adopted by Celtworld in Waterford, which illustrates Celtic legends of Ireland.

Celtworld

WHERE LEGEND LIVES.
Tramore, Co. Waterford, Ireland.
Tel: 010 353 51 86166. Fax: (051) 90146.

Crafts and Factory Visits

While the shopping sprees of American tourists for sweaters and crystal may be diminishing, sales of traditional Irish crafts and goods have grown to become a multi-million pound export industry. The craft industry in Ireland has blossomed with potters (Nicholas Mosse), glass (Simon Pearce), crystal (Tyrone, Galway and Waterford), fashion (Paul Costelloe) and leathermakers (Chesneau), to mention just a few. Department stores and duty-free shops display a large selection of Irish crafts; as well as these, the growth of craft outlet shops, many adjoining the actual craft workshops, reflect the high standards of product and keen interest in this market.

Tax incentives encourage people from overseas to buy — the refund of VAT on goods when leaving represents a saving of 17% on retail prices. A number of shops and outlets also handle substantial mail-order business worldwide.

Perhaps a surprising growth area as tourist attractions is factories. The large number of visitors to crystal factories may be expected; Waterford Crystal for example, had 97,718 visitors in 1991. Other products are now opening their doors to visitors: Bushmills had 52,625 visitors in 1990, while Movanagher fish farm showed 550 people around the premises in 1991. Other well-known industrial visitor attractions include the Guinness Brewery in Dublin, Jameson Whiskey Centre in Midleton, Cork, and Locke's Distillery, Kilbeggan. Some factories provide opportunities to sample products.

Other Places to Visit

Factories are not the only attractions where tourism is very much secondary to the main function. Trinity College Dublin, for example, has an estimated 9,000 students annually. The college also attracts thousands of visitors to see the famous Book of Kells, admire the architecture and stroll in the grounds which have featured in a number of films including *Educating Rita*. Another attraction at Trinity College is the Dublin Experience, a multi-media audio-visual show.

The same dual function or purpose is true of many stately homes throughout the country. The owners open part of their homes to a fee-paying public; they may allow visitors to wander throughout the house and gardens freely or they may provide tours. The cost of maintaining these houses is so great that any income or revenue earned helps contribute to the upkeep of the estate. Clonalis House in Co. Roscommon and Castle Matrix in Co. Limerick are two such examples.

While the stately homes are certainly of interest to many visitors, so too are the houses of famous Irish figures. In America, tourists are guided in buses past the homes of the wealthy and famous living in Hollywood, but in Ireland, houses of literary and political fame have been opened to the public. Parnell's house in Avondale, Co. Wicklow and Padraig Pearse's cottage in Rosmuc, Co. Galway are two such examples.

Events and Festivals

The growth and success of Irish festivals throughout the year has gained valuable publicity for the country. Festivals such as the Rose of Tralee, Féile, the Cork Jazz Festival and the Galway Oyster festival (ranked among the Automobile Association's top ten festivals in Europe) have gained international recognition. The influx of visitors to local festivals can contribute substantially to the overall revenue of most regions during the season. Almost every county has several

festivals, particularly during the summer period, with Irish music, song and dance featuring strongly, although literary weekends, agricultural fairs, crafts, theatre, and even matchmaking provide the basis of some of the most successful festivals around the country.

Among the regular events and festivals which have become tourist attractions are: Kilkenny Arts Festival, Listowel Writers' Week, the Merriman and Yeats Summer Schools, the Wexford Opera Festival, the All-Ireland Drama Festival in Athlone and the Belfast Festival at Queen's.

Some events and festivals have a distinctive Irish flavour. These include: the Fleadh Ceoil na hÉireann, the World Irish Dancing Championships, Siamsa Tíre in Tralee, set dancing summer schools, traditional ballads, and céilí seisuína throughout the country and, of course, the St Patrick's Day celebrations.

Night-time entertainment, in theatres, pubs and nightclubs, is attractive to tourists of all nationalities. Some venues like the Abbey Tavern in Howth have achieved international fame and many others, particularly those with Irish music and song, add much to the tourists' overall enjoyment.

The growth of the arts in Ireland has gone from strength to strength, with the choice of shows in Dublin and many regional cities and towns reflecting this. Towns and cities around the country have heritage walks and trails, such as the Georgian Trail and Literary Pub Crawl in Dublin which both entertain and inform.

Case Study: Giant's Causeway

The Giant's Causeway coastline extends from Fair Head to Magilligan Point, a total distance of 42 miles. It consists of the world-famous rock structures of dark basalt which were formed about 55 million years ago when the lava cooled. The 40,000 or so stone columns, most of which are hexagonal in section, extend at their tallest to 40 ft.

The Causeway is one of Ireland's most magnificent tourist attractions; this was recognised when it was awarded the status of World Heritage Site. It is also a National Nature Reserve. It is not surprising that the site is often referred to as the eighth wonder of the world.

Access to the Causeway, a National Trust property, is by way of a circular walk which takes the visitor through the rock formations and alongside breathtaking views of the cliffs, ocean and shoreline. In the

summer months a bus runs from the car-park of the Giant's Causeway Centre to the head of the Causeway.

The award-winning visitor centre, provided in 1986 by Moyle District Council, offers a varied and interesting account of the geology, history and wildlife on the Causeway coast. The centre includes an audio-visual display, tourist information centre, toilets, shop and tea room. Parking facilities for cars and buses are also provided.

The spectacular rock formations and breathtaking scenery have made the Giant's Causeway one of the most popular tourist attractions in Northern Ireland with about 350,000 visitors in 1990.

1. Identify the man-made developments to this natural attraction to cater for visitors.

2. What markets would be interested in this tourist attraction and why?

3. Suggest a marketing and publicity campaign at the site to encourage visitors to care for the area and protect the environment.

4. To reduce the numbers of people visiting the Causeway, a boat service is being launched to view the Causeway from the sea. Discuss the viability of the scheme.

Case Study: Bunratty Castle and Folk Park

Bunratty Castle and Bunratty Folk Park are located on the main Limerick to Shannon and Ennis road in Co. Clare, about 25 minutes drive from Limerick City.

Bunratty Castle was built around 1450 and today houses a collection of furniture and tapestries which reflect the design and layout of castles built in that period. Famous mediaeval banquets are held in the castle. Visitors are wined, dined and entertained by the Bunratty singers, accompanied by the music of the harp and fiddle. Since the introduction of the banquets in 1963, hundreds of thousands of visitors have enjoyed the evening's activities. Such was the success of the banquets, that an evening of Irish music, dance and singing was added to the programme; the popularity of this evening is reflected in the growing number of visitors annually (see Table A).

Bunratty Folk Park contains replicas of buildings of the 19th century from the region with original furniture and designs of that time. The house exhibits range from those belonging to the very poor to the more affluent farmers of the time and therefore reflect the social divisions. Skills of that period are demonstrated, with butter making and soda bread baking among the activities.

Bunratty Village Street takes the Folk Park a stage further and carefully recreates a typical Irish street scene at the turn of the century, complete with a post office, drapery, school house, craft shop and a village pub. McNamara's or Mac's pub is fully licensed and visitors to the park can experience the surroundings with the staff in period dress. The pub also opens in the evening, with locals and visitors enjoying the atmosphere and music.

Bunratty House was built in 1804 as a temporary residence for the family of the castle. However the comfort of the house by comparison was so great that the family never returned to the castle. The furnished Victorian house has been carefully restored so that visitors can easily visualise the way of life of that time. Alongside the house is the Talbot collection of farm equipment which also dates from the 19th century.

Table A Numbers of visitors at Bunratty					
	1987	1988	1989	1990	1991
Bunratty Banquets	62,060	59,047	61,241	60,140	53,507
Shannon Céilí	13,676	19,085	12,367	19,115	17,078
Bunratty Castle and Folk Park	179,262	191,219	242,170	271,897	271,273
Source: Shannon Development					

1. Discuss the problems associated with converting historical properties into tourist attractions.

2. Bunratty Castle and Folk Park offer a range of tourist experiences. Identify these and suggest new features that could be developed.

3. 'An ancient castle must be made weatherproof and safe for tourists so it is no longer the castle it once was.' Discuss.

4. Identify folk traditions or an aspect of folk history from your locality that could form the basis of a tourist attraction. Suggest how this could be interpreted and presented to tourists.

Case Study: Inishowen Peninsula

The Inishowen Peninsula in Co. Donegal lies between Lough Swilly to the West and Lough Foyle to the East and stretches to the most northerly point in Ireland, Malin Head.

The beauty of the region varies from the miles of magnificent beaches along the Atlantic coast to the cliffs and mountains in the centre of the peninsula. The 'Inishowen 100' is a scenic drive around the peninsula designed to show tourists and daytrippers the variety and beauty of the area. While the region, surrounded by water, is a haven to water sport and fishing enthusiasts, walks, golf, pony-trekking and cycling are also available.

MALIN HEAD
Garvan Isles
Ballyhillin
Crockalough
938
Glengad Head
GLENGAD
Knockmanagh 856
808
Glashedy Island
Tullagh Point
Doagh Isle
MALIN
Dunmore Head
Culdaff
Inis Eoghain 100
DUNAFF HEAD
BALLYLIFFIN
18
FANAD HEAD
Point
CLONMANY
Coolcross Hill
1657
856
Balbane Head
Raghtin More
Lenan Head
Gap of
Mamore
Gleneely
Crocknasmug
1076
Leel Point
CARNDONAGH
INISHOWEN HEAD
754
Murren Hill
Urris
Hills
931
Crockaulin
1074
Dunagree Point
PORTSALON
Glasmullan
Tullymore
1158
GREENCASTLE
Tamney
SLIEVE SNAGHT
2019
1058
Magilligan Point
Dunree
Head
FORT DUNREE
Slieve Main
1557
997
TruskMore
MOVILLE
Glencaw
1123 Hill
REDCASTLE
MAGILLIGAN
KNOCKALLA MOUNTAIN Knockalla Coast Road
KERRYKEEL
BUNCRANA
Some
881 Hill
Crockglass
1305
QUIGLEYS
POINT
1260
Binevenagh
Harkin's
Hill
Crockanaffrin
1137
Killygarvan
Point
Eskaheen
1377
Mountain
INIS EOGHAIN 100
RATHMULLAN
FAHAN
1589
Scalp Mountain
Longfield Bank
Keady
110
Mountain
Ray
Inch
Island
732
Inch
Muff
Ballykenny
Point Whale
Head
Carnaghan
BURNFOOT
Eglington
Airport
A2
BALLYKEELY
LIMAVADY
Ramelton
BRIDGEND
EGLINGTON
Grianan of Aileach
Donald's Hill
1318
DRUMSURN
Carn Hill
797
NEWTOWN-
CUNNINGHAM
Derry
Loughermore
1298
BOVENAGH
Big
Isle
N13
Altahullion
914 Hill
Benbradagh
MANOR-
CUNNINGHAM
808
CARRIGANS
NEW
BUILDINGS
DERRY

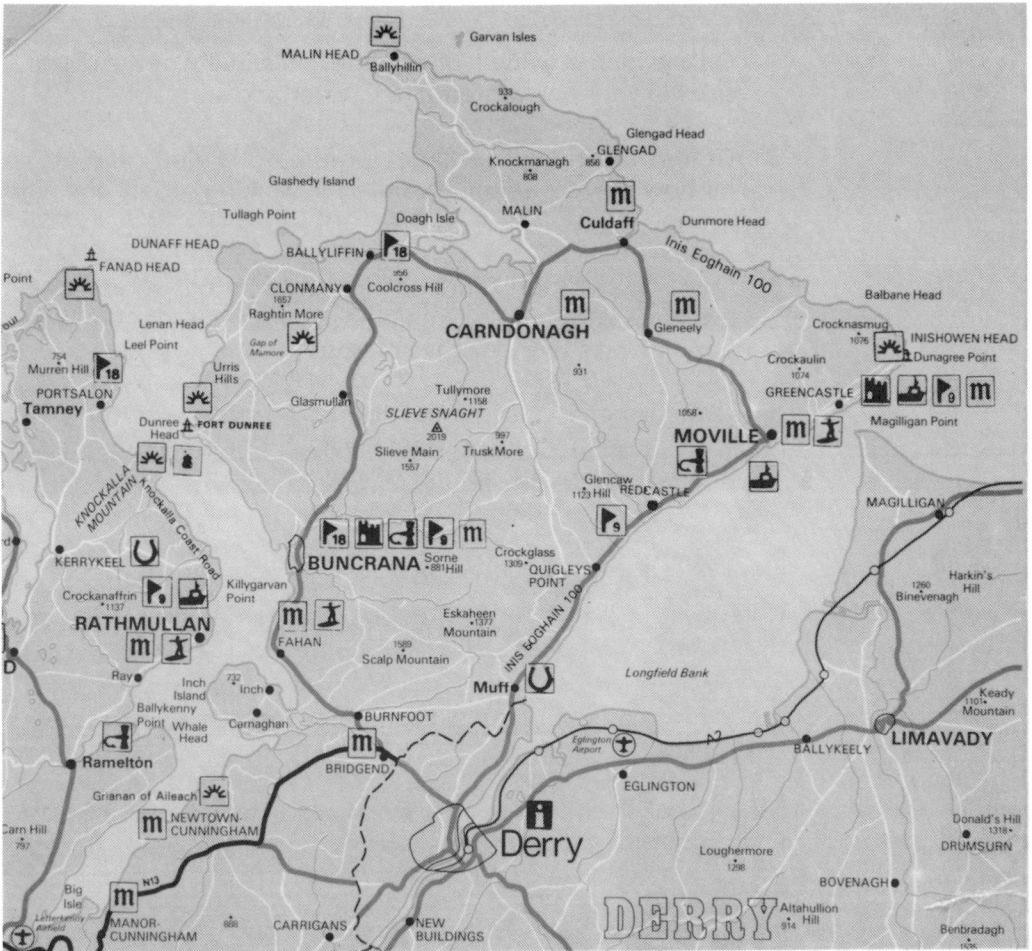

The history of the region is reflected in the range of historical attractions in the area. The Grianán of Aileach consists of a circular wall, or cashel, enclosed within three earthworks, probably built in the last centuries BC. Fort Dunree military museum, near Buncrana, is situated at the mouth of Lough Swilly and was built to withstand the threat of the Napoleonic invasion. The castle at Greencastle was built in 1305 strategically overlooking the mouth of Lough Foyle. The Donagh Cross in Carndonagh dates from the seventh century and is one of the very early Christian crosses outside mainland Europe.

The Vintage Car and Carriage Museum in Buncrana and the nearby Tullyarvan cultural and exhibition centre provide a history of the region and a craft shop where local craftsmen can sell their products.

The peninsula hosts a variety of festivals and fairs throughout the summer months from the agricultural fair in Carndonagh, and the literary Macklin Festival in Culdaff, to the sea angling festival in Moville which attracts competitors from around the world.

1. On the map provided, discuss the accessibility of the region. Consider in your answer road, rail, water and air.

2. Design a holiday package for the following markets in the Inishowen area: a fishing club, a hill walking society and a golfing group.

3. Contact your local tourist office and find out what literature is available on the Inishowen area. Do you consider the area to be popular with tourists? Give reasons.

4. Compare and contrast the tourist attractions in the peninsula with those in your local area. Which is more developed? What differences are there?

Student Questions and Assignments

1. Make a list of 20 tourist attractions in your area and divide them into man-made and natural tourist attractions. Find out what services and facilities are provided at each site. What are the opening hours and conditions? How many people visit the attractions annually?

2. 'The risk of damaging the environment is too high a price to pay for making a natural attraction available to the public.' Discuss.

3. Choose two contrasting international tourist attractions and identify reasons for their popularity and growth or decline as tourist attractions.

4. 'The success of a National Park depends on the siting of the interpretative centre and amenities as close to the attraction as is possible.' Discuss.

5. Develop a theme park concept for Ireland — similar to Euro Disney. Give reasons for your choice of theme, location etc. Draw up a marketing campaign attracting tourists having decided upon your target market.

6. Identify ten different Irish festivals and highlight the differing marketing and publicity techniques used to attract visitors.

7. The advantage of providing year-round leisure centres is that the host population as well as the visitors can avail of the facilities. Consider the leisure facilities in your local area and discuss the service they offer to both tourists and residents.

8. Discuss the role of the arts in Ireland as a tourist attraction.

6 *Environmental Tourism*

Objectives

At the end of this chapter the reader will be able to:

- identify the factors that contribute to Ireland as a 'green' destination

- demonstrate an awareness of the bodies responsible for conserving Ireland's environment

- appreciate the need for planned tourist development and explain the threats to Ireland's natural environment

- identify environment-related tourism products in Ireland

- understand the concept of rural and sustainable tourism.

Tourism is not only about a destination — it means a total holiday experience for the traveller. Today's tourists are sophisticated in terms of holiday expectations and have disposable income to spend satisfying these. The challenge for the tourism industry is to deliver a quality product which will appeal to a wide variety of holidaymakers.

The classification of destinations overleaf illustrates the different types of travel experiences provided in different settings.

One of the most important travel motivators is an interest in other people's culture — entertainment, food, drink, hospitality, architecture and hand crafts are all the outward manifestations of a national identity. 'Local colour' can make a destination unique and a holiday memorable. Tourists' experiences are enriched when they have opportunities to get to know local people and their way of life. Bord Fáilte, in promoting Ireland as a holiday destination, focuses particularly on Heritage, Environmental and Leisure tourism. These reflect Ireland's image as a green, unspoilt country with quality leisure facilities and a rich cultural heritage.

Ethnic Tourism	*Purpose*: To observe the cultural expressions and lifestyles of exotic peoples. *Typical activities*: Attending dances and ceremonies, demonstrations of traditional crafts, visits to native homes.
Environmental Tourism	*Purpose*: To appreciate natural and environmental attractions in remote areas (rural tourism and 'back to nature' holidays fall into this category). *Typical activities*: Camping, walking, pony-trekking, hostelling, photography.
Leisure Tourism	*Purpose*: To participate in sports, sunbathe and make social contacts in a relaxed setting. *Typical activities*: Golf, tennis, theme parks, skiing, swimming, night-clubbing.
Heritage and Cultural Tourism	*Purpose*: To experience a disappearing lifestyle and contemporary cultural activities. *Typical activities*: Folk music and dance performances, costume festivals, traditional arts and crafts, displays and demonstrations, mediaeval banquets, modern drama, film and dance.
Historical Tourism	*Purpose*: To appreciate the glories of the past, often city based. *Typical activities*: Guided tours of monuments, visits to churches, museums, galleries, re-creations of important past events.
Business Tourism	*Purpose*: To attend meetings, conferences and seminars. *Typical activities*: Business travel is frequently combined with other forms of tourism. Leisure activities, entertainment and sight-seeing frequently feature in conference programmes.

Irish Tourism and the Environment

Ireland's relatively unspoilt natural environment, with its great scenic beauty and the wide variety of flora and fauna constitutes one of its principal attractions. Green fields, rolling mountains and hills, isolated islands, unpolluted lakes and rivers are typical perceptions of Ireland.

IRELAND NATURALLY
Only the Best

A relatively unindustrialised country by European standards, the natural environment of Ireland's rural areas is particularly attractive to people from built-up urban areas of Europe and the US. Indeed, the significance of the environment to Ireland's tourism product is now even more important as the 'green' movement has created a deeper awareness worldwide of the value of landscape, flora and fauna in preserving the world's delicate ecological balance.

KEEP IRELAND
LITTER-FREE

Recent scientific research has indicated that the thinning of the earth's ozone layer due to environmental pollution has increased the risk of skin cancer. Public awareness of such risks, together with an increasing popular interest in cultural and leisure pursuits, have meant a decline in interest in sun-holiday destinations and a corresponding rise in numbers travelling to areas of environmental interest. With its unspoilt pollution-free countryside, Ireland is well-poised to appeal to this growing market.

The scenic beauty of Ireland's landscape is also reflected in the character of its towns and villages, which lie in harmony with the surrounding landscape in their situation, design and economic activity. Such towns give the visitor a focal point from which to explore, discover and understand the beauty of the rural scenery.

Ireland's Tourism Regions

Each of Ireland's regions has a distinct, natural character of its very own and displays an immense variety of flora and fauna. The South-West of the country, for example, is very much influenced by the warm temperatures of the Gulf Stream. The resulting mild oceanic climate promotes the growth of many types of plant and tree life not found elsewhere in Ireland. In the Killarney National Park area, distinctive ferns, mosses, arbutus and greater butterwort are found in abundance — flora more usually seen in Southern Europe. The great River Shannon winds its way through the heart of Ireland, through Carrick on Shannon, Athlone, Portumna, Dromineer and Killaloe before ending at Limerick City. Two of Ireland's best-known lakes, Lough Ree and Lough Derg are important features on the magnificent river as it meanders leisurely and majestically through the flat plains of the Midlands. The surrounding countryside with its eskers and bogs plays host to a rich variety of birds and wildlife. In addition, the landscape of the Shannon region featuring as it does impressive remains of monasteries and seats of learning reflects its political and cultural importance in Irish history of the Early Christian period.

Specific Interest Holidays

Bord Fáilte's five-year plan, Developing for Growth (Bord Fáilte 1989), to increase Irish tourism numbers has focused on the strengths of the environment as an area of future product development and market expansion. Ireland's clean, natural and unspoilt countryside makes it ideal for a wide range of outdoor recreational and leisure pursuits such as hill walking, golf, cycling, sailing, equestrian activities and angling which may be packaged and promoted as specific interest holidays.

Walking

Of all the outdoor leisure activities in which tourists participate those of walking trails and walking holidays stand out as areas which have seen rapid advance in its product development and marketing. Under the guidance of *Cospóir* — the National Sports Council, a Long Distance Walking Routes Committee has developed a nationwide network of signposted walking trails. About a dozen of these are already in operation and approximately the same number are in various stages of preparation.

Walking routes allow the tourist to experience the Irish landscape in a unique way. The visitor is brought closer to the countryside with the help of waymarked signs, specially designed maps and literature pointing out the natural and historical features which may be encountered en route. Among the most important of these nature trails are *The Kerry Way*, a 200 km circuit which starts and finishes at Killarney, the 90 km *Ballyhoura Way* from John's Bridge (the point at which O'Sullivan Beara crossed the North Cork river) to Limerick Junction, *The Wicklow Way*, a 132 km route from Marlay Park,

Co. Dublin to Clonegal, Co. Carlow and *The Táin Trail*, which encircles the Cooley Peninsula in Co. Louth for 14 km.

Bord Fáilte actively promotes the concept of walking holidays through its brochure *'Only the Best' Walking*. This booklet outlines the major trails in operation with lists of the accommodation available and places of interest along the way.

Ecology

Ireland's natural environment is being marketed under the theme 'Environment and Ecology'. Within this theme, Bord Fáilte has been active in developing holiday options for tourists interested in specific aspects of Ireland's natural landscape, flora and fauna.

This has involved co-operation with the Office of Public Works in the promotion of nature reserves and peatland areas. One aspect targeted for particular promotion has been that of the country's off-shore islands. The remote natural landscapes of these islands have remained essentially unchanged for centuries. Moreover, islands such as the Aran Islands, the Blaskets and the Skelligs feature bird and marine life habitats which are among the most important in Europe. Bord Fáilte promotes the island holiday concept through their 'Only the Best' brochure *Islands of Ireland*.

Rural Tourism

Connecting the product development themes of Specific Interest leisure pursuits and Environment and Ecology is the development of *Rural Tourism* (also known as *Agri-Tourism* or *Green Tourism*). Rural Tourism is part of an EC policy which encourages people to identify ways of supplementing farm incomes through alternative uses of the land. The background to the development of rural tourism, both in Ireland and in Europe, is the continued decline of rural income.

Within the last decade, this decline in income has meant a population drain from many regions together with a growing sense of community dislocation. Rural Tourism is being developed throughout the EC as a means of regenerating these economies and preserving rural communities and their way of life.

In Ireland, the National Co-operative for Rural Tourism was established in 1990 to market rural tourism on behalf of its members. The Board of the Co-operative is made up of representatives from Ireland's Rural Tourism Groups, in addition to representatives from nationwide rural organisations such as the Irish Farmers Association and Macra na Feirme. The Board of the Co-operative is advised by Bord Fáilte and Teagasc.

All Rural Tourism products developed by the National Co-operative for Rural Tourism are closely linked to Ireland's natural environment and the role of Irish farming. Holiday options within this area have been developed according to Bord Fáilte guidelines and fall into four categories:

(i)   rural holidays for the independent traveller

(ii) specialised agricultural tours for farmers, students, agricultural associations etc.

(iii) groups of general tourists who may include a visit to a farm on their holiday itinerary

(iv) island holidays.

Marketing Rural Tourism

Bord Fáilte research has indicated that the overseas market for rural tourism products is composed primarily of green conscious urban dwellers from continental Europe who wish to interact with a rural community while having a variety of environmental-based attractions and leisure activities to choose from.

In meeting the demands of this market, one of the most successful rural tourism products developed to date has been the *Irish Country Holidays*

IRISH COUNTRY HOLIDAYS

programme spearheaded by the National Co-operative for Rural Tourism and Bord Fáilte. Irish Country Holidays are comprehensive rural holiday programmes operated by community tourism co-operatives. They offer the opportunity to holiday in one or more rural communities and to avail of a comprehensive range of rural and environmental activities and attractions, from visits to working farms, equestrian activities, fishing, golfing, walking and cycling to boating, water sports and agricultural study tours.

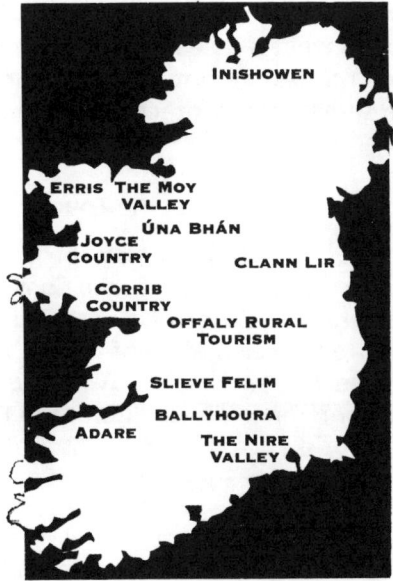

INISHOWEN

ERRIS THE MOY VALLEY

ÚNA BHÁN

JOYCE COUNTRY

CLANN LIR

CORRIB COUNTRY

OFFALY RURAL TOURISM

SLIEVE FELIM

BALLYHOURA

ADARE

THE NIRE VALLEY

WHAT TO DO

Farm Visits: Discover the rural way of life on a choice of dairy, cheese, deer, organic, fish, country garden/tillage and home bakery/horticultural farms.

Fishing: Enjoy Salmon, Wild Brown Trout and coarse fishing on the great Shannon and Blackwater rivers, or the many smaller rivers and on Lough Gur.

Golf: Experience the freedom of golfing on any of our five uncrowded parkland courses, or sharpen your skills on our excellent driving range, with tuition and equipment hire if required.

Outdoor Pursuits: Kilfinane Education centre offers an opportunity to try a range of activities - canoeing, rock climbing, hill walking, wind surfing, bowling, and croquet. Tuition and equipment provided.

Cycling: Pedal quiet country roads through small villages on a wide selection of routes on low-land or hilly terrain, with route maps provided. Bicycle hire.

Horse Riding: Trail rides, pony & trap rides, and lessons for beginner or experienced riders. Practice on a purpose built course before going fox hunting, in season, with the Scarteen or Limerick Hunt.

Walking: The long distance Ballyhoura Way follows the footsteps of the Irish Chieftan O'Sullivan Beara on his long march of 1603. Also a variety of loop routes or the Galtee Mountain climbs.

Entertainment: Village festivals; traditional Irish music, song and dance in local pubs, with opportunities to participate.

Leisure: Catch the spirit and excitement at Gaelic hurling and football games, greyhound racing or horse racing.

These attractions and activities are locally owned and run, thus ensuring that the income generated finds its way into the local economy. The entire Irish Country Holidays programme is underpinned by local community involvement to regenerate the local economy as well as retaining control of tourism development in areas of natural beauty and environmental significance.

Within a European context, the Irish Country Holidays programme represents what is called sustainable tourism, that is, carefully planned, locally controlled tourism development which encourages growth while at the same time protecting the natural environment and all its inhabitants.

Environmental Events in the Tourism Calendar

Other environmental tourism products now promoted to tourists include special events such as the *Connemara Bog Week* in May and the *Connemara Sea Week* in October. These are special study conferences devoted to the celebration of aspects of Connemara's natural environment. The *Burren Wildlife Symposium*, in Spring and Autumn is a special conference on wildlife in the Burren. For committed environmental tourists, accommodation is available at an increasing number of Irish Organic Farm Guesthouses.

Each of these farm guesthouses is a member of the Irish Organic Farmers and Growers Association and guarantees organically grown produce together with opportunities to visit working organic farms. Other environment-related tourism products include Outdoor Adventure Holidays, Arts and Crafts Holidays and Painting Holidays. Bord na Móna operate a successful Bog Railway Tour which takes the visitor through the bog landscape of Clonmacnoise and Shannonbridge.

PEATLAND WORLD

LULLYMORE, RATHANGAN, CO. KILDARE

Visitors Centre showing Flora and Fauna of Kildare Boglands

Museum showing the history and folklore of the Bogs

Threats to the Environment

Despite its relatively untouched condition, Ireland's natural environment is under continuous threat from a number of sources. Such environmental threats have been highlighted by the Irish Tourist Industry Confederation (ITIC) in a significant report 'Tourism and the Environment 1988'. The ITIC report concluded that the future success of Irish tourism depends greatly on the quality of its natural environment. Pollution from untreated sewage, agricultural pesticides, and chemical emissions from factories have grave consequences for flora and fauna as well as the landscape generally. Water contamination by agricultural slurry or pesticides has caused an increasing number of fish kills in some of Ireland's important rivers and lakes. Coastal marine and birdlife also need constant surveillance to offset the threat of pollution from large power-generating and chemical companies.

In recent years the phenomenon which has come to be known as Bungalow Blight has increased in rural areas. This is characterised by building isolated houses in areas of the countryside where they are totally unsuitable both in location and design. Concern at the escalation of Bungalow Blight, or ribbon development, has resulted in calls for tighter controls in the Planning Permission procedures.

Ireland can learn from the mistakes of other countries in this regard. The high rise, densely developed resorts on the Spanish costas, such as Benidorm, are examples of the lack of planning control.

Some believe that another threat to the environment is tourism itself. The fact of providing for tourism may mean permanently altering features which attract tourists. The restoration of the ancient monument at Newgrange did not meet with universal approval; nor did the construction of interpretative centres at several Irish beauty spots. Inevitably, places like the Cliffs of Moher and many of the castles and abbeys of Ireland must be rendered safe for visitors.

Again the presence of large numbers of visitors can lead to the destruction of the environment. Rare flora are trampled under foot and fauna, such as nesting birds of prey, can die out due to the destruction of their habitats.

Positive measures can be taken to arrive at an accommodation between the environment and tourism. Damage through pollution to urban landscape may be identified and repaired in time. Paths for walkers may be provided to concentrate the depredations of the public and leave the rest of a mountainside, a wilderness or a forest relatively free to nature. In the last resort it may be necessary, as at Stonehenge, to exclude visitors and thus reduce the threat to the environment.

Who Protects our Environment?

Ireland's environment is protected through a number of bodies, organisations and laws. The Department of the Environment is the government department with primary responsibility for the protection of Ireland's natural environment. It institutes legislation in accordance with EC directives on environmental protection including planning legislation and legislation on water, air and other pollutants. The Department of the Environment is responsible for the functioning of Ireland's local authorities — Corporations, County Councils, and Urban

District Councils. Local authorities play an important part in safeguarding the environment within their local areas.

Environmental Protection Agency

A government action programme (Environment Action Programme January 1990) for the environment has recently been launched to address environmental issues facing Ireland in the future. A key element of the programme is the creation of a special Environmental Protection Agency (EPA) with wide-ranging power to control developments which are potentially harmful. One of the EPA's most important powers will be the monitoring of recognised procedures for Environmental Impact Studies (EIS). An EIS is a detailed study which must be carried out before any major construction development, to establish its potential impact on the environment.

ENFO

Another significant government initiative on the environment has been the Department of the Environment's information service — ENFO. Located in Dublin, ENFO provides the public with a comprehensive information service on all aspects of the environment. The Agency has particularly targeted the Irish educational system for the dissemination of principles of environmental protection and preservation. Other bodies in the Republic of Ireland which aim to protect and create a greater awareness of the natural environment include the following:

Environmental Body	Purpose
Office of Public Works	The State body charged with the protection of Ireland's natural heritage
An Taisce	National Trust for Ireland
Irish Wildlife Federation	To conserve Irish wildlife and their habitats together with the promotion of conservation awareness
Irish Wildbird Conservancy	To conserve the habitats of Ireland's wildbird species
Irish Peatland Conservation Council	Concerned with the conservation of bogs of particular importance
Tree Council of Ireland	Promotes the propagation, planting, conservation and management of trees in Ireland

Case Study: Rural Tourism, The Ballyhoura Experience

Ballyhoura is a rural region situated at the boundary conjunction of counties Limerick, Cork and Tipperary. Not traditionally regarded as a tourist area, Ballyhoura lies in the heart of the Golden Vale, one of the principal dairy-production areas of Ireland. It is bordered to the south by the rolling wooded hills and unspoiled, fertile valleys of the Galtee and Ballyhoura mountain ranges. To the north it is an area of dairy pastures and green hills inhabited by farming communities.

Though Ballyhoura is an area of outstanding natural beauty, in the last decade it has suffered from a shrinking agricultural economy, low farm incomes, rural population decline and increasing village dereliction. In an effort to combat the downward trends in the agricultural economy and the negative effects on the rural community of the area, the Ballyhoura Fáilte Society was established as a community based tourism co-operative in 1986. The founding of the Society was spearheaded by concerned local community groups like the Kilfinane Development Association and Macra na Feirme, together with assistance from Shannon Development and the Youth Employment Agency.

The aim of the Society was to realise the rural tourism potential of the Ballyhoura region through sustained, planned development and local community co-ordination. With offices located at Kilfinane, Co. Limerick the Society set up a rural tourism development sub-committee incorporating community and statutory organisations.

In 1989, the Ballyhoura region was chosen for a Bord Fáilte/ Teagasc/Macra Community Agri-Tourism Pilot Project selling Irish Country Holidays on the German market. This pilot project motivated the development of a rural tourism framework in the area through:

(i)   special training schemes for local product providers

(ii) market-led local holiday products

(iii) the operation of a central marketing, sales and reservations service.

Training consisted of vocational courses in hospitality skills, language training, craft and business planning. Training content was specially developed by CERT, Teagasc, the VEC, FÁS and the Kilfinane Education Centre and augmented by local media and study tours. Irish Country Holiday products were identified among existing products which would be packaged, marketed and promoted, and a wider range of products was developed in co-operation with local individuals, community groups, clubs and statutory bodies. The success of the 1989 pilot Irish Country Holidays programmes contributed significantly to the establishment in 1990 of the National Rural Tourism Co-operative (Ireland) Ltd.

The marketing of Irish Country Holidays began in earnest with the branding of the product and the publication of a brochure in English, French and German. The potential visitor was seen as being a continental European urban dweller in search of an environmentally-based holiday. The Irish Country Holidays product consists of a total experience rural holiday including countryhouse or farmhouse accommodation, leisure and recreational activities like walking, fishing, cycling, visits to local attractions and the opportunity to visit a working family farm. An information pack on what to see and do in the area and the services of the local rural tourism group are also provided.

Under the umbrella title of Irish Country Holidays, Ballyhoura Fáilte Society has developed a number of special interest holiday options including:

— agricultural study tours of local farms

— educational tours for school groups and historical societies centred around the attractions of Ballyhoura country

— a range of cycling tours of the region

— a range of activity holidays centred on Kilfinane Education Centre

— language training courses

— youth riding holidays and trail riding products.

The growth in visitor numbers to the area encouraged local interest in the Ballyhoura Rural Tourism project so that additional accommodation capacity, a riding school, farm trail, bicycle hire, golf facilities, a farm restaurant and canoeing were developed in the period 1990–91. More recent tourism development has focused on the need to improve the tourism infrastructure in the Ballyhoura area, particularly in the areas of signposting, literature and additional products.

Under the guidance of the Society several significant new tourism products are in various stages of development. These include development of a long distance walk — the O'Sullivan Beara Way from West Cork to

Leitrim, of which Ballyhoura will provide 90 km of way-marked routes. European Regional Development and local authority funding has been secured for the development and promotion of the Ballyhoura Mountain Park, and a Golden Vale Cycle Route and Drive.

The Ballyhoura Irish Country Holidays programme has gone from strength to strength. In 1991, tourism receipts in the area almost doubled those for 1990. The average stay on an Irish Country Holiday was 12 nights and on other special interest holidays 8 nights in 1990.

Side by side with its co-ordinated product development strategy, rural tourism in Ballyhoura is integrated in the intensive Bord Fáilte and Shannon Development marketing and promotion. This has been responsible in no small way for the continued success and growth of the Ballyhoura rural tourism product.

The Ballyhoura Fáilte Society sees continuous challenge in the future to achieve increased occupancy and product quality for the tourism development of the area. Its long-term planning strategies not only envisage an increase in tourism revenue in the area by IR£1.1m in 1991–93 but aims at restructuring the rural economy in the area, preserving rural communities and increasing public awareness of the countryside.

The Society does, however, realise that rural tourism alone is unlikely to achieve the necessary wealth creation to regenerate the area; so through its development sub-committee, Ballyhoura Development Board, it has developed a multi-sectored plan. In 1992, the Society was successful in gaining funding under the EC Leader Programme for its integrated strategies in tourism, local education and training, town and village renewal, agricultural and small business development.

Source: Carmel Fox, Ballyhoura Fáilte Society

1. Why has Ballyhoura Fáilte Society developed rural tourism in the region?

2. List some of the achievements of Ballyhoura Fáilte Society in developing the Irish Country Holidays programme.

3. Why do you think it is necessary to provide special training schemes for local product providers?

4. List the holiday options in Ballyhoura available to tourists under the Irish Country Holidays programme.

5. What are the long-term aims of Ballyhoura Fáilte Society in relation to tourism development?

Student Questions and Assignments

1. Describe the particular environment of your locality and identify existing or potential tourism-related amenities and activities.

2. List the principal legislation which protects the Irish environment. Why is this essential for tourism development?

3. Develop a leaflet for a walk or trail, making reference to the stages and distance of the route, attractions to be seen, equipment needed by the walker and any potential dangers.

4. 'Rural Tourism is important both to agriculture and tourism.' Explain.

5. Describe the profile of the typical potential customer for the Irish Country Holidays product.

6. What is meant by the term Sustainable Tourism?

7. Develop an original idea for an environmentally-based holiday in Ireland.

8. Find out about the EC Blue Flag scheme and identify beaches in Ireland currently awarded the Blue Flag.

7 Heritage Tourism

Objectives

At the end of this chapter the reader will be able to:

- identify the principal areas of Irish heritage product development

- understand the purpose of heritage interpretation as a means of facilitating the visitor, understanding and enjoyment

- appreciate the potential of Irish heritage as a tourism product

- examine general trends in heritage tourism

- distinguish between national, local and personal heritage and between natural and man-made heritage.

Heritage Tourism refers to the tourism markets and tourism industry which have evolved around a country's heritage. It incorporates all facets of natural and man-made heritage which are categorised as tourist attractions, together with literature, maps, trails and related consumer merchandise.

Heritage tourism is a worldwide industry and is part of what is classified in international tourism terms as *cultural tourism*. While heritage tourism revolves around the cultural attractions of the past, cultural tourism relates to contemporary cultural activity such as art, architecture, literature, music, dance, drama, film design etc. Research shows that over one third of tourist arrivals into the European Community are made up of 'cultural tourists' i.e. 'tourists travelling with the intention, wholly or partly, of increasing their appreciation of Europe's cultural resources'.

The aspect of cultural tourism in greatest demand by the EC's cultural tourists falls into the category architectural resources and includes famous buildings, churches, medieval towns and gardens. Art is the second most popular followed by music, drama, pilgrimage, dance, language and literature.

National and Local Heritage

Visitors with no Irish connections value Ireland's national heritage as a means of experiencing the highest achievements of the culture they come to see. This accounts for the popularity of such attractions as the Rock of Cashel, Dublin Castle and the Book of Kells. In contrast to national heritage, *local heritage* celebrates ordinary people and their way of life.

Bunratty Folk Park is one of Ireland's major tourist attractions and celebrates 19th-century life through the reconstruction of typical houses, farms, shops, schools etc. Here, the visitor can see and appreciate the way of life of people of all social classes. Unlike *national heritage* which values the 'important' past, local heritage values the legacy of the ordinary, everyday past.

The heritage of the past can be of importance at a personal level also. This is reflected in the growth of interest in genealogy, heraldry and clan rallies.

Diversification of Bord Fáilte Activities

Ireland's popularity as a cultural tourism destination is far behind that of major EC cultural tourism destinations like France, Italy and Spain. However, Ireland has always relied on its heritage and culture as a key component of its tourism product. While the Irish Tourist Board's early activities concentrated on the development of amenities in scenic areas and seaside resorts of Ireland, from the early 1950s onward their planning and promotional activities began to focus on the tourism potential of Ireland's history and culture.

The diversification of the Board's activities at this time stemmed from the provisions of the 1952 Tourism and Traffic Act which widened the scope of the Board's activities to protect and promote Irish heritage i.e. historic buildings, sites, shrines and places of scenic interest.

In addition, the Act empowered Bord Fáilte to facilitate visitors to such attractions by providing and improving means of access.

The 1952 Tourism and Traffic Act marks the recognition by the Irish government of the value of Ireland's heritage and culture to tourism. Bord Fáilte and the Office of Public Works co-operated closely, and all improvements carried out by Bord Fáilte are subject to OPW approval.

Irish heritage played a significant part in the Irish tourism product throughout the 1960s and 1970s. Greater protection continued to be afforded to monuments and scenic sites, particularly through the 1964 Local Government Planning and Development Act, which laid down guidelines for development in areas of historic and cultural interest and placed a greater onus on individual local authorities to protect their local heritage. A number of new heritage tourism attractions were developed. For example, Bunratty Castle, Co. Clare, was restored and opened as a major tourist attraction by Shannon Development in 1960.

Developing Heritage Tourism Products

Bord Fáilte Survey of International Travellers which was initiated after 1972 began to give a clearer picture of visitor trends in relation to Irish heritage attractions. It indicated that all Ireland's overseas tourists visited heritage attractions while on holiday in Ireland. Information for the period 1980–88 showed that the most popular heritage attractions for holidaymakers were areas of historical and cultural interest followed by stately homes and gardens, national and forest parks, museums and art galleries.

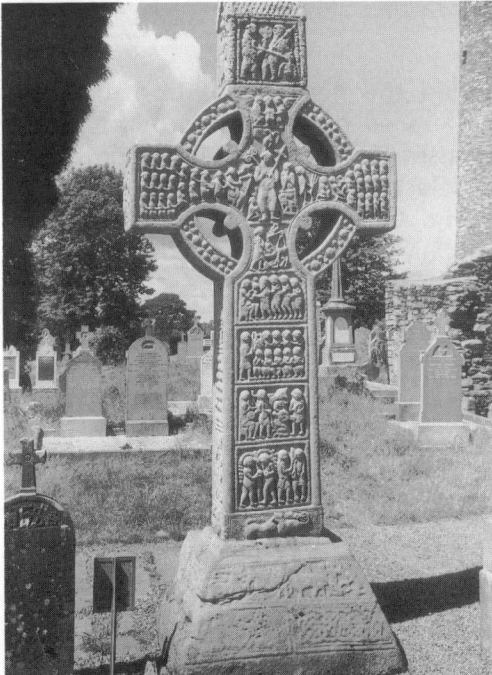

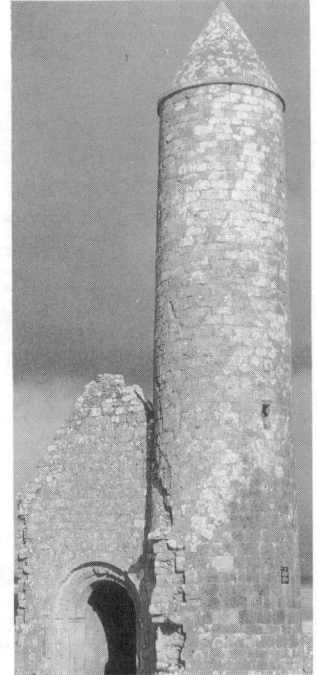

St Muireadach's Cross, Monasterboice (left) and the Round Tower at Clonmacnoise (right)

111

The response to growing demand for heritage tourism products was led by the Irish government in the National Development Plan 1989–93. For the government, Ireland's heritage and culture was seen as one of the areas with the greatest potential for tourism development. Tourist organisations quickly endorsed the government's policy in relation to the role of Irish heritage in developing the Irish tourism industry. The Irish Tourist Industry Confederation study 'Doubling Irish Tourism: A Market-Led Strategy', highlighted the potential of Irish history and culture as a major marketing opportunity for tourism. As part of its strategy for doubling Irish tourism numbers up to 1992, Bord Fáilte targeted Ireland's heritage for development and marketing abroad. In addition to developing, promoting and presenting individual heritage attractions, Bord Fáilte isolated specific areas of Irish heritage for intensive product development.

The Ardagh Chalice

These included the heritage of Christian Ireland, Gardens and Genealogy. Detailed market and product profiles were drawn up, designed to assist tour operators in promoting specific Irish heritage products. A selection of colourful and informative visitor guides to Christian Ireland, Gardens and Genealogy has been produced by Bord Fáilte in the 'Only the Best' series produced in a number of languages.

Heritage Towns

Finally, Bord Fáilte's most innovative and ambitious project in relation to the development of heritage in Ireland was the launching of the Heritage Towns programme in 1989. This outlined plans to develop between 23 and 30 of Ireland's most historic towns as heritage attractions. Each of the heritage towns has focused its development programme around a particular theme or set of themes which exemplify the town's history and culture.

Carlingford, Co. Louth is designated as a mediaeval heritage town; Cobh in Co. Cork, centres its development on the town's past as a point of emigration. Before any town is awarded its Heritage Town status, it must first complete a series of related infrastructural works including a conservation plan for historic buildings, landscaping, signposting and a traffic management programme. All heritage towns will feature a range of visitor attractions in addition to facilities from accommodation and catering to interpretative centres and car parking.

In 1991, almost 4.5 million visitors visited 88 fee paying heritage attractions in the Republic of Ireland generating IR£11.5m. Almost one third of these visits (1 million) were made by Irish people. These figures, when added to the 136,000 visits made by Northern Ireland residents indicates a strong interest in and demand for heritage tourism products in the Irish market. In the same period over half a million visits to heritage attractions were made by British tourists.

Natural and Man-made Heritage

Irish Heritage covers many aspects of Irish culture and history. It is most readily divided into Natural Heritage and Man-made Heritage. The former category includes all facets of Ireland's unique and relatively unspoilt natural heritage of mountains, forests, lakes and wildlife. Ireland's natural heritage is seen at its best in the country's five national parks at Killarney, Connemara, Glenveagh, the Burren and the Wicklow Mountains.

Ireland's man-made heritage includes a wide variety of attractions. These range from sites and monuments dating from the earliest period of Irish history to places and buildings of historical significance in the 20th century. Historic houses, castles, monuments, gardens, museums and interpretative centres are all being promoted. Most of Ireland's 700 important monuments come under the aegis of the Office of Public Works. Many have special visitor centres with interpretative aids such as guided tours, audio visual shows and exhibition areas. Much of recent EC funding for the development of Ireland's heritage tourism has gone towards the provision and up-grading of visitor facilities at monument and park sites.

Not all sites and buildings of historic interest are under OPW care. The National Museum, the National Gallery and the Irish Museum of Modern Art fall within the responsibility of other state organisations. Many of Ireland's historic cathedrals and churches continue in use as places of worship and are under the care of church bodies — such as St Patrick's Cathedral and Christ Church Cathedral in Dublin, St Mary's in Limerick and St Canice's in Kilkenny.

Others may be stand-alone heritage attractions which contain few or no original treasures and are concerned with interpreting the heritage of a town or a region. Important examples include the recently developed Geraldine Tralee Centre which takes the visitor in a time car trip through a reconstruction of the Town of Tralee complete with inhabitants sights, sounds and smells in the year 1450. The Lismore Experience is an interpretative centre located at the heart of the Co. Waterford town and co-ordinates all aspects of Lismore's history

and culture that have achieved its designation as one of the Bord Fáilte Heritage Towns. Celtworld in Tramore, Co. Waterford interprets the heritage of Ireland's myths and legends through characters, creatures and situations brought to life with state-of-the-art technology such as holograms and laser displays.

Interpretative Centres

The newest type of heritage attraction in Ireland is the interpretative centre. These are specially built visitor centres with displays on aspects of heritage and culture. Interpretative sites contrast with monuments and museums in that they facilitate a greater degree of visitor participation through the use of audio-visual facilities and sophisticated visual media such as reconstructed scenes from the past, the use of actors, 3D displays and sound effects. These interpretative centres can be found at historic monument sites facilitating greater visitor understanding and enjoyment. Examples include centres at Glendalough, Co. Wicklow, Killarney National Park, Co. Kerry and King John's Castle Visitor Centre, Limerick.

Genealogy

The development of genealogy and clan rallies as heritage tourism products illustrates and reflects an interest in their personal heritage by the large number of overseas visitors. Bord Fáilte estimates the size of this potential market to be up to 80 million people of Irish descent worldwide. As part of a co-operative project involving genealogical research organisations both North and South of the border, and as a result of funding from the EC and the International Fund for Ireland, both Bord Fáilte and the Northern Ireland Tourist Board have implemented a scheme for the development of 30 heritage research centres all over Ireland. These centres have begun the computerisation of all parish registers, genealogical and local history records in a process which will eventually enable tourists to trace their ancestry through any one centre.

Tracing your **Ancestors**

I R E L A N D

The tourism potential of genealogical ties with Ireland has been harnessed further through the organisation of Clan Rallies for visitors who hold particular Irish surnames. Such Clan Rallies give them a means of searching out the history and tradition of their clan name and meet other people of that clan while in Ireland. The potential of genealogical tourism was further realised in 1992 with the first Irish Homecoming Festival — aimed at tourists who have come to Ireland because of ancestral ties.

Heritage Bodies

The Office of Public Works (OPW) is the principal guardian of Ireland's man-made and natural heritage: it is responsible for the conservation, protection, restoration, presentation and promotion of Ireland's National Monuments, Parks, Gardens, Wildlife and Waterways. The OPW holds a National Heritage Day each September to widen public awareness of Ireland's unique heritage. The National Museum of Ireland is the state institution charged with the guardianship of Ireland's archaeological and historical artefacts and treasures. Under the terms of the National Monument Acts all finds made at monument sites must be reported within four days to the keeper of Antiquaries at the National Museum. The National Heritage Council is a government-appointed council of fourteen members whose task is to aid the government in drawing up policies for the protection and preservation of Ireland's heritage.

Bodies and organisations responsible for the heritage of Northern Ireland include the Department of the Environment (NI), the Historic Monuments Council (NI) and the Ulster Museum, Belfast. The archaeological heritage of Northern Ireland is protected under the terms of the Historic Monuments Act, (NI) (1971).

Trends in Heritage Tourism

A number of trends have accompanied popular demand for heritage tourism. Firstly, visitors wish to have a *participative* experience with heritage rather than simply being passive bystanders. In consequence, newer interpretative heritage attractions and many of the interpretative centres built adjoining existing monuments and parks focus on visitor interaction with the aspect of heritage being presented.

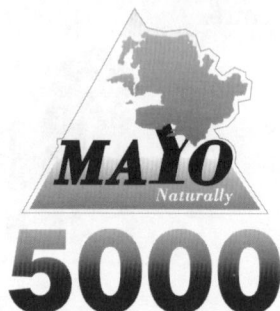

Both the Lismore Experience and Celtworld feature sophisticated hands-on displays where visitors can use those displays which have particular information in which they are interested. The use of scale models at Boyle Abbey and Glendalough Visitor Centres and even entire reconstructions like Bunratty Folk Village and Geraldine Tralee are designed to help the visitor imagine particular aspects of heritage in a vivid and realistic way.

Another trend emerging in Irish heritage tourism is visitor demand for additional on-site facilities which render a visit to a heritage attraction an experience of 1–2 hours' duration. Many of the newer heritage centres have visitor facilities such as restaurants, shops, and play areas for children. As a leisure activity, heritage attractions are becoming increasingly packaged with a variety of facilities so as to ensure a complete consumer experience for the visitor.

Inherent in the development of increasingly consumer oriented heritage attractions is the risk of damage or destruction of heritage itself. The potential harm excessive visitor presence could cause to Ireland's irreplaceable heritage has given rise to major controversies in relation to planned OPW interpretative centres in the Burren and Wicklow Mountains, National Parks, the Great Blasket Island, National Historic Park and the Boyne Valley Archaeological Park.

Concerned bodies, groups and individuals contend that packaging unique aspects of our heritage through these interpretative centres will draw more visitors, cars and pollution into these sensitive areas of history, landscape and culture. Some groups such as An Taisce and the Burren Action Group have succeeded in raising public awareness of the need for careful and phased development of heritage tourism. Only a wider realisation that our heritage is a non-renewable resource will ensure that heritage is developed and promoted in a sensitive and meaningful way.

Case Study: Kilkenny

Kilkenny city, located in the heart of County Kilkenny on the River Nore, has traditionally been one of Ireland's most important heritage tourism destinations. The city has been fortunate in retaining its mediaeval structure and buildings. These buildings give visitors the opportunity to experience Kilkenny's remarkable history which dates back to the pre-Norman period.

Among the city's most important mediaeval buildings are St Canice's Cathedral and Round Tower which date back to the period of 12th-century Church reform and the Anglo-Norman invasion. Kilkenny Castle, a massive stone castle dating from the 12th century was the stronghold of Kilkenny's most famous family — the Butlers of Ormond. It dominates the entire city from a rocky promontory overlooking the

River Nore. Other significant mediaeval buildings include the Shee Almshouse dating back to 1381 which is now the site of the tourist office, the Tholsel (1761) which was the seat of the city government, the Dominican 'Black' Abbey (1225) founded by William Marshal and Rothe House (1594) a splendidly preserved merchant's house.

These aspects of Kilkenny's man-made heritage together with its network of mediaeval streets convey a vivid impression of the city's past political, cultural and economic significance. Not only was Kilkenny a major Anglo-Norman stronghold from the 12th century, it became a focal point in Anglo-Irish politics in the Middle Ages and was the seat of Anglo-Irish parliaments.

The famous Statutes of Kilkenny enacted in 1366, were an attempt to reverse the merging of Irish and Anglo-Norman cultures, which made the Norman settlers 'more Irish than the Irish themselves'. Kilkenny was one of the key Anglo-Irish towns until the mid 17th century. The formation of the Confederation of Kilkenny in 1641 began an eight-year revolt during which Kilkenny was the capital of Ireland. This peak of Kilkenny's glory was brought to an end by Oliver Cromwell and his armies to whom the city surrendered in March 1650.

Kilkenny's importance as a heritage tourism destination has earned it a designation as one of Bord Fáilte's Heritage Towns. Within the framework of the heritage town programme, existing heritage attractions will be promoted in an integrated way and the visitor infrastructure will be upgraded and extended — all within Kilkenny's heritage tourism theme 'A Mediaeval City'.

Kilkenny has been a centre of cultural and artistic activity for many years. The internationally renowned Kilkenny Design Centre located in the former stables of Kilkenny Castle specialises in traditional Irish craftmanship, such as metalwork, pottery, textiles and candle-craft. Products from the Kilkenny Design Workshops are sought after, not only in Ireland, but all over the world and the centre attracts a great number of visitors annually.

The Kilkenny Arts Festival is now one of Ireland's best known cultural festivals. During the month of August visitors participate in a wide range of cultural activities and events such as recitals, concerts, readings, street theatre and music.

Other features which complete Kilkenny's role as a tourism destination include angling, equestrian, golf, leisure centres, traditional enter-tainment, wildlife and a town trail. The local community's commitment to Kilkenny's tourism future is borne out by the fact that the city is a former overall winner of the Bord Fáilte Tidy Towns Award and is indeed, among the top yearly entrants in this prestigious competition.

Kilkenny's future as a heritage tourism destination seems assured. The city's historic monuments will benefit from ERDF funding. Among them, Kilkenny Castle together with its 23 hectares of grounds, is now a National Historic Park. Construction and restoration work continues on the castle, together with the provision of additional visitor facilities at the site.

1. Under what theme and for what reason has Kilkenny been designated one of the Bord Fáilte Heritage Towns?

2. What features can Kilkenny draw on in relation to its development as a heritage town?

3. Other than the importance of its historic buildings, what attracts tourists to Kilkenny?

4. When did Kilkenny win the Bord Fáilte Tidy Towns Award? Why do you think the Tidy Towns competition is important?

5. Design a heritage town trail for Kilkenny or your own town, carefully marking all buildings and areas of historic and cultural interest.

Case Study: Carlingford, Co. Louth

Carlingford is a small and lively town of 650 inhabitants lying at the foot of Sliabh Foy on the shores of Carlingford Lough. Its name Carlingford — city of the pool — suggests Viking origins. In the mediaeval period Carlingford flourished as a prosperous merchant town, dominated by the fortress called King John's Castle which commemorated the English King's visit there in 1210.

Carlingford boasts more mediaeval remains than any comparable town in Ireland. These include:

— King John's Castle, a 13th-century fortress on the shores of Carlingford Lough, around which the town grew.

— the Dominican Abbey, dating to 1305, which was built outside the town wall.

— Taaffe's Castle, a fortified 15th-century townhouse.

— the Mint, also a 15th-century townhouse, which is a National Monument situated on Tholsel Street, the main mediaeval street of Carlingford.

— the Tholsel, one of the few mediaeval town gates surviving in Ireland.

— Holy Trinity Church, containing a mediaeval tower which it is believed was one of the four towers on the town wall.

The quality and character of these buildings, together with Carlingford's beautiful natural setting, have resulted in its designation as one of the Bord Fáilte Heritage Towns. The background to Carlingford's development as a heritage town is unique among all the towns involved in the programme. For while all other heritage towns are being developed by local authorities, the Carlingford programme is being planned and developed by the local community.

Within the last few years, local initiative has seen the growth of a community movement which aims to stimulate Carlingford's economic life. One of the first results of community action came in 1988 when Carlingford won the National Tidy Towns Award. In the same year, a history of the Carlingford Lough area was produced by a local heritage committee. These encouraging achievements led to the formation of a plan to restore Carlingford's mediaeval buildings and develop them commercially, and in May 1990 the Carlingford Lough Heritage Trust was formed.

The dedicated 22-member committee of the Heritage Trust then set about obtaining funding for their ambitious project. Its aim was to secure funds which were being made available as a result of increased government commitment to heritage tourism.

In 1990, Carlingford, designated a Heritage Town by Bord Fáilte, became eligible for both European Regional Development funding and the International Fund for Ireland grants for tourism development in border areas. About this time, it also received an ESB Community Enterprise Award of IR£10,000. The Heritage Trust felt the necessity for professional direction in the development of Carlingford's Heritage

Town Programme and appointed a manager to co-ordinate the programme. Funded by FÁS, a secretary was employed and an office set up in the local courthouse.

Stage One of the Carlingford Heritage Tour Programme was due to be completed by mid-September 1992 and involved the following projects:

— the flood-lighting of King John's Castle

— the restoration of Holy Trinity Church and Tower to be used as an interpretative centre. A map and history of these are also being produced

— production of a town trail and guide

— repair of the Tholsel.

Conservation of the Dominican Priory is being carried out by the Office of Public Works.

While EC funding pays for 75% of these projects, the Carlingford Heritage Trust faces the difficult task of raising the remaining 25% cost. By 1992, the Trust had succeeded in raising some IR£13,000 through draws and special events. Fund-raising remains difficult and has not been made easier by the general economic recession and competition from other worthy causes.

carlingford lough
heritage trust

Some of the major expenditure involved in the programme goes towards staff costs. These include workers of all kinds from builders' labourers and artists to stained glass window restorers and accountants. Only the heritage manager and secretary are employed on a full-time basis. Other expertise and labour is used when required. Where possible, the Heritage Trust utilises local expertise and labour. To date this has included a local building contractor and labourers, a local graphic artist, art student, tour guide, architect and accountant, as well as craftspeople and painters.

Carlingford
Medieval Monuments
and Historic Sites

1. Holy Trinity Church
2. Dominican Friary
3. Millstone
4. Birthplace of D'Arcy McGee
5. Market Square
6. Site of Spout Gate
7. Viewing Point for Town Wall
8. King John's Castle
9. Medieval Houses & Stone Head
10. Birthplace of Fr. Murray
11. Taaffe's Castle
12. D'Arcy McGee Memorial
13. The Mint
14. The Tholsel
15. Ghan House

Town Wall

Old Shoreline

Water Mill

0 ——————— 250
metres

Based on OS manuscript town plan, 1835

The success of the Heritage Trust in regenerating Carlingford as a Heritage Town has resulted in a number of benefits. One of these is growing private sector investment in the programme. The owner of a local grain store which adjoins Holy Trinity Heritage Centre is in the process of converting it to a museum, restaurant and market area. Another entrepreneur has begun the development of the nearby Ghan House as a top class equestrian centre and cookery school.

In spite of the necessity for constant fund-raising, Carlingford Heritage Trust is confident that the town's success as a mediaeval heritage town is assured. Elements of the second stage of the programme are already being undertaken and will further consolidate Carlingford's past and enhance its future. These include:

— the development of a site in Tholsel Street as a housing project

— the undergrounding of all electrical and telegraph wiring to further enhance the town's mediaeval character

— the establishment of a public library

— the restoration of the Dominican Abbey Mill Pond and mill race

— the development of a harbour amenity.

The achievements and objectives of Carlingford's Heritage Town programme are underlain by a strong desire on the part of the Heritage Trust Committee not only to make Carlingford a unique tourism attraction, but — as they put it — 'to leave Carlingford in better condition than they found it'. This admirable sense of community spirit surely accounts for Carlingford's remarkable achievements.

Source: Carlingford Lough Heritage Trust

1. Why has Carlingford received its heritage designation?

2. List and describe three mediaeval monuments in Carlingford.

3. What is significant about Carlingford's development as a heritage town?

4. List four of the achievements of the Carlingford Lough Heritage Trust.

5. From what sources has Carlingford received funding for its heritage town development?

6. What sort of difficulties does the Heritage Trust encounter in raising funds? Why?

7. What does the desire of the Carlingford Lough Heritage Trust — 'to leave Carlingford in better condition than they found it' — indicate in terms of the town's tourism development?

Student Questions and Assignments

1. 'Heritage celebrates only those elements of the past which we want to remember.' Discuss.

2. Find out what aspect of Irish heritage is celebrated at the following attractions:

    a   Rock of Cashel, Co. Tipperary

    b   Fort Dunree Military Museum, Co. Donegal

    c   Newgrange, Co. Meath

    d   Dunmore Cave, Co. Kilkenny

    e   Kilmainham Gaol, Dublin

    f   The Skellig Experience, Valentia Island, Co. Kerry

    g   Celtworld, Tramore, Co. Waterford

    h   Number Twenty Nine, Lower Fitzwilliam Street, Dublin

    i   Irish National Heritage Park, Co. Wexford

    j   Céide Fields, Co. Mayo.

3. Carry out a study on a heritage attraction in your locality with reference to:

    a   historical and cultural importance

    b   numbers of visitors received

    c   admission fees, if any

    d   visitor interpretation and other facilities

    e   possible threats to the future of the attraction.

4. Try to find out the names of as many heritage attractions as you can which have received EC funding for tourism development. Identify the positive and negative consequences for Irish heritage that may result owing to the availability of such funding.

5. Choose an historical event from Ireland's past and design an effective means of interpreting this scene to the public within a heritage centre. Describe the materials and presentation formats to be used.

8 Leisure Tourism

Objectives

At the end of this chapter the reader will be able to:

- demonstrate an awareness of the significance of leisure in the context of tourism

- list the reasons for the growth and development of tourism related leisure facilities

- identify and list key tourism leisure amenities

- identify the leisure preferences of Ireland's main tourist markets.

We live in an age of great change. Changes in society have had a profound effect on people's lifestyles. One of the most significant developments has been in the area of leisure. It is now a growing and dynamic industry, accounting for almost one third of all consumer spending, creating many new jobs and generating millions of pounds in revenue.

Although leisure has expanded rapidly in recent times, it is not a new phenomenon and elaborate discourses on the topic can be traced back to the height of classical Greek culture in the writing of Plato and Aristotle. The English word 'leisure' comes from the Latin *licere* meaning 'to be free'. The English words 'licence' and 'liberty' are derived from the same root. Over the years it has had varying but related meanings associated with it: 'freedom from restraint', 'opportunity to choose', 'time left over after work and obligatory duties', and 'to be at ease'.

In 1987 a report on Irish tourism was prepared by Price Waterhouse for the Department of Tourism and Transport. The objectives of the study were to assess past performance and to make recommendations for future development. It found that Ireland was not maximising its tourism potential; three main reasons were put forward for this:

1. Irish tourism compared badly with its competitors in relation to the range and standard of its facilities.

2. Ireland was not price competitive.

3. There were major weaknesses in the marketing strategy for Irish tourism products.

In 1988 Bord Fáilte launched development plans to increase revenue and employment from tourism. The strategy adopted focused on product, competitiveness, promotion and distribution. It particularly identified activity and special interest holidays as having considerable growth potential. The practical effect of this focus on the marketing of the Irish tourism product can be seen in the Bord Fáilte Discover Ireland Brochure for 1992. The contents page lists the following:

Cruising holidays
Adventure holidays
Angling
Banquets and entertainment
Children's organised activity holidays
Cycling
Fitness/health
Golf
Gourmet weekends
Horsedrawn caravans
Horse riding
Painting
Pitch and putt
Sightseeing
Stately Houses and Gardens
Swimming
Tennis
Walking
Walking and cycling
Wildlife and leisure holidays in general

This reflects the trend towards activity and other involvement holidays as people seek healthier lifestyles and cultural activities. The growing level of environmental or green consciousness in the last decade has also made people more selective in their choice of holiday destination. Ireland's low population density, lack of heavy industry, low levels of pollution, the quality of Irish food, and the generally relaxed pace of life are all important factors in attracting foreign visitors. Another health related factor which has operated in Ireland's favour is growing concern over the incidence of skin cancer, due to over-exposure to the sun.

Types of Activity Holiday

Walking

Every county in Ireland offers excellent opportunities to the walker. The countryside is beautiful and relatively unspoiled by industrial development or pollution.

Table 1 Overseas Holidaymakers — Trip Characteristics (detail)					
	Total% O'Seas	Britain	Mainland Europe	North America	Other Areas
Package Hiking/ Hill walking	30%	26%	45%	18%	30%

Source: Tourism Facts, Bord Fáilte, 1991

German and French visitors are particularly keen walkers; hiking is commonly recognised as the German national pastime. Although the British constitute the biggest single market for hill walking, many of them visit friends and relatives and therefore spend less per head than some other segments of the overseas market. This may be seen in the 1990 average spend figure which was IR£186 for the British visitor and IR£309 for the German visitor respectively.

Some county-based studies give an indication of how significant walking has become as a high choice holiday activity; one such is the Pierse, O'Leary and O'Donnchadha study of 'Tourists in North Kerry 1991'. (See Table 2)

Thirty-eight Irish-based companies specialise in walking holidays. These are mainly to be found in the scenic areas of Dublin, Wicklow, Waterford, Kerry, Clare and Donegal.

Table 2 Holiday Preferences

Activity	First Choice	%
Walking	227	38.7
Cycling	124	21.1
Sightseeing/touring	92	21.1
Visits to archaeological sites	61	10.4
Golf	38	6.5
Fishing	32	5.5
Shopping	7	1.2
Water sports	3	0.5
Pony trekking	2	0.3

Source: Tourists in North Kerry 1991

Angling

Ireland has a hugely significant resource in its rivers and lakes — over 14,000 km of river feed over 4,000 loughs, about 1,500 of which hold brown trout, sea trout or salmon — with the cleanest water in the EC, according to Bord Fáilte/Angling Ireland. Ireland is the finest game angling holiday resort in Europe. Sea angling, including shore angling, inshore angling and deep sea angling, is well organised and inexpensive.

Seventy-five commercial firms were identified in a recent CERT report in the area of angling and fishing. However, employment is mainly indirect and seasonal. Direct employment occurs in bait and tackle shops, boat hire and guiding, with indirect employment in accommodation services such as B&Bs and hotels.

Ireland has been host to many major international fishing competitions and in 1992 five major events were organised:

- The Irish Wet-Fly Master's Open Competition, on Lough Corrib at Easter

- The Lough Conn Brown Trout Wet-Fly Angling Festival at Whit weekend

- Lough Melvin Trout Wet-Fly International at the end of June

- The World Cup Brown Trout Wet-Fly Angling Championship at the August Bank Holiday

- The Rosses International Angling Festival in September.

The international flavour of these competitions underlines the significance attached to Irish angling. Angling schools have been set up throughout the country, for example, in Kerry, Cork, Waterford, Galway, Mayo, Cavan and Wicklow. Fishing is a popular up-market sport in a number of our principal markets, such as Britain and Germany. During the 1989–90 season, 150,000 visitors came to fish and 90,000 cited it as having influenced their choice of destination.

Cycling

Ireland is a cyclist's paradise. The roads are relatively safe and the volume of traffic low compared with other countries.

Cycling/hostelling holidays available include bicycle hire, with youth hostel overnight accommodation vouchers, handbooks and maps. Another package offers rail transport to a starting point, along with all of the above. There are guided cycle tours available in West Cork, Kerry, Galway, Mayo, Sligo and Donegal with B&B accommodation en route. Others prefer to choose their own route and accommodation.

Table 3 Overseas Holidaymakers — Trip Characteristics 1990 (detail)					
	Total %	Britain	Mainland Europe	North America	Other Areas
Cycling	7%	6%	14%	4%	3%

Source: Tourism Facts, Bord Fáilte, 1991

Cycle touring groups and individual cyclists have become a notable feature on Irish roads over the past decade. Doubtless this has been encouraged by the international success of Irish racing cyclists. However, much remains to be done to raise the profile of leisure cycling and make it a popular activity among tourists.

There are sixty-eight bicycle hire centres around the country. The heaviest concentrations of these are in Dublin, Kerry, Clare, Galway and Mayo. They employ about 215 people of whom 155 are full-time.

Golf

The *Golfer's Guide to Ireland* lists 250 clubs. Of these over 100 are 18-hole, and the remainder 9-hole courses. This changes constantly with the addition of new courses and the upgrading of others from 9 to 18 holes. Golf in Ireland has been expanding steadily for over 100 years; with so many courses to choose from, it is one of the world's most respected golfing countries, with celebrated clubs such as Ballybunion, Lahinch, Portmarnock, Sligo, Tralee and Waterville.

In its marketing drive, Bord Fáilte divided Ireland into six golfing regions and selected golf clubs that are particularly well equipped for the tourist. By travelling from one to another the golfer can vary the golfing experience from day to day. Golfing holidays are marketed by Irish golf holiday specialists and packages can be arranged to fit particular needs, from a golfing holiday for beginners to a tournament circuit of the great links.

Equestrian

Trail riding or trekking, residential equestrian centres, hunting, horse-racing, and horse-drawn caravans, are just some of the equestrian activities available in Ireland. The most popular, the trail-ride, is an ideal way to experience the Irish countryside, progressing along country lanes, forest tracks, beaches and mountain routes.

The principal sporting and social event of the equestrian year in Ireland is the Kerrygold Dublin Horse Show followed closely by the Millstreet International Show. Other shows include the Connemara Pony Show and the Ballinasloe Great October Fair. Horse-racing meets at Punchestown, Leopardstown, the Curragh and at numerous other racecourses throughout the country are very popular.

irish
NATIONAL
STUD

There are 78 registered horse-riding establishments in operation in the country as well as some which are unregistered.

Cruising

Ireland's rivers are among the cleanest in Europe; with no commercial traffic they provide an idyllic location for tranquil cruising holidays. Main cruising areas are the Erne Systems, the Shannon and the Grand Canal which connects Dublin with the Barrow and Shannon.

Sailing

Being an island, Ireland has a long sailing history. The most popular sailing area is between Cork Harbour and the Dingle Peninsula which offers no less than 143 small harbours.

Adventure Sports

Outdoor adventure sport in the early 1970s was very much a minority interest. Its enthusiasts were a committed group who participated without resources. The representative body for this interest sport is the Association for Adventure Sports (AFAS) who set up the first Outdoor Pursuit Centre in Ireland in Tiglin, Co. Wicklow in 1972. Tiglin is now the National Adventure Centre. Another centre, Achill, was set up in 1973 by Co. Mayo VEC; since then a steady flow of developments, commercial and public has raised the numbers to 19 centres by 1990.

Leisure Preferences of Main Source Markets

Germany

German tourists visit Ireland chiefly for angling, hiking and walking, cycling, history and culture. Angling is very directly related to the choice of destination and for German people, Ireland is an angler's paradise. This is no doubt influenced by the German perception of Ireland as a green and unspoilt land, and they stay for a relatively long period (15.5 nights, 1989).

Britain

Twenty-six per cent of British visitors chose walking for part or all of their holidays compared with 45% from the Continent. However, British numbers were significantly greater than those from any other country. There are also more British tourists seeking fishing and golf. In fact British fishermen and anglers have been a common sight in Ireland since the mid 1980s. Only 2% of British visitors participate in horse-riding and 4% in cycling. The figure for cycling is particularly low in comparison to those from the Continent of whom 14% chose cycling.

North America

American visitors come to Ireland for golfing, hiking and walking holidays and to visit historic sites. With the exception of golf, American tourists are not particularly conspicuous in active outdoor leisure pursuits. A lot come to visit friends and relatives or on structured bus tour packages. The American visitor is significantly older than the visitor from mainland Europe, 52% of American tourists being over 45 years of age, compared with 19% of German and 17% of French.

Although their length of stay is near the bottom of the list in terms of bed nights, American visitors spend more than any others in Ireland at IR£375. In America there is a strong domestic market for active outdoor pursuits but the active vacationer tends not to come to Ireland to pursue this interest.

France

French tourists visit Ireland for angling, walking and hiking, cycling, historical and cultural activities. They do not come in search of sun or because of family associations. The French tend to holiday in Ireland to experience the cultural heritage, meet the people and explore the landscape. French walkers on average stay for 11 days, walking for 8 of them. Three-quarters are on their main holiday and 40% are under 25 years of age and another 43% are between 25 and 34 years old; 64% are from the white collar sector and 26% from the professional/managerial socio-economic group. Ireland does not attract French families with children; these have averaged only 11% of the French total over the years 1986–1989.

The Hotel Leisure Centre

It is predicted that almost 70% of all hotels will have indoor or outdoor leisure facilities by the year 2000. Research carried out by CERT showed that of those hotels that did not offer leisure facilities, 66% of Grade A and 61% of Grade B had plans to develop them. Most hoteliers (89%) with leisure facilities reported increased room occupancy of the order of 10% which they attributed directly to the provision of extra facil-ities. Bord Fáilte has been promoting the development of leisure facilities in hotels since the early 1980s as part of a major drive to increase the revenue-earning capability of Irish tourism. Hotel leisure centre facilities are expensive. Typical examples of recent developments, without inde-pendent food facilities, range from between IR£400,000 and IR£750,000. As operating costs frequently account for 70% to 80% of income and the return on capital employed as low as from 3–6%, very careful attention must be paid to determining a project's viability from the outset.

Grant aid and the availability of generous tax breaks have influenced many hoteliers to embark on developments in the leisure area. The European Regional Development Fund grants range from 10% to 50% of project costs. An applicant must establish the potential of the project to attract foreign tourists. The International Fund for Ireland grants are directed mainly at border counties and can be up to 50% of project cost. In 1989 alone IR£4m was invested by the IFI in leisure facilities in border counties.

Conservative estimates predict that total spending on hotel-based leisure facilities will amount to around IR£200m by 1994. Hotels have been influenced by the public's growing interest in personal fitness and appearance. In response, facilities including swimming pools, weights gyms, bicycle ergometers, treadmills, step machines, rowing machines, dance studios and fitness testing, all provided with expert tuition, are now taken to be an essential client service rather than an exceptional and rare treat.

Case Study: Mount Juliet Golf and Country Club

Mount Juliet is a Golf and Country Club on 1,500 acres situated near Thomastown in Co. Kilkenny. It was built in the 19th century as a family-owned manor house. When it was sold it was extensively renovated and opened as a hotel in October 1989. It is now positioned as a top quality country club with almost everything the outdoor enthusiast could ask for. Facilities include a parkland golf course designed by Jack Nicklaus — 7,200 yards long (6,584 metres) — and it plays to a 72 par off the championship tees. Mount Juliet is hosting the Carrolls Irish Open Golf Championships in 1993 and 1994.

There is a unique 3-hole teaching academy at Mount Juliet on 60 acres; again designed by Nicklaus, it consists of par 3, 4 and 5 holes. It is designed to allow the novice and the experienced player to improve and fine-tune their games. Professional tuition and the unhurried atmosphere of the academy combine to offer the best possible environment for mastering the game.

Traditional country sports like fishing, hunting, shooting and riding are also on offer. The River Nore runs close to the manor house and is excellent for salmon and brown trout. Excursions to the coast for groups wishing to go deep sea angling are also arranged.

Clay Target Shooting is an increasingly popular sport at Mount Juliet. It is not subject to seasonal factors and can be enjoyed all year round. Archery is also available at the Clay Target area.

Facilities for equestrian sports at Mount Juliet are also very extensive. The Iris Kellett Equestrian Centre offers basic tuition, show jumping, dressage, trail riding and a Cross Country Jumping Academy. Mount Juliet is home of the Kilkenny Hunt. Guests may join this hunt or one of the neighbouring hunts if they wish. Polo is also played.

Sport and Hunting theme breaks are available during the season from November to March.

Mount Juliet estate has a number of walking trails traversing its open pasture and woodland. To add interest to the walks, a treasure hunt has been designed to help participants explore and absorb the main features of interest along the pathways.

Bicycles are available to guests, as is a hard tennis court for those wishing to play. A new leisure centre, opened in November 1992, includes a swimming pool, whirlpool, exercise room, sauna, steam room and solarium. Massage, aromatherapy and the services of a beautician are also available.

Since its opening in 1989 the task of marketing Mount Juliet has been progressing. Initially, most clients were Irish, but as overseas marketing effort began to bear fruit, US and European visitors accounted for about 15% and 50% respectively, with the remaining 35% coming from the home market during the Summer season. The Winter season is dominated by domestic weekend and short breaks.

A large proportion of clients are members of incentive groups, being rewarded for particular achievement within their companies. Many companies use Mount Juliet to entertain prospective customers and to secure business contracts.

1. Find out the current tariffs and fees at Mount Juliet Golf and Country Club. How do these compare with similar up-market establishments?

2. How has Mount Juliet maximised its natural location?

3. How important is incentive and business travel to luxury hotels?

4. Design a six-day golfing circuit for a group of international business people. Include suggestions for accommodation, dining and entertainment near each course.

Case Study: Cruising Holidays on Lough Erne

Boat rental on Irish waterways has grown annually in recent years. While the Shannon and the Erne are the two principal waterways, many smaller lakes and inlets offer boat hire and excursions. The Upper and Lower Lough Erne system stretches for almost 70 km, from Belturbet, Co. Cavan, to Belleek in Co. Fermanagh. With the opening of the Erne-Shannon link, the Erne and Shannon together will become one of the longest inland waterways in Europe.

Interest in cruising holidays is strongest in the German market, though the domestic market within Northern Ireland remains strong. The beautiful countryside and the wide range of water activities available in a pollution-free environment strongly appeal to the Continental market.

The Northern Ireland Tourist Board (NITB), have recognised the potential in cruiser hire and provided grants and funding to promote the industry. Amenities of various kinds, theatres, shops and pubs are all easily accessible from the numerous jetties along the waterway and it is estimated that total tourism spending in Fermanagh as a result of the cruiser industry is about IR£2m.

Occupancy in 1991 fell slightly due to uncertainty about the Gulf War. Non-Northern Ireland resident numbers dropped but the domestic market increased. This was due in part to greater availability because of the decrease in other markets.

Table 4 A Erne: Cruiser Weeks Sold

	1987	1988	1989	1990	1991	%Change 1990/91
NI Residents	652.0	639.0	552.0	414.5	438.5	+5.8
Non NI Residents	916.5	980.0	1219.5	1541.5	1484.5	-3.7
Total Boat weeks sold	1568.5	1619.0	1771.5	1956.0	1923.0	-1.7

Table 4 B Erne: Cruiser Occupancy Rates

	Low	Mid	Standard	High
	Before April 23 After Sept. 25	24 April–14 May 4 Sept–24 Sept	15 May–18 June 21 Aug–3 Sept	19 June– 10 Aug.
Total Weeks Booked	234.5	383.5	549.0	756.0
Occupancy Rate%	33.2	70.9	87.3	92.6

Table 4 C Erne: Country of origin of Hirers — 1991

	No. of Weeks
Germany	941.5
Northern Ireland	438.5
Switzerland	376.5
Holland	48
Great Britain	45
Republic of Ireland	23.5
Austria	23
France	8
Portugal	8
Belgium	3
Denmark	2
Canada	1
Isle of Man	1
Hong Kong	1
Scotland	1
South Africa	1
USA	1
Total	1,923

1. Study Table A and Table C. Suggest why the industry is more attractive to non-NI residents than the domestic market.

2. What spin-off benefits or multiplier effect does the cruiser industry present to Fermanagh? To Northern Ireland?

3. What effect will the Erne-Shannon Link have on the cruiser industry throughout Ireland?

4. 'Polluted and over-crowded waterways will result from the development of the cruiser industry in Northern Ireland.' Discuss.

5. Suggest reasons why the American market is slow to avail of cruising holidays. Consider in your answer location, cost and marketing.

6. What problems might the Northern Ireland cruising industry face in marketing abroad, and what steps might they take to overcome these?

Tourism and the Economy

9

Tourism encompasses many economic sectors — so many, in fact, that the tourist industry's contribution to Ireland's economy is often underestimated. In particular, tourism:

- contributes substantially to Gross National Product (GNP)

- supports a significant level of employment

- has the potential to support more jobs

- earns high added-value foreign exchange

- generates exchequer revenue

- assists regional distribution of income and jobs.

Over the 1960–89 period, tourist arrivals in Ireland (including visitors from Northern Ireland) rose from 1.4 million to 3.5 million. Ireland's share of world tourist arrivals thus fell from 2.0% to 0.8%, and of European tourist arrivals from 2.7% to 1.3%.

During this 30-year period, the main decline in Ireland's market share occurred in the 1960s and 1970s. The downward trend stabilised during the 1980s and has improved since 1986: Ireland's share of world tourist arrivals rose from 0.75% in 1986 to 0.84% in 1989, and of tourist arrivals in Europe from 1.17% to 1.34%.

Tourism Revenue

Income generation is determined first and foremost by the scale of expenditure by out-of-state visitors, on accommodation, food, transport and so on after their arrival in Ireland, and on the access fares they paid to Irish carriers.

It is important to distinguish between expenditure by visitors to Ireland (export tourism) and spending by domestic tourists. Export tourism is worth more to the domestic economy because it represents a flow of money into the country, while part at least of domestic tourism represents a transfer of income and expenditure from one sector of the economy to another.

Overseas tourist numbers grew from 2,098,000 in 1987 to a record 3,096,000 in 1990 and then fell back slightly by 2.6% to 3,015,000 in 1991. However it is estimated that a new record figure of just over 3.1 million overseas visitors will be achieved in 1992. The associated tourism revenue (i.e. excluding that derived from domestic holiday-makers and visitors from Northern Ireland) increased from IR£504.3m in 1987 to IR£795.8m in 1990; then, despite the slight drop in numbers, increased by a further 7.6% to IR£855.9m in 1991. For 1992, overseas revenue was estimated to have grown by about 8% to some IR£920m.

Table 1 Tourism Numbers and Revenues

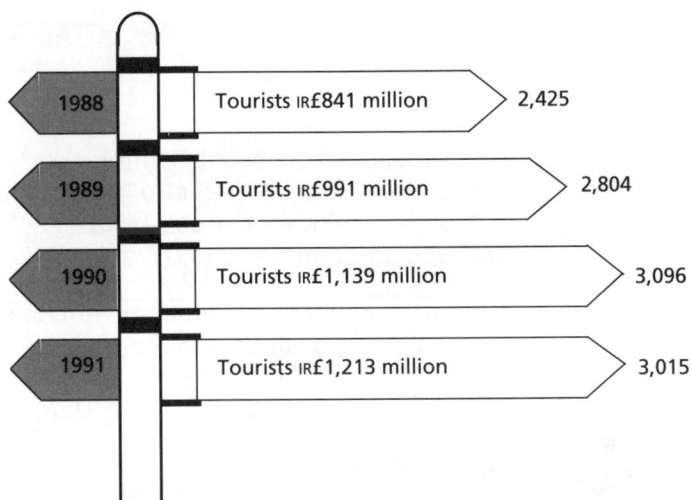

Year	Tourists	Number
1988	Tourists IR£841 million	2,425
1989	Tourists IR£991 million	2,804
1990	Tourists IR£1,139 million	3,096
1991	Tourists IR£1,213 million	3,015

Source: Bord Fáilte

Table 2 Foreign Exchange Tourism Earnings 1985–90

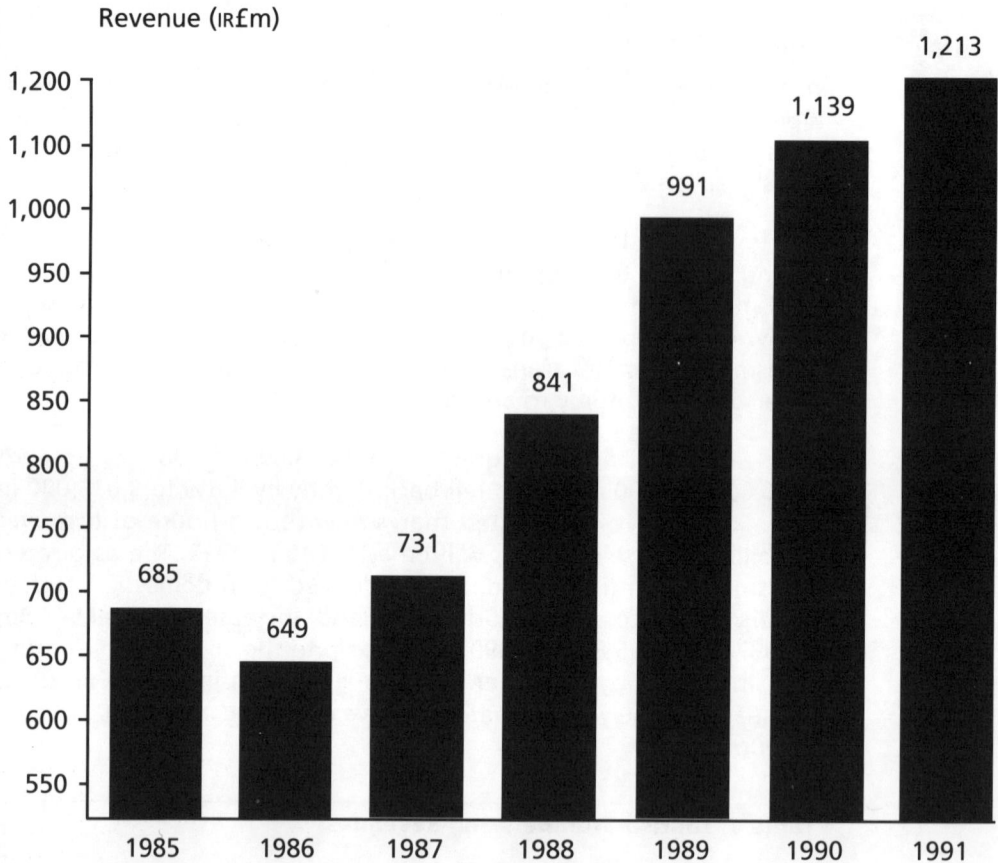

Revenue (IR£m)

Year	Revenue (IR£m)
1985	685
1986	649
1987	731
1988	841
1989	991
1990	1,139
1991	1,213

Source: Bord Fáilte

When tourists from Northern Ireland, day visitors from all markets and carrier receipts are also taken into account, total foreign exchange earnings increased from IR£731m in 1987 to IR£1,213m in 1991 and an estimated IR£1,310m in 1992.

After adding revenue from home holidays and other domestic (non-business) trips, total tourism revenue increased from IR£1,021.7m in 1987 to IR£1,717.8m in 1991, the latter figure being an increase of 10.7% on the 1990 figure of IR£1,551.7m.

The Economic Benefits

Summarising the economic benefits of tourism to the Irish economy, Bord Fáilte states:

— Foreign and domestic tourism expenditure amounted to IR£1,717.8m in 1991, representing approximately 7.3% of Gross National Product (GNP). (See Glossary)

— A significant proportion of foreign tourism spending within Ireland goes to the exchequer in taxation. In 1991, the exchequer received approximately IR£326m from foreign tourism and a further IR£149m from domestic tourism, a total of IR£475m.

— Tourism revenue accounted for 7.3% of all exports of goods and services in 1991, compared with 7.1% in 1990.

— Tourism makes an important contribution to employment. By its nature, tourism is highly labour intensive because it relies so much on personal service. Furthermore, much of the employment generated by tourism is in areas otherwise economically under-developed.

— In recent years, tourism has sustained significant additions to total employment in Ireland. In 1991, Bord Fáilte estimated that there were 87,000 full-time job equivalents attributable to tourism, compared to 82,000 in 1990.

— Foreign tourism accounted for 2,000 of these additional jobs, and domestic tourism for the remaining 3,000.

Tourism Statistics

It is important to add a cautionary note on the statistics relating to tourist numbers, revenue, employment, contribution to Gross National Product, and so on, however reliable the source. This is because tourism is not a neatly defined economic activity such as agriculture or industry, because there are changes in data collection methods, and sometimes definitions from year to year, and because various organisations may have differing views as to what should be included. In particular, they may adopt different positions on whether not only direct and indirect income should be included but also induced income, and they may then use a different tourism multiplier to determine, for example, tourism's contribution to GNP or employment statistics.

A brief explanation of these terms has been given by Brian Deane of Bord Fáilte:

1. Some businesses (e.g. hotels) are the *direct* recipients of tourist expenditure.

2. These businesses buy goods from other firms in Ireland (e.g. foodstuffs, computers): this may be termed an *indirect income effect.*

3. Increased direct and indirect income is spent, some on goods and services produced in Ireland: this may be termed an *induced*

income effect. This expenditure becomes income for others in Ireland (for example, wages, salaries and rents).

Thus one tourist's spending can lead to successive increases in direct and indirect income, and in expenditure out of that income, which would lead to a new and higher level of income and employment and so on; so the tourist's expenditure is multiplied, hence the term multiplier effect .

The multiplier effect does not, however, maintain its momentum. It is dampened by a number of leakages. Imports give rise to leakage: for example, wages and salaries, rents, interest and profits paid to non-residents. Savings, since they are not spent, also constitute leakage. So does taxation: some argue that, in the longer term, taxation should be taken into account and treated as part of the overall income-expenditure process.

Thus, the tourism multiplier, the amount by which direct tourism income should be multiplied to establish total income from tourism, actually adopted can vary widely, from 0.5 to as high as 2.0, depending on the level of indirect and induced incomes included. Table 4 shows tourism revenues and contributions to GNP for the years 1985–90, as calculated by Tansey Webster and Associates for the ITIC report, 'A Study of the Economic Impact of Tourism in Ireland: 1985–90' (1991).

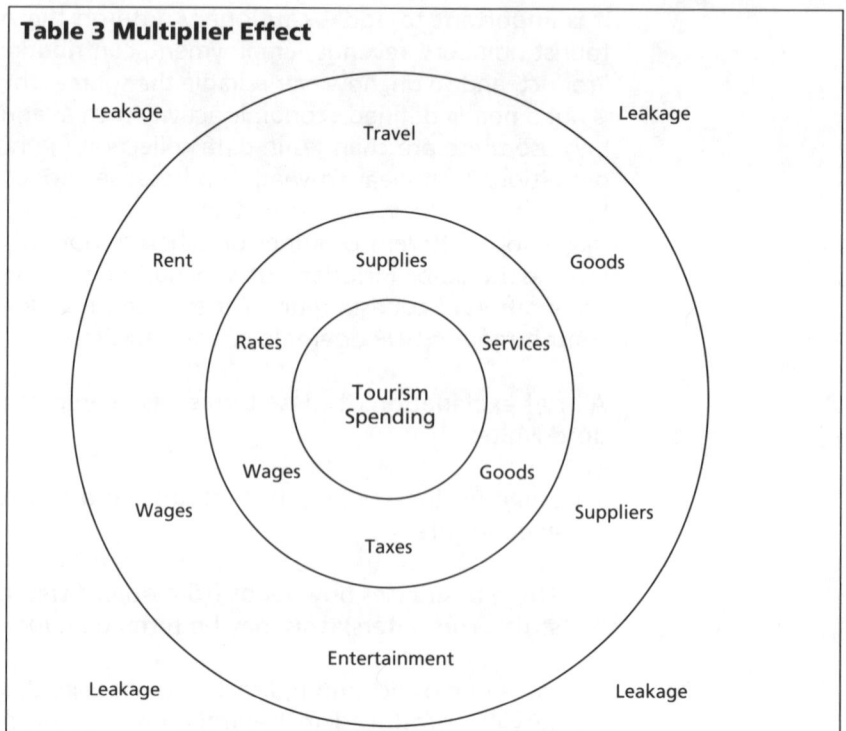

Table 3 Multiplier Effect

Table 4 Tourism Revenue and GNP (IR₤ million at constant 1985 prices)

	1985	1986	1987	1988	1989	1990
GNP	15,725	15,615	16,332	16,866	17,608	18,664
Tourism Revenue of which:	954	834	953	1,052	1,161	1,319
— Foreign	685	625	682	768	870	968
— Domestic	269	209	271	284	291	351

GNP IMPACT (with GNP multipliers shown in brackets)

	1985	1986	1987	1988	1989	1990
Foreign Tourism:						
— Direct (0.64)	438	400	436	492	557	620
— Direct + Indirect (0.77)	527	481	525	591	670	745
— Direct + Indirect + Induced (0.99)	678	619	675	760	861	958
% of GNP	**4.3**	**4.0**	**4.1**	**4.5**	**4.9**	**5.1**
Domestic Tourism						
— Direct (0.61)	164	127	165	173	177	214
— Direct + Indirect (0.81)	218	169	219	230	236	284
% of GNP	**1.4**	**1.1**	**1.3**	**1.4**	**1.3**	**1.5**
Total Tourism						
— Direct	602	527	601	665	734	834
— Direct + Indirect	745	650	744	821	906	1,029
— Direct + Indirect + Induced	896	788	894	990	1,097	1,242
% of GNP	**5.7**	**5.0**	**5.5**	**5.9**	**6.2**	**6.7**
GNP growth rate %	−0.4	−0.7	4.6	3.3	4.4	6.0
Growth rate of Tourism's GNP Contribution %		−12.1	13.6	10.8	10.6	13.1

Sources: CSO; Bord Fáilte, Tansey & Webster Associates

The way in which tourism revenue can benefit other sectors, through direct, indirect and induced income, may be illustrated with a few examples suggested by Bord Fáilte in 'Tourism in the Irish Economy'.

— If only 20% of the three million visitors had one steak during their stay the demand created for beef cattle would amount to 21,000, or 8% of the beef herd killed for domestic consumption.

— If each visitor staying in serviced accommodation (i.e. excluding self-catering and staying with relatives) used an average of one egg per day — in sweets, cakes, confectionery, sauces, or eaten as part of a meal — the total egg consumption by tourists would be equivalent to the output of over 156,000 hens, almost 10% of the national flock.

— If visitors made 1.3 million taxi trips with a minimum half-hour journey each, that would be equivalent to one year's employment for over 320 taxi drivers working 40 hours a week for 50 weeks of the year.

— If 75% of female visitors made one visit to the hairdresser during the average 11-day stay they could be supporting the employment of over 170 hairdressers.

— If each visitor went to the theatre once, this would more than keep a 350-seat theatre booked to capacity for over one year of nightly performances.

Similar analogies can be made with other sectors; clearly, many people depend on tourism for an important proportion of their livelihood — often without realising it.

Employment in Tourism

For the reasons outlined earlier, and also due to the fact that four different basic approaches have been used in recent years to measure tourism employment, no definitive figure can be given for employment in Ireland's tourism industry. For example, figures given include 157,000 by CERT in 1992 + 87,000 by Bord Fáilte in 1991. The discrepancy is accounted for by different methods of calculating employment statistics.

The four basic methods of measuring tourism employment are:

— *Input-Output Method*, which derives both the direct and indirect employment effects of 'out-of-state' tourism expenditure (including carrier receipts) based on the usual assumptions on which input-output tables are constructed. (Bord Fáilte uses this method.)

— *Direct Survey Method*, which probably gives the best estimates of *direct* employment, but cannot measure indirect or induced employment effects. (CERT uses this method.)

- *Proportional Method*, which establishes the proportion of total expenditure in each expenditure category derived from tourism and applies this proportion to total employment in the relevant sectors.

- *Macro-economic Model*, in its application to tourism employment estimation, is only suitable for measuring the effect of incremental 'out-of-state' tourism revenue on existing employment.

Table 5 Direct and Indirect Employment Supported By Tourism (1985–1990)

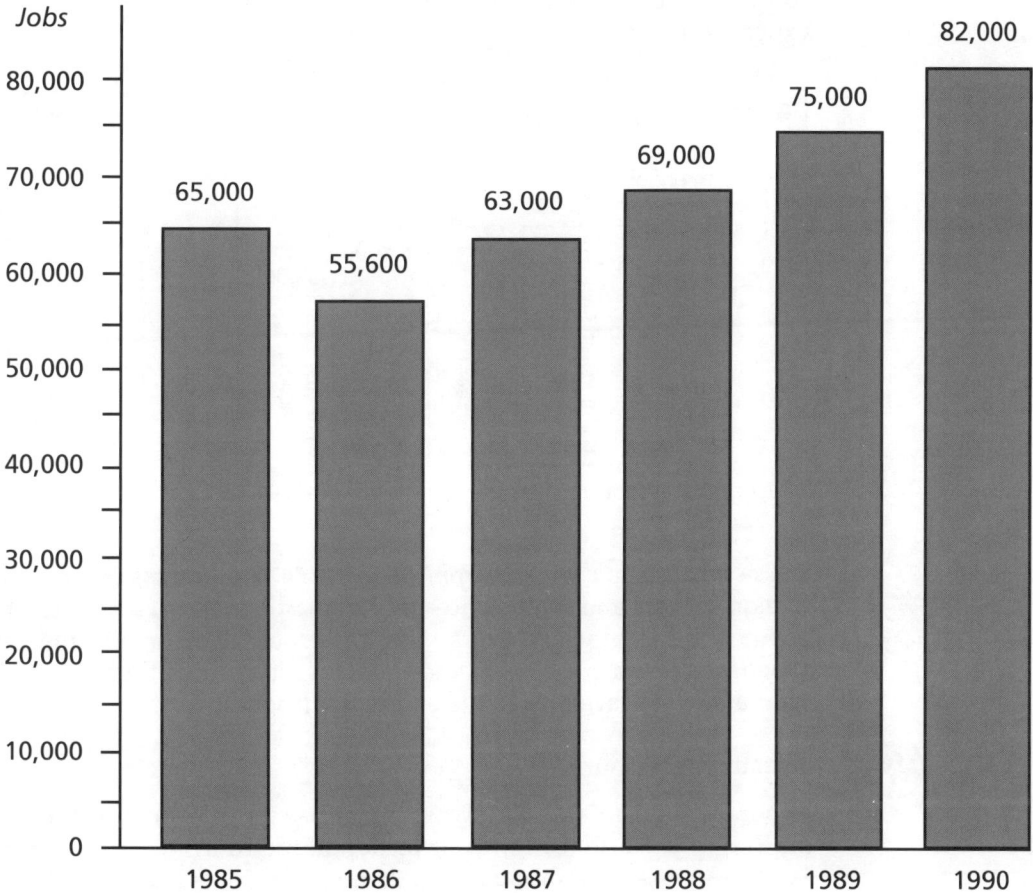

Courtesy ITIC

Exchequer Revenues

Tourist spending in Ireland is an important source of tax revenue for the exchequer, both directly, through Value Added Tax (VAT) and excise duties on expenditure by tourists, and indirectly, through the various taxes on economic activity arising as a result of tourist expenditure, such as income tax/PRSI from employment, corporation tax, local government rates on hotels and other tourism-related facilities, and so on.

From 1987 to 1990, for example, the estimated tax revenues from direct and indirect sources have represented around 27% of total tourism revenue, including carrier receipts and domestic tourism expenditure (see Table 6).

Table 6 Comparison with other industry — numbers employed

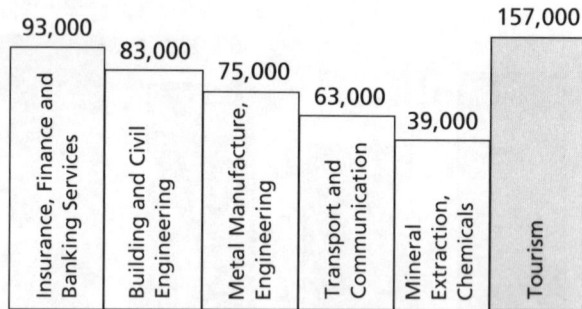

Insurance, Finance and Banking Services	Building and Civil Engineering	Metal Manufacture, Engineering	Transport and Communication	Mineral Extraction, Chemicals	Tourism
93,000	83,000	75,000	63,000	39,000	157,000

Figures rounded to nearest '000 (Based on 1990 Eurostat figures)

The estimated tax revenue for 1990 of IR£427m (over IR£300m from foreign tourists and the balance from domestic tourism) accounted for about 5% of total exchequer receipts from taxes on income and expenditure and social insurance contributions; thus there is a substantial flow of revenues to the exchequer from tourism.

Investment in Tourism

Although there are no official comprehensive statistics on investment in tourism — because it is difficult to define the tourism sector — Bord Fáilte estimates that about IR£1,000m will be invested in tourism in Ireland in the ten years from 1989 to 1998, and that projects worth over IR£500m had already come on stream by the end of 1992.

This rate of investment was a substantial increase on earlier years; for example, Department of the Environment statistics for new construction and repair and maintenance in the tourism sector show expenditure of IR£91.8m in 1990 compared with only IR£41.6m two years previously.

An even more dramatic rise occurred in the capital grant payments made by Bord Fáilte and Shannon Development for tourism facilities

Table 7 Tourism Employment by Region

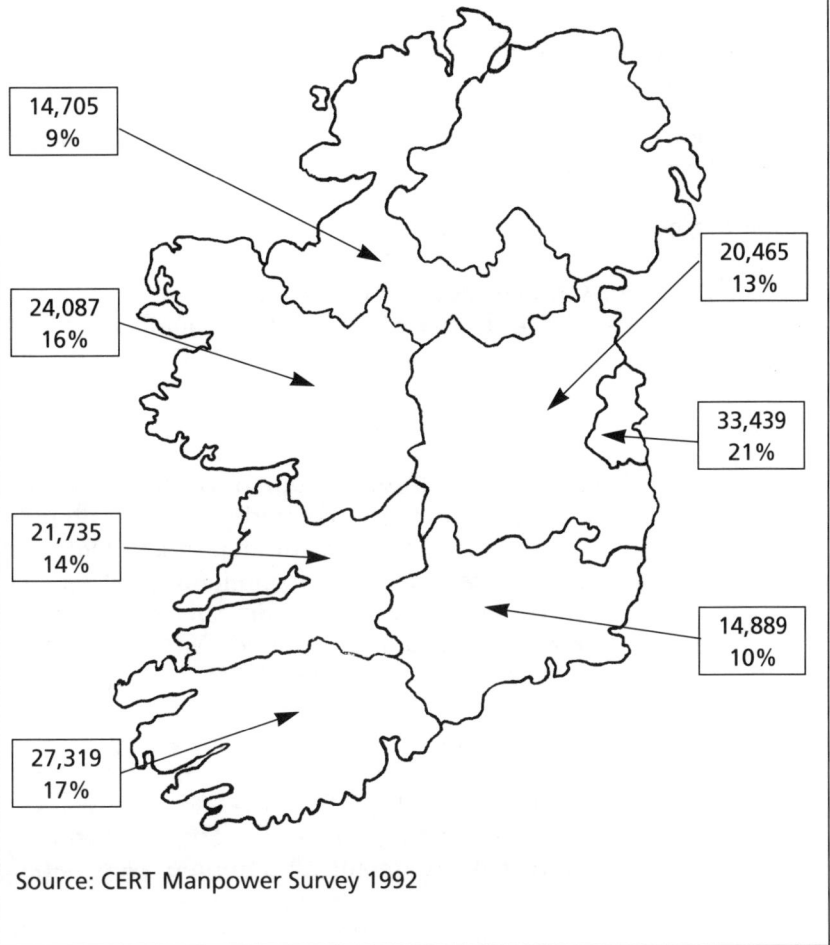

14,705
9%

20,465
13%

24,087
16%

33,439
21%

21,735
14%

14,889
10%

27,319
17%

Source: CERT Manpower Survey 1992

and accommodation. In 1985, grant payments totalled IR£2.8m towards a total tourism-associated investment of IR£14m. In 1990, however, IR£10.3m in grants supported a total investment of IR£51.6m. The substantial increase in grants and investment in 1990 and subsequent years resulted principally from the introduction of European Regional Development Fund (ERDF) support for tourism in that year.

This funding was part of the five-year growth plan for Irish tourism, the National Development Plan 1989–93, which aimed to double overseas visitor numbers to 4.2 million, increase revenue by IR£500m, and create 25,000 new jobs. Clearly, a substantial and sustained increase in investment in the industry was essential, and it was forthcoming from a variety of sources.

Table 8 Tourism Expenditure and Exchequer Revenues from Tourism (IR£ million)				
	1987	1988	1989	1990
Out-of-state Tourism Expenditure and Carrier Receipts	731	841	991	1,139
Domestic tourism expenditure	291	311	331	413
Total Tourism Revenue	1,022	1,152	1,322	1,552
Estimated tax revenues	283	317	364	427

Sources: CSO; Bord Fáilte; Tansey Webster estimates

A total investment by the government, European Community and the private sector of at least IR£300m was planned. The European Structural Fund was to contribute IR£147m, matched by IR£32.7m from public bodies (including IR£15.4m on training) and at least IR£120m from the private sector, both international and national.

In 1987, the Business Expansion Scheme (BES) was extended to include tourism. This created a further potential for investment for the National Development Plan of IR£320m from the private sector. The International Fund for Ireland grant schemes were expected to contribute a further IR£12.6m towards tourism development in the border counties and Co. Sligo, with grants up to 50% leading to a total investment of some IR£50m.

The ERDF grants are administered by Bord Fáilte and Shannon Development; they are given to the private sector for investment in priority, product-related infrastructural work, the development of amenities aimed specifically at attracting additional overseas tourists and revenue to Ireland, and for improved marketing.

In their report for the Irish Tourist Industry Confederation entitled 'A Strategic Framework for Tourism Enterprises' published in 1992, economic consultants Tansey Webster & Associates looked at how this investment was being made and concluded: 'Never before has so much investment been made or planned in the Irish tourism product in such a short time. As a result, a significant expansion and upgrading in the quality of the product has been effected. High quality leisure facilities have been added to the accommodation base to provide the all-weather facilities demanded by the modern tourist. Our cultural and heritage infrastructure has been upgraded and new sports facilities — particularly golf — are coming on stream rapidly.'

A summary of most of the projects approved for grants in excess of IR£25,000 was prepared in February 1992 by Bord Fáilte. This showed the scope and depth of investment in new tourism products. Over 170 projects that were completed in the previous two years, in progress or committed to start, included:

- 7 hotel conference facilities

- 31 leisure facilities

- 23 activity products, including cruisers, marinas, equestrian centres, activity centres, angling vessels, and the restoration of the Ballina-more – Ballyconnell Canal

- 22 golf developments

- 5 special interest products, comprising three language centres, a National Ecology Centre, and the National Genealogy Centre network

- 6 museums

- 14 visitor information projects, including improvements to the Tourist Information Office network, signposted touring routes, and signposting at historic sites

- 24 interpretative centres

- 5 historic houses and gardens

- 5 new hotels

- 23 heritage projects, including heritage centres and 15 heritage towns

- 5 literary/cultural projects

By no means was all of the investment ERDF-related or confined to government or native private enterprise sources: several were multi-million-pound independent, internationally funded projects. Examples of these include the Dublin Conrad Hotel by the USA-based Hilton Hotel Group, further development of the Trabolgan Holiday Centre near Midleton Co. Cork by the UK-based company Pontins (following its purchase of the Dutch-owned enterprise), the Sheen Falls Lodge in Kenmare by a Scandinavian private investor, and the development of the Waterville Lake Hotel in Co. Kerry by Club Med of France, the world's fifth largest tour operating company.

Investment Incentives

A variety of grant aid and other investment incentives has been made available to investors in tourism products.

ERDF: Grant aid under the ERDF schemes is assisting the development of facilities aimed specifically at attracting foreign tourism revenue including: marinas, cruising, water, field and adventure sports, angling, equestrian, golf, walking, cycling, language learning, visitor attractions, interpretative centres, heritage and cultural attractions, genealogy projects, health farms, leisure and conference facilities, visitor information, and marketing. The level of grant aid varies from 25% to 50% for private sector projects and from 50% to 75% for public sector projects.

Inter-reg Programme: The objective of the European Community's Inter-reg Programme is to develop and promote cross-border projects for the purpose of increasing visitor numbers and extending the tourist season. The scheme is administered by Bord Fáilte and offers levels of assistance of 50% for private sector and revenue-earning public sector projects, and 75% for non-revenue public sector projects.

Agri-Tourism Grant Scheme: This scheme, administered by Bord Fáilte on behalf of the Department of Agriculture and Food, provides grant aid of up to 50% for a wide range of rural tourism projects including leisure facilities, accommodation and community sponsored amenities. The objective of the scheme is to provide incentives to farmers and other rural dwellers towards the cost of providing facilities which will enhance the attractiveness of an area for tourists and meet clearly identified tourist demands.

International Fund for Ireland: Bord Fáilte administers the following schemes on behalf of the IFI: Accommodation Amenities Development, Tourism Amenities Development, Hotel and Guesthouse Improvement, and Community Sponsored Amenities Development. The schemes apply to projects in the border counties of Cavan, Donegal, Leitrim, Louth and Monaghan, as well as Sligo.

Business Expansion Scheme: This scheme allowed owners and promoters of certain tourism businesses to raise investment finance at less cost than from traditional borrowing sources by securing outside investors who could obtain significant tax relief on their investment, up to a maximum of IR£75,000, at the investor's highest rate of income tax.

The BES was originally planned to operate until 1991. By August 1991, 277 companies had received approval for BES funding, of which 145 were hotel projects, representing a total investment of over IR£320m. Up to the end of the 1991/92 tax year, actual investment in BES funded tourism projects amounted to IR£85m, of which around IR£63m was raised for 63 hotel projects. The BES was extended until 5 April 1993, subject to some amendments.

Capital Expenditure Tax Relief: Three types of relief applied to capital expenditure for tourism development in 1992:

— Initial allowance was a once-off deduction granted for the accounting period in which the expenditure on new premises or plant is incurred.

— Writing down was available over a number of years on new or newly acquired premises and equipment.

— Accelerated Capital Allowance (Free Depreciation) enabled an owner to obtain an immediate tax deduction for a substantial part of the capital expenditure incurred on new premises or plant. However, the accelerated capital allowance rate was progressively reduced from its initial 100% to 50% and then 25% from 1 April 1991, and finally zero from 1 April 1992.

The Operational Programme for Tourism 1989–93 will, it is expected, be followed by a second five-year programme for the years 1994–98. By October 1992, the various tourism interests had submitted their individual proposals for such a programme to the government, for incorporation into a national plan for submission to the European Community.

Student Questions and Assignments

1. Describe how tourism can impact on a local economy.

2. Find out the most up-to-date figures for the regional distribution of tourism revenue and analyse the regional variations.

3. Why are some countries more dependent than others on tourism as an earner of foreign exchange?

4. Trace the multiplier effect from a tourism facility in your region. Identify reasons for leakage and suggest methods of preventing such leakage from occurring.

5. Why is out-of-state tourism more valuable in economic terms than domestic tourism?

6. Identify tourism enterprises in your region that have benefitted from investment incentives or grants. Select one scheme, explain the qualifying conditions and assess its effectiveness in terms of supporting tourism development.

7. Explain the term GNP. Research and compare the contribution of tourism to the GNP of any five countries.

8. Explain how currency exchange rates can affect the attractiveness of a holiday destination. Is a strong *punt* good or bad for Irish tourism?

References

1. *Tourism and the Economy* by Tansey Webster and Associates. Published by the Irish Tourist Industry Confederation, 1991.

2. *A Strategic Framework for Tourism Enterprises* by Tansey Webster and Associates. Published by the Irish Tourist Industry Confederation, 1992.

3. *Scope of the Tourism Industry in Ireland.* Research Report published by CERT, 1993.

4. *Tourism Facts 1991*, published by Bord Fáilte, 1992.

10 Tourism and Employment Opportunities

Objectives

At the end of this chapter the reader will be able to:

- understand the nature of work in the tourism industry

- identify tourism related education and training opportunities available in Ireland

- identify the range of job categories within tourism and the skills required

- understand the role of CERT.

Tourism is a growing industry which offers long-term career prospects and opportunities for advancement to people who enjoy meeting its many challenges. A labour-intensive industry, it includes jobs calling for widely differing abilities and qualifications. As in almost all fields, the career structure is in pyramid form and jobs range from unskilled, through clerical and technical, to management and professional.

Naturally any work involves much that is routine and ordinary, but most tourism jobs also include variety in the challenges and experience presented. It can be an exciting career field for anyone who wants more than a regular nine-to-five job, enjoys meeting people, and likes taking responsibility within a team which is constantly working to achieve higher quality standards.

Tourists, whether they be on holiday or on business, want to relax and enjoy themselves. Even the slightest hitch can mar an otherwise pleasant experience. Their pleasure and enjoyment is due to the hard work of those who serve them, whether during their travel, arriving at an hotel or theatre, eating out or going to a cabaret. Those who work hard are not only those who meet the tourists, but also the many behind the scenes. The higher the standards, the harder the work of everyone involved so as to ensure as smooth and professional a service as possible.

For those who work in the industry there is considerable satisfaction in meeting these challenges. There can be a particular glow after having dealt well with a potentially problem guest and customer relations skills are extremely important for everyone working in tourism. Pushing a buffet trolley down a crowded train, answering the hundredth irritated passenger awaiting a late ferry or refusing yet more refreshment to an inebriated customer at the end of a long day can test patience. But each of these, and more, must be cheerfully met by staff, because every job in tourism is about the customer's enjoyment and comfort.

Jobs may be in direct or indirect employment. Someone directly employed in tourism is in one of three main sectors:

— travel and tourist services

— accommodation and catering

— tourist attractions and other facilities.

Thus people who work for organisations in the business of providing tourists with transport or information, with somewhere to eat or sleep or with things to see and do are in direct employment.

Indirect tourism employment includes the jobs of those who make goods or provide services for the organisations directly catering for tourists. Making hotel towels, preparing chilled potato chips for restaurants, working in a staff recruitment agency or selling and servicing electric hand driers are all occupations which depend indirectly on tourism.

Before considering the skills, qualifications and attributes needed in someone intending to work directly in tourism, it may be useful to meet some people already employed in the industry.

Careers in Tourism

Hotel Receptionist

Deborah O'Gorman has been a hotel receptionist with Jurys Hotel, Dublin since 1989 when she was 20 years old. She has also had work experience in hotels in the USA and Germany. After leaving school, Deborah took a one-year course in reception and secretarial skills, part of which comprises work experience for one-day per week for six weeks and one week full-time — in her case, at the Ashling Hotel, Dublin.

Deborah then worked in a hotel in Atlantic City, New Jersey, for ten months, on the front desk and the switchboard. On returning home she got a job with Jurys: as she did not have the full two years' experience required she became a trainee for three months and received on-the-job training.

Deborah says: 'I began in April 1989 and love my job, particularly meeting and greeting people, helping them plan their activities, and so on. Sometimes I wonder what a nine-to-five job would be like, but by this stage I have got to like shift work!

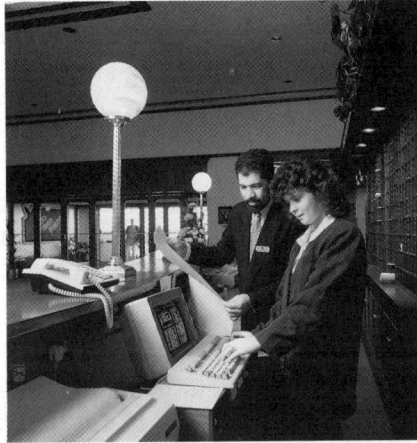

'Last year I took a German course supported by the EC, which involved one day a week for ten weeks followed by two weeks in a German hotel doing waitressing, housekeeping and kitchen work. I have just completed a French course organised by CERT — again one day a week for ten weeks.

'I would like to continue working as a hotel receptionist for quite a while yet — there are possibilities of becoming a supervisor at some stage — and I certainly see my long-term career within tourism.'

Tour Guide

Martine Lavery has been working part-time as a tour guide throughout Ireland since she undertook a CERT National Tour Guide certificate course in 1990. A Belgian, she is married to an Irishman, speaks seven languages and combines work as a tour guide and as a translator.

Martine says: 'It was a spur of the moment decision to take the tour guide course, and since completing it I have been working mainly with general visitor tours and incentive tours, as well as some conferences. The training was wide ranging and covered Irish history, geography, literature, and tourism attractions, as well as practical issues such as first aid and customer handling skills.

'Once you start as a tour guide you always want to know more and you develop a compulsion to keep abreast of everything you need to know. That includes the answers to the general questions that many visitors ask, such as the cost of housing and food in Ireland, average wages, levels of Social Welfare payment and so on.

'I would say that the mid-20s is a good age to start as a tour guide. You really need to have some experience of travel to other countries and cultures, have to become aware of what makes a good — and bad! — tour guide, and have to have learnt how to cope with people, particularly when they may be difficult or demanding.

Travel Adviser

David O'Flaherty of Cork was 21 years old when he undertook a sales and marketing course, during which he developed a wish to work in a retail travel agency.

David says: 'After two months of theory, the marketing course required participants to find three months' work experience; I enquired in several travel agencies in Cork, and was lucky to get a position with Classic Travel in the city. That was August 1989.

'Apart from in-house training, I have undertaken Aer Lingus day courses on ticketing, and have been on a number of educational trips to European countries organised by Irish and British tour operators. There is a graduated series of Aer Lingus courses that I could undertake, as well as IATA/UFTAA courses run in co-operation with the Irish Travel Agents Association.

More Jobs in Tourism

It is not possible to review every job in tourism in Ireland, but here are just a few:

Tourist Information Office Staff

TIO staff provide information about their areas to visitors who call to the office or telephone. They may also deal with questions relating to other regions of Ireland, including Northern Ireland. Tourists also come to a TIO to book accommodation, usually in that particular region but often in others too. The TIO charges for these services and also have books, pamphlets, souvenirs and local crafts on sale. When the office is not busy correspondence must be attended to, and stocks of leaflets and brochures checked and ordered. Most offices have a permanent staff augmented by temporary staff during busy seasons; staff working hours can change according to season, however, particularly during the high season.

Ferry Manager

Ferry managers are responsible for the smooth service of people and vehicles on the short sea journeys from Ireland to Great Britain and France. Obviously, ferries based in Great Britain tend to recruit staff there and those based in Ireland tend to have Irish-based staff. There are managers for every aspect of the operation of a ferry, including catering, shops and traffic operations. There are also managers behind the scenes for personnel, concerned with sea-going and shore-based staff, and sales and marketing, who generate passenger and freight traffic. Still others look after engineering and technical services.

Managers who go to sea must enjoy sea travel even in difficult weather conditions; those who remain on shore must understand life on board. Vacancies for Ferry Managers do not often arise. When they do, they may go to people who have already been working with the company on shore or at sea, as they often have the appropriate qualifications.

Air Cabin Crew

Air stewards or stewardesses may seem to travellers to be waiters and waitresses, but they are much more than that. Highly trained in emergency and safety procedures as well as first-aid, they are also trained in customer care. The number of crew on a flight depends on the kind of aircraft and sometimes other factors. Each person is scheduled to undertake duty at certain times ahead. In practice, long haul flights are allocated to the more senior staff while new staff usually serve on short haul routes.

Members rostered to the crew of a particular flight attend for briefing before it and are allocated their duties. Food stores are monitored and other checks made to ensure all is in order. When the passengers board they are helped, if necessary, to find their seats and stow hand baggage. Special attention is given to children travelling alone and disabled passengers.

Competition often is keen for jobs as air cabin crew. People start on temporary or short-term contracts during busy seasons and permanent staff are recruited from among these.

Car Hire Staff

Car hire companies employ people in three main areas: reception, marketing and as chauffeurs.

Most car hire is self-drive. Customers are met at their arrival point, which may be an airport or city office, and are received by a receptionist — though the job title may depend on the size of the office. This person must have a knowledge of the cars being hired out, and of the company's documentation, customer records and insurance arrangements. Ability with languages is often an asset.

Sales representatives deal with advance bookings and liaise with corporate customers in their areas; they have to monitor the availability of vehicles particularly if customers leave them back to other 'depots'.

Chauffeurs are still requested by some customers, and a good knowledge of Ireland is usually required of them. Companies with more than one location may employ drivers to move cars from one depot to another to suit customer needs. Car hire in Ireland is a seasonal business and personnel vacancies occur therefore often during the summer season.

Tourism Assistant

This is a general job title for which other titles are used in visitor attractions such as heritage centres, managed historical sites such as castles, craft centres, holiday centres and other places where tourists need information and assistance to help make their visits enjoyable. The jobs often call for multiple skills which may include guiding visitors, selling souvenirs, guide books, entrance tickets or providing coffee and snacks.

These jobs are found by application to the individual attraction. Many attractions are seasonal so they may have no permanent jobs to offer. Others which are open year-round often recruit their permanent staff from those who have worked temporarily with them.

Chef

Chefs are employed in hotels, restaurants and industrial or contract catering kitchens; in hospitals and at sea they are known as cooks. In large kitchens preparing haute cuisine, the hierarchy of chef positions may be seen:

— the head chef plans menus, buys supplies and trains new staff as well as preparing food

— the sous-chef is a senior chef who may work anywhere in the kitchen

— the chef de partie runs a particular part of the kitchen such as pastry, or fish

— a commis chef is a trainee chef undergoing training in all areas of the kitchen

— a short-order chef prepares fast food or simple dishes.

Being a chef involves more than cooking: a chef is concerned with food production that is on time and at a controlled cost. Food preparation in top restaurants still uses traditional methods and involves much hard work and unsocial hours, but increasingly, machines are being used to handle more routine functions. There is plenty of scope for individual flair as a chef, and successful men and women in this field are much sought after.

Bartender

There are many kinds of job in the general area of bartending. Most are in the public houses around Ireland in cities and towns and in rural areas. Others are more specialised such as the small number engaged in cocktail bars where an outgoing personality and presentation skills are preferred. Others again are in multi-skilled situations such as small hotels where serving drinks goes with other job elements.

There is a range of job knowledge which largely depends on the kind of bars in which the bartender works. Knowledge of various table wines, for example, develops more in a small hotel or restaurant dining room or in a wine bar than in a public house bar; the range of cocktails is usually limited in bars, too. However in each case a bartender has to ensure that tables and the bar are kept clean and prepared for customers, used glasses washed, dried and restored, and stocks of ice, lemon and so on are maintained. Bar work calls for good personal qualities including the ability to cope with peak pressures, to stay cheerful, deliver orders and handle cash accurately.

Accommodation Operations

Hotels employ accommodation assistants and they are supervised by an accommodation manager. The accommodation assistant does a great deal of cleaning in guest rooms and corridors and sometimes other areas of an hotel; beds have to be made and, of course, linen changed when the guests have checked out. During their stay, guests' property is not re-arranged, but at the end of their stay rooms must be checked to ensure that nothing has been left behind. In smaller hotels, the role of accommodation assistant may be combined with other duties such as preparing and serving breakfast.

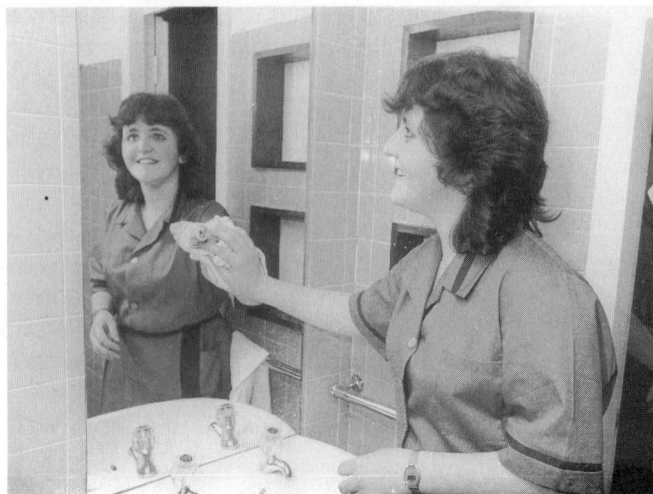

The accommodation manager is responsible for the effective running of guest accommodation including cleaning, laundry and general maintenance. This involves supervising members of the team, including the accommodation assistants and ensuring that stocks of linen and other requisites are maintained. In a small hotel these duties may be combined with others.

Job Numbers

It is difficult to calculate precisely the number of jobs in the tourism industry because it is difficult to isolate the components of the industry. Relatively few of the jobs are exclusively devoted to handling tourists; for example, every hotel is open to local people for food and drink. A hotel may be family and owner managed, employ a high proportion of family members, have a large number of part-time and seasonal workers and, in many sectors, employ a high proportion of young workers. As in all business sectors, there is a failure rate, so it is difficult to keep track of and maintain records of the industry.

The CERT Manpower Survey undertaken in 1992 found that over 157,000 people were employed in tourism with a further 24,000 working in industrial and hospital catering. The report predicted an overall 3% increase in employment for 1993. See Table 1 for a breakdown of employment by sector. Table 1 also shows that up to 85% of employment was permanent.

GETTING AHEAD IN YOUR CAREER
PLAN YOUR CAREER PATH THROUGH PROFESSIONAL TRAINING

The tourism and catering industry offers you a chance to carve out your own career path. You can move up the career ladder by taking advantage of the many training options offered by CERT along the way.

Your career should not stop when you take up your first job on leaving training college. You will be able to follow advanced courses while working or by returning to college for short periods. This training, added to experience in your job, can help you to take up a position either as a supervisor or a manager.

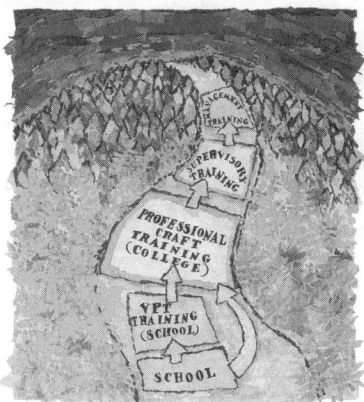

CAREER LEAFLETS
This brochure is intended as a brief introduction to the many training courses offered through CERT. For more detailed information, please see individual course leaflets available from CERT Recruitment.

CERT House, Amiens Street, Dublin 1.
Telephone (01) 742555 Telex 90161 CERT EI Fax: (01) 742821

THE GROWING INDUSTRY

Table 1 Numbers employed by sector (1992)				
Types of Establishment	Permanent	Seasonal	Occasional	Totals
1. Hotels and Guesthouses	25,664	5,420	2,377	33,461
2. Restaurants	17,991	1,902	—	19,893
3. Fast Food Outlets	6,266	956	—	7,222
4. Carriers	1,083	507	—	1,590
5. Licensed Premises	68,269	4,688	—	72,957
6. Self-Catering Accommodation	916	238	—	1,154
7. Non-food and Accommodation Sectors	9,974	6,987	—	16,961
8. Leisure	2,941	381	79	3,401
Totals	133,104	21,079	2,456	156,639*

Source: CERT Manpower Survey (1992)
*Direct employment figures including assisting relatives

As further study will show, people are employed in many sectors of the tourist industry and these are just some of them:

State Organisations
Government Departments
Bord Fáilte
Shannon Development
CERT
Local Authorities

Access Transport
Aer Lingus
Ryanair
B & I
Irish Ferries
Stena Sealink
Isle of Man Steam Packet
Brittany Ferries

Internal Transport
Car Hire Operators
Taxis

Coach Touring and Private Coach Hire
Domestic Air Carriers
Licensed Boat Services
Internal Ferry Services
Iarnród Éireann
Bus Éireann
Dublin Bus
Other Local Bus Operators

Accommodation

Hotels
Guesthouses
Town Homes
Country Homes
Farmhouses
Caravan and Camping
Touring Caravan Operators
Tent and Camping Equipment Hirers
Youth Hostels
Self-catering Accommodation

Travel Facilitation

Aer Rianta
International and Regional airports
Ports and Harbours

Dining and Entertainment

Restaurants
Public Houses
Night Clubs
Theatres
Festivals and Events

**Leisure and Recreation
Activity Facilities**

Cabin Cruising
Pleasure Cruises
Sailing Tuition,
Boardsailing,
Canoeing
Yacht Charter
Other Water Sports
Horse Drawn Caravanning
Horse-Riding Establishments
Golfing
Deep Sea Angling
Boat Operators
Historic Houses, Castles and Gardens
Nature Walks
English Language Tuition
Other Summer Schools and Camps
Museums
Art Galleries

	Genealogy
	Irish Craft-making
	Greyhound Racing
	Horse Racing
	Sports and Social Clubs
Tourism Services	Incoming Tour Operators
	Tour Operators and Retail Travel agents
	Youth and Student Organisations
Other Services	Banks
	Bureaux de Change
	Local Tourism Initiatives
	Centres of Pilgrimage

Training and Qualification

Whilst there are plenty of jobs in the tourism field, there are even more people seeking them. A prospective employer has to differentiate between applicants for a position and is likely to do so on the basis of one or both of two factors:

— experience

— training and qualification

For junior positions in tourism, especially temporary or part-time ones, previous experience in appropriate work is obviously helpful: the employer will not have to lose too much time in making the new person a useful member of the team. The difficulty for a new job-seeker may therefore lie in finding the first job.

After that the employer can evaluate job applicants on the basis of any training they have undertaken and qualifications in the form of certificates, diplomas and degrees they have obtained. Not only does the training and education concerned add to the applicant's body of experience and knowledge, but the time and effort spent helps to impress on a prospective employer that the applicant is well-motivated and hard working. So clearly it is in the long-term interests of those intending to work in tourism to avail of opportunities which add to any initial training and experience gained.

CERT

CERT is the state tourism training agency. It was founded in 1963 as the Council for Education, Recruitment and Training, charged with responsibility for raising standards in hotels, catering and tourism. CERT's goal is to ensure the highest operational standards in the tourism industry by providing a professionally trained workforce and support services for businesses. It has two operating divisions:

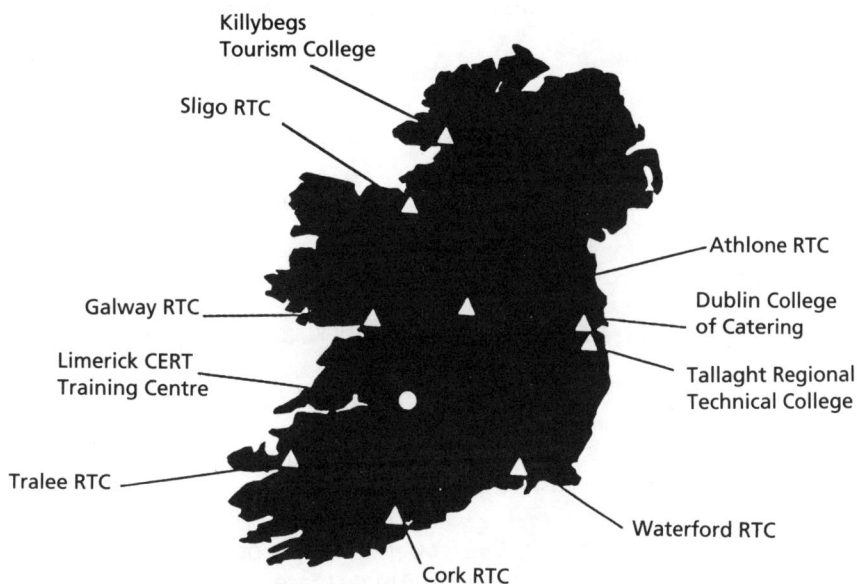

Killybegs
Tourism College

Sligo RTC

Athlone RTC

Galway RTC

Dublin College
of Catering

Limerick CERT
Training Centre

Tallaght Regional
Technical College

Tralee RTC

Waterford RTC

Cork RTC

Training Centres

— Industry-based Training

— Education, Placement and Research

Through its Industry-based Training division it provides a range of courses and seminars for job-seekers and people in the industry and consulting services for tourism businesses.

The Education, Placement and Research division is responsible for education and training leading to certification by the National Tourism Certification Board (NTCB), for research of many kinds — often with EC support — and for the preparation of tourism teaching resources and seminars for teachers in schools and colleges.

CERT advises government on manpower and training needs for tourism and develops training programmes and structures to meet those needs. It enjoys a unique partnership with the tourism industry and educational bodies which enables it to target its training effectively. CERT Council represents tourism employers, trade unions, education and government.

Among CERT's other services are:

— courses in European languages for tourism

— return to work programmes

— a specialist wine and spirit appreciation certificate programme

— training for Tour Guides and Tourist Information Office staff

— overseas placements

— overseas consultancy

— research and planning

— publication of training materials and guides and study manuals for schools and colleges.

In 1992, CERT opened its purpose-built National Training Centre and Headquarters in Amiens Street, Dublin. It also operates full-time training centres in Cork and Limerick. In addition, CERT leases seasonal hotels throughout the country to supplement the training facilities provided in these three centres and in the hotel and catering colleges.

In 1992, CERT trained 11,500 hotel, catering and tourism personnel. Linkage with the industry helped to maintain strong employer

CERT

demand for CERT graduates and 100% final placement was commonly achieved.

The National Tourism Certification Board

The National Tourism Certification Board (NTCB) operates under the auspices of CERT and the Department of Education. Most college trainees on CERT programmes now follow national courses designed by CERT and certified by the NTCB. Those qualifications are recognised by all EC member states.

CERT Training Opportunities

Third-level training courses are available all over the country in CERT centres and catering colleges, including the Dublin College of Catering, Killybegs Tourism College and Regional Technical Colleges in Athlone, Cork, Galway, Sligo, Tralee, Waterford and Tallaght.

For those who wish to obtain a qualification in Hotel Management whilst working in industry, CERT, in conjunction with the Irish Hotels Federation and Irish Hotel and Catering Institute, offers the Trainee Manager Development Programme. This 4-year programme is designed for candidates who have secured a position as trainee manager in a hotel affiliated to this scheme. The list of affiliated hotels is available from CERT.

(See Figure 1 for the range of professional training courses funded by CERT.)

Full details of current courses on offer, together with their entry requirements, course locations and qualifications, are given in the 'CERT Career Guide' — and all courses include foreign language training.

VPT Courses

Training for a career in tourism can begin from as early as 15 years of age by taking a *Vocational Preparation and Training* (VPT-1) course in second-level school or in community training workshops and Youthreach programmes. VPT-1 courses are for early school leavers of 15–18 years of age and comprise vocational skills related to hotel, catering and tourism, work experience, and general education.

There are two VPT-2 Certificate courses, both certified jointly by CERT and the Department of Education. They are offered by selected second-level schools around the country to students who have completed one of the above courses, and who are at least 16 years of age. The *VPT-2 Hotel, Catering and Tourism* course enables students to acquire basic skills and work experience in food preparation, food and beverage service, accommodation services, hospitality and tourism studies, plus art, craft and design.

The *VPT-2 Tourism* course covers a selected vocational skills area within tourism, such as agri-rural tourism, tourism and leisure or tourism and travel reception skills.

Tourism Awareness Programme

Another option introduced in 1992 for 16 to 18-year-olds is the *Tourism Awareness Programme*, a joint educational project co-ordinated by CERT in conjunction with the Department of Education and the Travel and Tourism Programme in Ireland. The module, which has the active support of leading tourism companies (including American Express Ireland, Jurys Hotels, Great Southern Hotel Group, Bord Fáilte, and Forte Ireland), is a 150-hour programme for second-level schools and is designed as an introduction to tourism at home and abroad.

CHEF COURSES

- Professional Cookery
- 2-day Release Professional Cookery
- 1-day Release Professional Cookery
- Cooks Skills Development

WAITER/WAITRESS COURSES

- Food & Beverage Service — Diningroom training only
- Food & Accommodation Service — Diningroom and Accommodation training combined
- Food & Beverage Service — 1-day Release

ACCOMMODATION/HOUSEKEEPING COURSES

- Accommodation Service

MULTI-SKILLED COURSES

- Hospitality Skills

TOURISM COURSES

- Tourism Skills
- Advanced Tourism Business Studies

BARTENDER COURSES

- Bar Service

RECEPTION COURSES

- Hotel Reception
- Hotel Reception Skills

SUPERVISORY COURSES

- Supervision of Bar Service Operations
- Supervision of Food Service Operations
- Supervision of Accommodation Operations

MANAGEMENT COURSES

- Trainee Manager Development Programme

TOUR GUIDE COURSE

- Part-time programme for over 25s. Check with CERT regarding availability.

More Qualifications for Tourism

The NTCB certificates provide recognised qualifications for people in a variety of fields. There are however many other ways in which people may follow tourism-related courses and obtain degrees, diplomas and certificates. Among the categories of programmes and courses available are:

— Degree

— Diploma

— National Certificate

— Post Leaving Certificate Courses (PLCs)

Other Courses

Degree Programmes

- Hotel and Catering Management — B.Sc. (Mgt)
  Dublin College of Catering — 4 years

- Hotel and Catering Management — B.A.
  Galway Regional Technical College — 4 years

- Hospitality Management — B.A. (Hons)
  University of Ulster (Jordanstown) — 3 years

- Hotel and Tourism Management — B.A. (Hons)
  University of Ulster (Magee) — 3 years

Diploma Programmes

- National Diploma in Business Studies — Hotel and Catering Management (NCEA)
  Athlone Regional Technical College — 3 years

- National Diploma in Business Studies — Hotel and Catering Management (NCEA)
  Galway Regional Technical College — 3 years

- National Diploma in Business Studies — Hotel and Catering Management — Block Release (NCEA)
  Galway Regional Technical College — 4 years

- Shannon Hotel School Diploma (Diploma graduates have option of reading for a degree in hotel management at UCG)
  Shannon Hotel School — 4 years

- Diploma in Hotel Management (DIT)
  Dublin College of Catering — 3 years

- Diploma in Catering Management (DIT)
  Dublin College of Catering — 3 years

- National Diploma in Business Studies Recreation and Leisure
  Waterford Regional Technical College — 3 years

- BTEC National Diploma in Hotel Catering and Institutional Operations
  Northern Ireland Hotel and Catering College Portrush — 2 years

- BTEC National Diploma in Travel and Tourism
  Coleraine Technical College — 2 years

- BTEC First Diploma in Hotel and Catering Studies
  Northern Ireland Hotel and Catering College Portrush — 1 year

- Diploma in Hotel Reception and Front Office Practice
  Northern Ireland Hotel and Catering College Portrush — 1 year

- Diploma of Higher Education in Hospitality Management
  University of Ulster (Jordanstown) — 3 years

- BTEC Higher National Diploma Hotel, Catering and Institutional Management
  University of Ulster (Jordanstown) — 2 years

- BTEC National Diploma in Leisure Studies
  Fermanagh College of Further Education — 2 years

- BTEC National Diploma in Hotel Catering and Institutional Operations
  Fermanagh College of Further Education — 2 years

- BTEC Higher Diploma in Hospitality and Tourism Management
  Belfast Institute of Further & Higher Education — 3 years

- BTEC National Diploma in Hotel, Catering and Institutional Operations
  Belfast Institute of Further & Higher Education — 2 years

- HCIMA Certificate in Hotel and Catering Management
  Belfast Institute of Further & Higher Education — 2 years

National Certificate Courses

- National Certificate in Business Studies — Front Office Administration (NCEA)
  Athlone Regional Technical College — 2 years

- National Certificate in Business Studies — Hotel and Catering Supervision (NCEA)
  Athlone Regional Technical College — 2 years full-time or 3 years block release

- National Certificate in Business Studies — Hotel and Catering Supervision (NCEA)
  Cork Regional Technical College — 2 years

- National Certificate in Business Studies — Hotel and Catering Management — Sandwich (NCEA)
  Galway Regional Technical College — 2 years

- National Certificate in European Hospitality Administration
  Galway Regional Technical College — 1 year

- National Certificate in Business Studies — Tourism (NCEA)
  Cork Regional Technical College — 2 years

- National Certificate in Business Studies — Language and Marketing/ Tourism (with major in French or German)
  Sligo Regional Technical College — 2 years

- National Certificate in Business Studies — Languages and Marketing/ Tourism (with major in French or German)
  Tralee Regional Technical College — 2 years

- Certificate in Business Studies — Bar Management
  College of Marketing and Design — 2 years

- Certificate in Hotel Reception (NCEA)
  Dublin College of Catering — 1 year

- Certificate in Travel and Tourism (NCBS/IATA)
  Dublin College of Catering — 2 years

- Certificate in Hotel and Catering Supervision (DIT/IHCI)
Dublin College of Catering — 2 years

- Certificate in Business Studies — Recreation and Leisure Studies
Cork Regional Technical College — 2 years

Plc Courses

Course Title	Venue
Travel and Tourism	Athlone Community School
Agri-Tourism and Catering	Moyne College, Ballina
Tourism/Business Studies	Ballinamore Vocational School, Co. Leitrim
Certificate in Hotel and Catering Management	Ballyfermot Senior College
Diploma in Hotel Reception and Tourism Studies	Ballyfermot Senior College
Diploma in Travel and Tourism	Cavan College of Further Studies
Linguistic Secretary/Tourism	Cork School of Commerce
Reception/Tourism	Cork School of Commerce
Irish Heritage and Tourism	Scoil Stiofáin Naofa, Cork
Leisure and Recreation Management	Scoil Stiofáin Naofa, Cork
Marine Leisure Management	Scoil Stiofáin Naofa, Cork
Business Administration/ Tourism Awareness	Croom Community College
Hotel and Catering Supervision	Crumlin College of Business and Technical Studies
Tourism and Reception Studies	Crumlin College of Business and Technical Studies
Tourism and Reception Course	Ennis Vocational School
Recreation and Leisure Studies	Ennistymon Vocational School
Leisure and Recreation	Inchicore Vocational School
Leisure and Recreation in Tourism	Inchicore Vocational School

Sports and Leisure Management	Inchicore Vocational School
Secretarial and Tourism Studies	Kildare College of Further Studies
Travel and Tourism	Limerick Senior College
Secretarial/Tourism Awareness	Longwood Vocational School Co. Meath
Secretarial Reception and Tourism	Lucan Community College
Tourism and Travel	Moate Business College
Leisure Management	Monaghan Institute of Further Education and Training
Certificate in Hotel and Catering Management	Moyne Community School, Co. Longford
Certificate in Tourism and Reception	Moyne Community School, Co. Longford
Leisure and Recreation Management	Moyne Community School, Co. Longford
Tourism	Senior College, Sallynoggin, Co. Dublin
Travel/Tourism	Stillorgan Senior College
Languages/Tourism Secretarial Course	Whitehall House Senior Secretarial College
European Studies/Tourism Awareness	Mercy College, Woodford, Co. Galway

The above list of courses operating in 1993 gives some indication of the upsurge in interest in tourism careers but is not necessarily all inclusive. For instance, there are also a number of private colleges offering courses in tourism.

Travel and Leisure Courses ▬▬▬▬▬▬▬▬▬▬

Some of the non-food and accommodation sectors of the tourism industry have their own training opportunities, either in full-time or part-time courses or in-house training. For example, training courses for tour operators and retail travel agency staff are organised by the Irish Travel Agents Association. Standard and advanced courses are arranged on a modular basis and lead to IATA/UFTAA Certificates, the world standards in the industry established by the airline and travel agency bodies. Both standard and advanced courses are offered by the Dublin College of Catering and standard courses by Stillorgan Senior College and Coláiste Ide in Finglas. The ITAA also has its own training programmes for staff and management already working in the industry.

The Irish Travel Trade College in Dublin offers courses for prospective travel agency staff, existing staff and management. All courses are operated in association with City and Guilds, the Association of British Travel Agents and Speedwing, and have internationally recognised certification.

In addition to the leisure courses already listed, the Institute of Leisure and Amenity Management offers a part-time Certificate Course in Leisure Management in a number of centres around the country. The syllabus is specially adapted for the Irish leisure industry and gives participants an overview of the industry as well as knowledge of several specialist sectors.

Student Questions and Assignments

1. Identify and assess the employment opportunities provided by the tourism sector in your own area.

2. Select a career area within the tourism industry and explore the related training opportunities open to school leavers in Ireland. What do the courses involve? What is the application procedure? What are the entry requirements? What qualifications are awarded? What are the job prospects on completion?

3. 'Service not servility' — why do you think jobs involving customer service often have a poor image in Ireland?

4. Interview a tourism professional from your locality and write a profile on them and their job.

5. Evaluate the pluses and minuses of a career in tourism.

6. Discuss in small groups the personal qualities that you think would be desirable for anyone working in the tourism industry.

7. Select two vacancy notices for tourism staff from a newspaper and draft letters of application. Research the general working conditions for the occupations selected.

8. Develop proposals for encouraging more young people to consider careers in tourism and for increasing levels of professionalism within the industry generally.

11 *Tour Operations*

Objectives

At the end of this chapter, the reader will be able to:

- describe the role and function of the different parties involved in incoming and outgoing travel

- describe the key components of the travel product: air and sea carriers, coach and rail travel, car hire and accommodation

- explain how the product providers structure, price and package their travel services

- understand basic travel terminology

- demonstrate an awareness of how package holidays are put together.

The tourist industry in every country includes those organisations and products which service the needs of outward tourism. This chapter discusses some of the products which are available for people who wish to travel out of Ireland, in particular transport and accommodation and the tour operators that package these into inclusive holidays abroad; the structure of the travel trade and its handling of these products are dealt with in the next chapter.

Obviously, whether the prospective traveller is planning a holiday, to go abroad on business or to visit friends and relations, the first need is transport. For almost everyone the choice of transport is between air and sea travel.

Air Carriers

Air carriers serving outward tourism are the same as those serving inward tourism: some aspects of air travel have already been dealt with in an earlier section on access transport. But some of the operating detail needs to be examined here in connection with outward tourism, including the issues of timetabling and the various fares on offer.

There are many considerations which lead an airline to acquire planes for its operations. Aircraft require a substantial investment and new planes are ordered only after careful research into the viability of new and existing routes. Most busy routes are shared by international agreement and several airlines may be servicing them. The amount of traffic can vary for different reasons including the health of the economy and changes in public requirements; fare levels, which may need to be adjusted for totally independent reasons such as the politics of the Middle East, can also exert pressure on demand. So planes must be bought to serve a market which is uncertain.

Assuming that the outcome of the viability studies was to acquire more aircraft to increase the number of flights, provide more capacity on existing routes or to serve new destinations, an airline must apply to the authorities for licences to operate them. In Ireland the relevant authority is the Department of Transport, Energy and Communications. The Department has to study the markets and decide whether or not to agree on the viability of the proposal. Government regulation is discussed further in the next chapter.

Once it has bought an aircraft on the best available information the airline has to ensure the plane is kept busy. Even the cost of staffing it must be subordinated to turning it around into the air again after each journey. For example, in the winter Delta Air Lines may consider there is only enough traffic to fly between Atlanta and Ireland twice a week. Flight and cabin crews have a full day's work on the flight in one direction, so the crews that operate a plane from Atlanta to Ireland must rest when they arrive; the plane returns to Atlanta with the crews that have been resting in Ireland. In the low season this is expensive for the airline because the crews that are resting would have been ready to work again after one day but they must be paid to wait in Irish hotels for half a week.

With substantial investment in an aircraft and crews on the payroll, the airline must try to find as much work for them as possible to pay the costs. So it will seek additional business, perhaps on scheduled routes that may be only marginal or accept charters if necessary below the normal prices. It must do so subject to the regulating authorities. One important restriction up to now has been that an airline could only operate to and from its country of origin. For example Aer Lingus could not decide to operate a daily flight from Rome to Vienna. A flight would have had to operate from its country of origin which meant it could only operate Dublin — Rome — Vienna and back to Dublin. This ensured that the airlines of all countries got a share of the market. However, within the EC this is being changed.

Clearly there is great complexity in programming the use of an aircraft to ensure it is not only working all day, and if possible some of the night as well, but that it is in the right place at the right time for all of its work and similarly that there are crews to operate it; at the same time it must be given time on the ground for obligatory maintenance checks and overhauls. Thus timetables are most important.

From GALWAY (GWY) Continued

To GLASGOW (GLA)
123456-	0630	1155	EI053	SF3	0715 DUB	1050	EI224	F50
....-6	1615	1915	EI057	F50	1700 DUB	1810	EI234	F50

To KERRY COUNTY (KIR)
123456-	0630	1310	EI053	SF3	0715 DUB	1205	EI022	SF3
1234567	1300	1615	EI055	SF3	1345 DUB	1510	EI024	SF3

To LEEDS BRADFORD (LBA)
12345-7	1300	1925	EI055	SF3	1345 DUB	1820	EI368	SF3

To LONDON (LON)
123456-	0630	0910 LHR	EI053	SF3	0715 DUB	0800	EI154	737
1234567	1300	1645 LHR	EI055	SF3	1345 DUB	1535	EI172	737
....-6	1615	1950 LHR	EI057	F50	1700 DUB	1840	EI178	737

To MANCHESTER (MAN)
123456-	0630	1000	EI053	SF3	0715 DUB	0910	EI622	737
12345-7	1300	1640	EI055	SF3	1345 DUB	1550	EI668	737
....-6	1615	1940	EI057	F50	1700 DUB	1850	EI216	737

To MILAN (MIL)
1.-4...	0630	1415 LIN	EI053	SF3	0715 DUB	1040	EI676	737

To NEWCASTLE (NCL)
123456-	0630	1000	EI053	SF3	0715 DUB	0845	EI302	SF3
12345-7	1300	1910	EI055	SF3	1345 DUB	1755	EI308	SF3

To PARIS (PAR)
123456-	0630	1020 CDG	EI053	SF3	0715 DUB	0745	EI522	737
12345-7	1300	1940 CDG	EI055	SF3	1345 DUB	1705	EI528	737

To SHANNON (SNN)
12345--	0630	1210	EI053	SF3	0715 DUB	1125	EI083	SF3
.-3.-6	0630	1115	EI053	SF3	0715 DUB	1030	EI133	747

To ZURICH (ZRH)
1..5.-	0630	1135	EI053	SF3	0715 DUB	0825	EI664	737
12345-7	1300	2000	EI055	SF3	1345 DUB	1550	EI668	737

From GLASGOW (GLA) GMT

To CORK (ORK)
12345--	0910	1315	EI223	F50	1020 DUB	1230	EI523	737
....-6-	0910	1400	EI223	F50	1020 DUB	1305	EI046	F50
123456-	1245	1600	EI225	F50	1355 DUB	1505	EI036	F50
12345-7	2005	2245	EI235	F50	2115 DUB	2200	EI048	737

To DUBLIN (DUB)
123456-	0910	1020	EI223	F50	NONSTOP			
1234567	1245	1355	EI225	F50	NONSTOP			
1234567	2005	2115	EI235	F50	NONSTOP			

To GALWAY (GWY)
123456-	0910	1240	EI223	F50	1020 DUB	1150	EI054	SF3
....-6	1245	1545	EI225	F50	1355 DUB	1455	EI056	F50

From GLASGOW (GLA) Continued

To GALWAY Continued
12345-7	2005	2250	EI235	F50	2115 DUB	2200	EI058	SF3

To KERRY COUNTY (KIR)
123456-	0910	1310	EI223	F50	1020 DUB	1205	EI022	SF3
1234567	1245	1615	EI225	F50	1355 DUB	1510	EI024	SF3

To KNOCK (NOC)
1234567	1245	1620	EI225	F50	1355 DUB	1530	EI016	SF3

To NEW YORK (NYC)
123456-	0910	1615 JFK	EI223	F50	1020 DUB	1230	EI105	747

To SHANNON (SNN)
123456-	0910	1310	EI223	F50	1020 DUB	1230	EI105	747
12345--	0910	1215	EI223	F50	1020 DUB	1125	EI083	SF3
12345-7	2005	2245	EI235	F50	2115 DUB	2200	EI097	F50

To SLIGO (SXL)
123456-	0910	1305	EI223	F50	1020 DUB	1215	EI064	SF3
1234567	1245	1510	EI225	F50	1355 DUB	1420	EI066	SF3

From KERRY COUNTY (KIR) GMT

To AMSTERDAM (AMS)
12345--	1400	1900	EI023	SF3	1500 DUB	1630	EI608	737

To BIRMINGHAM (BHX)
....-6	1400	1710	EI023	SF3	1500 DUB	1600	EI274	F50
12345-7	1635	1915	EI025	SF3	1735 DUB	1820	EI272	737

To BRISTOL (BRS)
12345--	1400	1910	EI023	SF3	1500 DUB	1755	EI286	F50

To BRUSSELS (BRU)
12345--	1400	1900	EI023	SF3	1500 DUB	1630	EI636	737
......7	1635	2205	EI025	SF3	1735 DUB	1940	EI634	737

To DUBLIN (DUB)
1234567	1400	1500	EI023	SF3	NONSTOP			
1234567	1635	1735	EI025	SF3	NONSTOP			

To EAST MIDLANDS (EMA)
12345-7	1635	1945	EI025	SF3	1735 DUB	1835	EI356	SF3

To EDINBURGH (EDI)
12345--	1400	1915	EI023	F50	1500 DUB	1805	EI258	F50

To FRANKFURT (FRA)
......7	1400	1840	EI023	SF3	1500 DUB	1540	EI656	737

To GALWAY (GWY)
12345-7	1635	2250	EI025	SF3	1735 DUB	2200	EI058	SF3

Days of Service :	1 = Monday	2 = Tuesday	3 = Wednesday
	4 = Thursday	5 = Friday	6 = Saturday	7 = Sunday
	* Indicates following day	§ 2 days later	

Timetables

There are many factors to be taken into account when preparing a timetable: one of the most important is that a timetable must attract passengers, indeed apart from ticket cost it is the most important factor. For example, there would be no point in offering a business person a first flight from Dublin which arrived at its destination at four in the afternoon when the working day was over. On the other hand a person going away for the weekend might prefer to leave at these times.

The airline must take into account the needs of potential customers, and the service available from its competitors, before it arranges its timetable. If it is to maintain a good name for reliability on the market, once a flight is timetabled at a certain time, the airline must meet the obligation to operate it whether the aircraft is full or empty. Hence the term *scheduled* flight.

Particular difficulty arises when a flight is delayed or does not leave at its scheduled departure time, for reasons such as adverse weather conditions, air traffic control or a technical fault; obviously these are outside the control of the airline. They cannot be planned for in advance and when a delay occurs it is unlikely that there is a spare aircraft sitting idle that can be used as a substitute. So when flights are tightly timetabled, a delay in one flight can lead to subsequent delays in flights to be operated later by the same aircraft. This can be a cause of frustration to passengers, particularly business people who may themselves have detailed programmes to meet.

Ticket Pricing

Over 800,000 tickets for scheduled flights are sold each year on the Irish market. Each one involves a choice of fares and conditions from among a wide range of options available to suit the public's many different tastes and expectations.

When an airline sells tickets on its scheduled services its principal objective is to sell as many as possible so as to maximise its *load factor*. Load factor is the percentage of seats occupied by fare-paying passengers. On each flight the airline aims to reduce the risk of the aircraft's not leaving full. A carefully prepared timetable can help reduce that risk but so too can the pricing of the tickets. Flights fill up with passengers, each with different needs and budgets to adhere to, so the pricing and conditions of their tickets are arranged to suit those needs and in turn reduce the risk of a low load factor.

The ideal is a plane full of people paying the highest fare. The business traveller going abroad on a trip wants complete flexibility to leave when it is most convenient and to return when the business is completed. If the business takes less or more time than expected the business person wants to be sure that, if the airline does not have a suitable flight available on which to return, the ticket may be used on any other airline offering an acceptable service. The ticket for this person is a high risk ticket to the airline as it can never be sure when and if the passenger will fill one of the seats; so this is the most expensive kind of ticket. To justify its cost, which may be two or three times that of some low-cost fares, the airline may often provide better quality in-flight service to this class of traveller such as more refreshments, better meals, free newspapers, or lower-density seating.

- *High risk, high cost seats = first class or business class tickets*

- *Low risk, low cost seats = economy, APEX, PEX, stand-by tickets*

On the other hand there are people who know exactly when they intend to travel. Such reservations represent low risk for the airline because from the moment the booking is made, sometimes months in advance, there is a guarantee that those seats will be occupied. As a rule the further in advance and the firmer the bookings, the lower the price at which seats may be sold.

Most airlines offer several kinds of low-cost ticket, each with different sets of conditions, so as to attract different markets and in many cases there is a limit to the number of such seats on any one flight; these arrangements are useful for attracting potential travellers at relatively low risk. For example, PEX and APEX fares may require the traveller to accept that if the journey is not undertaken on the specified date, the ticket will no longer be valid and the cost will have been lost. However, some airlines recognise that such harsh conditions are not good for public relations so instead they may offer an option to upgrade the ticket to a higher cost level, in effect a fine which the traveller finds acceptable rather than lose the original cost completely.

At the other end of the low-cost scale are *stand-by seats* which are sometimes sold at the last moment before a flight; these ensure some revenue for the company when one or more seats would not have been occupied. People who wait for stand-by tickets accept the chance that they may not be able to travel.

Because of the wide range of fares and conditions, any one flight may carry passengers who enjoy similar in-flight service at very different prices.

Airports

Airports are not owned by airlines, though in some countries airlines may provide their own terminal facilities. Airports are usually provided by national or local government, but some have started life as companies' private airstrips or even, as in the case of Connaught Regional Airport, as independent private enterprises. There is normally a body or company to administer an airport and ensure it is run, preferably, as a profitable business. In the Republic of Ireland, Aer Rianta runs the principal airports including Dublin, Shannon and Cork. It provides facilities for the airlines and charges for them.

Facilities provided by airport authorities to airlines may include: check-in desks, flight information displays, parking spaces for aircraft, and transport to aircraft by airbridge or minibus. Airports also provide security services including passenger and baggage screening, airport police and fire service.

Large airlines may provide their own staff to handle passengers and their baggage, as well as the staff and equipment for apron services including transfer buses and the many services which meet each incoming flight to prepare it for the next one. If an airline has a low frequency of flights from an airport it may arrange for the staffing of check-ins and other services from large airlines (such as Aer Lingus in Ireland) or from specialised contractors such as Servisair (in the UK). Each airport charges fees to the airlines which operate flights to and from it. The most important of these is the landing charge which usually varies according to the size of the aircraft and often the time of day; at a major airport such as London Heathrow one landing can cost an airline several thousand pounds.

Airports provide many facilities for passengers; these include restaurants and lounges, shops, duty-free shops, car rental desks, car parks and so on. In practice these facilities are usually put out to tender; they are seen as such worthwhile business concessions that a company must be substantial if it is to submit a winning tender. As a result these facilities are valuable sources of revenue to the airport authority. Aer Rianta has chosen to operate its duty-free shops in Ireland and generates much of its income from them.

Sea Carriers

The mainstay of sea transport is the carriage of goods or freight. A section of the business has been developed to attract and handle passengers particularly on relatively short journeys of a few hours or overnight. These are the ferries that ply between Ireland and Great Britain and the Continent, between Italy and Greece, and within countries such as the various islands of Denmark or Greece. However, passenger traffic is a minor and seasonal end of the whole sea transport industry and most carriers combine freight and passenger services to ensure that they operate at a profit.

One of the advantages of sea transport to travellers is that they can take with them their own means of land transport; this gives them more freedom as to how and where they spend their time once they reach their destinations. They can even take along their own accommodation in the form of frame tents, caravans or camping vans. One of the most popular routes on the Irish market for this type of travel is the Rosslare/Le Havre service which every year attracts families who choose to tour in France or further afield on the Continent. Cross-channel travel by sea is usually cheaper than that by air so it may be favoured by passengers with low travel budgets. Often carriers combine their services with rail tickets so that travellers can reach their final destinations using one ticket; for example a passenger can travel on a ferry service to the UK with an onward connection to London by rail included in the cost of the ticket.

Brittany Ferries

However, there are obvious disadvantages to travel by sea. Naturally a carrier is restricted to fixed ports of call which are not always based near capital cities or tourist regions. Because there is no universal standard for ship and shore ramps for cars and passengers, each route must be served by particular ships which are compatible with shore facilities. Equally a carrier cannot easily set up a new route without having arranged for the provision of expensive shore equipment. The time involved in many sea journeys deters some passengers and the limited timetable with its uncertainty when there are bad weather conditions is a disadvantage too. However, sea carriers update their facilities all the time to maintain market share or, better, to capture a greater share of the market; many ferries are being designed as mobile holiday centres with facilities on board which compare to those of good grade resort hotels, including live entertainment, discos, cinemas and electronic games rooms in addition to upgraded cafeterias, restaurants and lounges.

Stena Sealink
L I N E

The most obvious advantage to travelling by ferry is low cost. For example, a family with three or four children wanting to take an annual holiday at a foreign destination would have to make a substantial outlay for air fares, hotel accommodation and car hire. Taking the family car on a ferry may bring a holiday on a camping site on the Continent within easy reach.

IRISH FERRIES

Travel by ocean liner, for example from Europe to America, Africa or Australia died out when air travel boomed after the 1939–45 war. However, one area of liner travel has grown since the development of long distance air travel: this is the sea cruise. Cruises leave ports in the developed countries of the world headed for the picturesque parts of the Mediterranean, the Caribbean and Scandinavia. Many cruises combine air and sea travel as planes carry tourists from their own countries to ports of call near the cruising area; for example Genoa and Miami are popular ports from which to cruise, and often the vacation is enhanced with some days at a holiday resort on land.

Coach Travel

Coach companies have developed their section of the market to suit the requirements of the transport and tour passengers they attract. Obviously a journey abroad by coach includes sea transport for part of the journey, but by buying the tickets in bulk from sea carriers, coach companies can reduce their costs and therefore charge low fares. Thus coach travel is attractive to passengers with a restricted budget. However another important attribute for the traveller is the leisurely pace of coach travel which enables passengers to take in the sights on their journeys.

To ensure that their services reach every possible or potential section of the market, coach companies offer a variety of services. Low cost travel to popular destinations such as London is available to the individual traveller who requires the cheapest means of transport. Coach companies can also put together trips to special events such as football matches and sell seats to the public. They provide, too, for the needs of groups offering road/sea packages to any destination in the UK and many places on the Continent; group bookings usually involve special interest groups intending to attend conferences or events abroad.

While there is at least a possible risk of loss through having vacant seats on scheduled coach services abroad, group bookings present little risk to the operator as the coach as a whole is sold and any risk of vacancies is taken by the organiser of the outing. Similarly with transport to special events, the coach operator can estimate in advance the demand for a product and so may take little risk when organising a trip.

Some coach companies organise packaged tours to the Continent which range from budget ones based on camping accommodation to tours with overnights in top grade hotels. These normally attract tourists interested in travelling around rather than settling at one destination; with the added attraction of a driver/guide they are assured of assistance and information on the places they visit. Some people are attracted by the fact that although the passengers book individually they become members of groups on holiday.

Rail Travel

Some tourists choose to travel by rail on the Continent and further away. Many of these are students who take advantage of the excellent InterRail and other rambler fares available in most countries. In Ireland these are available through USIT.

Perhaps the most well-known rail service abroad is the Orient Express. This was revived by private enterprise by arrangement with several of the national railways on the Continent. It is aimed at the tour market and offers luxury accommodation and food which may be combined with holidays in Italy or France, and with return air travel. Its success has been followed by luxury train adventures in many other countries.

Rail travel can come into its own in the new fast trains on the Continent. For example, in France the TGV trains provide fast intercity services which rival internal air carriers on some routes. A person intending to travel from Ireland to the Alps, for instance, could find the journey can be accomplished most speedily and comfortably by flying to Paris and continuing by TGV to the destination.

Driving Abroad

Car hire is a component of the international travel trade which retails its products through a worldwide network. Large companies such as Hertz, Avis, InterRent and Budget have offices or franchises in most capital cities in the developed world; they are also to be found in popular tourist resorts.

Car hire brochures are available through travel agents and through their local offices in Ireland; price structures tend to vary from one country to another rather than from one destination to another. They cater for the needs of everyone offering vehicles ranging from small two-door cars to minibuses.

Practices vary from one country to another and are not necessarily common within one particular international car hire firm. In some countries most weekly car hire is provided on an unlimited mileage basis, so the tourist need not watch the odometer; but in others there may only be a certain allowance of kilometres free or even no allowance at all. Kilometre charges on an average journey can then be very high.

Car hire charges do not necessarily include all the costs that will be incurred. One of the most important additional costs is *Collision Damage Waiver insurance* — known as CDW. This is called optional but if the traveller does not take it he or she will be liable for the first part of the cost of any damage to the car, however it happens; in addition he or she will probably have to pay a deposit when taking the car. So it may be regarded as essential cover. Car hire companies may also offer other insurances; these should be examined with care as the risks may have been covered in the normal travel insurance or may not be required by the tourist.

Fly-drive is a popular form of package. This provides at least an airline ticket and a period of car hire for a combined fare that is less than the ticket and car would cost separately. The car hire terms of these packages are normally the same as the terms for hiring a car in the country concerned; thus the combined fare may not provide unlimited mileage and will not include optional items such as CDW cover.

Some people favour bringing their own cars on holiday abroad. Apart from the convenience of leaving home without having to touch the baggage until arrival at the destination, many perceive it as a cost saving. There are of course disadvantages: there are many details to be attended to including the proper service of the vehicle for its long journey, extending the insurance and ensuring the headlights can be adjusted; drivers may need to be prepared for hours at the wheel over unfamiliar roads.

Some of the worry can be avoided by acquiring the Automobile Association's (AA) Five-Star Insurance; this offers a number of essential benefits which ease the preparation. Any driver can run down the battery, run out of petrol or incur a breakdown; the AA Five-Star package includes cover for these eventualities so that the unexpected will not add to the holiday cost. The AA also prepares detailed routing instructions for a fee.

Whether the driver has hired a car or brought the family car, driving abroad can extend the experience of the Irish driver. Motorway networks are common in Great Britain and on the Continent; they enable fast travel over long distances but require planning and driving discipline, as motorway services including petrol and food are often at long intervals. Driving on the right side of the road on the Continent can be challenging at first, especially if driving a right-hand drive car. Rules in relation to drink and driving are often stricter abroad than in Ireland.

Accommodation

Unless the passenger is travelling to a destination with local contacts he or she will need accommodation upon arrival. For the business traveller this normally means hotel accommodation central to the area they are intending to do business in. A booking for this type of accommodation can be made through one of the international hotel groups, such as Trusthouse Forte, Hilton, or Sheraton, or through a company like Utell which has a worldwide network for hotel bookings.

The person who is travelling abroad on vacation also needs accommodation. This is of course available with package holidays in which the traveller will join a group going to the chosen sun, skiing or special interest destination. However some people prefer to travel independently; some packages are designed specifically for this market and in some cases the holidaymaker can enjoy the cost benefits of group travel on a charter flight while having accommodation at a hotel or resort away from the crowd. This kind of service is provided by tour operators, though their principal business is inclusive packages.

Besides the option of being booked into an hotel or resort the independent traveller may use one of the *hotel voucher schemes*. Vouchers for the required period abroad are bought before leaving home ; often the traveller has to book the first night but after that is free to book ahead day by day as required, subject to availability of course. Among these schemes is France Acceuil.

Tour Operators

Tour operators are companies that buy in bulk the components of the travel trade such as airline seats, accommodation and excursions and package them to be retailed through travel agencies or direct to the public. A tour operator can work on a small scale, packaging weekend breaks to London for example, or on a much larger scale with brochures containing an array of destinations at sunny — and other — resorts. Tour operators represented in Ireland range from large operators like Abbey Sun and Joe Walsh Tours, to specialist operators like Arrow Tours. The small tour operator may conveniently be differentiated from the travel agency putting together its own packages as its products are either available through other travel retailers or are regularly advertised to the public.

Whether large or small the principle is the same: the tour operator buys in bulk from airlines and hotels, combines the components and offers the packages for retail sale. By buying in bulk they pay less for seats and rooms than the public and their added margin covers their running costs and provides a profit. They can be compared to wholesalers in any trade, buying in bulk and distributing the product for retail sale. This is a simplified explanation of the role of the tour operator, but this will now be examined in more detail.

The process may be illustrated with a simple instance, say, a weekend break from Dublin to London. A tour operator calculates that there is demand for this type of short holiday and puts together an attractive package for retailing to the public. To compete with other tour operators packaging the same kind of product this operator must make it cost effective and competitive with existing prices. First, purchasing costs must be reduced as far as possible. If the tour operator will buy seats only every now and then from the airlines, they must be bought at full retail fares. However if the tour operator undertakes to sell a certain volume of seats a week or month it will be possible to negotiate better rates from the airline, thus reducing the cost of the air fares. Similarly the hotels: after selecting those they believe most likely to be able to sell, the company negotiates reduced rates with these hotels. The more bookings they can give the hotels, the lower the bed rates become.

When the two main components for a package holiday or weekend break, transport and accommodation, have been arranged other requirements can be organised such as transfer from the airport to and from the hotels. If the tour operator is a small company, the reservations with the airlines, hotels and taxi companies will have been made by its own staff ; but if it were selling about 40 packages a week it would not be cost effective to contact the hotels each time it got a booking nor to update the number of taxis needed. At that level of business it would usually employ the services of a *ground handling agent* to do the work.

Ground Handling Agents

Most tour operators employ a ground handling agent to look after the tour operator's interests at a destination. For a handling fee the agent does the administrative work, such as making hotel bookings, and organising taxis or coaches for the transfer of the clients at that destination.

The handling agent normally has excursion programmes available to tour operators. For example, for the London weekend the handling agent can supply a half-day tour of the city to the tour operator's clients, a city lights tour, a theatre visit or a day trip to Oxford or Brighton. The excursion may be included in the operator's package or be an option to be taken up if required by the client.

The handling agent probably looks after the interests of a number of tour operators; this can be an advantage to the tour operator when the handling agent is negotiating rates with hotels and coach companies. For example, if a handling agent represents three tour operators each requiring five rooms in the same hotel, the handling agent seeks fifteen rooms. This buying power allows the handling agency to negotiate a further reduction in rates to the advantage of the tour operators it is representing; this method of bulk buying can apply to taxis and coaches too. Clearly, it would not be sensible for directly competing tour operators to use the same handling agent: their products would not be differentiated in their market, so the three tour operators in this example may be based anywhere in the world.

For the small tour operator this process carries little risk: the various component products are paid for as they are used. This is the reason many travel agencies become involved in tour operating on a small scale. This trade supplements their existing income and at the same time does not involve a large financial outlay.

Medium-sized, and some larger tour operators, buy in bulk but in larger numbers. For example, a tour operator may hope to sell about sixty seats a week of a weekend in Paris and is prepared to take on the risk normally carried by the airline and hotels. So the tour operator will book a block of seats on the aircraft, assuring the airline that they will pay for them whether they are used or not; so the airline makes a further reduction in the fares. In the same way on the hotel rooms, the hotel reduces its rates because it is guaranteed a number of occupied rooms.

There are many different kinds of booking; for example, the airline (or the hotel) agrees to a price presuming that it is to receive a certain number of bookings. But if the tour operator has difficulty retailing all the seats booked in advance, it may be necessary to return some of the seats; these may be released back to the ai line within a certain time period for re-sale by the airline. So ther is a variation in costs for different types of booking. When block booking seats, tour operators can buy on a 100% *guarantee basis*, when they will either use or pay for the seats they reserve, or on a *release basis*, when if they have not sold the seats within a certain time period they will release them back to the airline. The same principles apply to accommodation. In this way the risk is shared between the tour operator and the airline or hotel but, as with airline tickets, the greater the risk the better the price.

Large Tour Operators

Large tour operators buy in bulk well in advance; this is a complex business with very high risk. Their packages are those with which the public is most familiar from brochures on the shelves of travel agencies offering many kinds of sunny destinations and winter holidays. The packages are put together to suit all tastes among destinations, accommodation, and climate. An example will serve to demonstrate how the tour operator arrives at its choice of accommodation, airlines, timetables and costs.

Flights

A tour operator based in Ireland decides that in the coming year it will have the capacity to sell approximately 150 seats a week to Mallorca; this will call for seats on an aircraft and accommodation to go with these seats. Being confident that it will sell that number of seats it is willing to take the risk and buy the seats in the cheapest way possible; and the cheapest way to do this is to charter an entire aircraft rather than buy blocks of seats from the airline. In this way the operator undertakes to fill the aircraft or at least to pay for the aircraft even if it is not fully loaded.

So the first task is to find a suitable aircraft. As discussed earlier in this chapter, aircraft can operate only to and from their country of origin, so the tour operator's choice is restricted to that of an Irish or Spanish airline. Obviously the size of the aircraft determines its cost, but in negotiation with the airline other factors such as the timetable of the flight will play an important part. Tour operators in large countries can have a wide choice of airlines to approach including some that specialise in the operation of aircraft for charter. In Ireland there is a limited choice of airlines to be approached. When the tour operator is satisfied with the cost and timetable availability of an aircraft a charter is agreed for a schedule with, say, one flight weekly on Fridays at 22.00 hours starting and finishing on specified dates.

Accommodation

When the weekly flight to Mallorca with capacity for 150 seats has been confirmed, the tour operator is in a position to turn to the requirement for hotel and apartment accommodation to go with these seats. On most flights those travelling will be a mix including couples, families of two or three children, and groups of friends with from two to ten people, so the task is to find accommodation to suit these combinations. Also among the people on the flight there will be passengers who prefer self-catering to hotel accommodation, others who want to be near the beach, and those who want to be located near the main thoroughfare for shopping and night life. For those who stay at hotels, meal options need to be discussed such as bed and breakfast only, *half-board* (breakfast and one main meal) or *full-board* (all meals); sometimes vouchers may be provided for local restaurants.

To suit the likely requirements of passengers, the tour operator will specify various kinds of accommodation. Through market research and experience, tour operators are aware that the most common passenger booking is for two people travelling together, but the variations on this can change from month to month; for example, in the summer months the number of passengers travelling in families and groups increases. So with the assistance of a ground handling agent who knows the destination, the tour operator buys accommodation based on these estimates.

Just as the tour operator had some choice of cost and risk in relation to flights for the holidaymakers, so there is a choice with accommodation. This can be block booked with a 100% guarantee to secure better rates while accepting a greater share of the risk. Alternatively, accommodation may be taken on a release basis as discussed earlier. Once the flights and accommodation have been costed, and costs established for details such as coach transfers to and from the airport, the tour operator may then decide on the retail price of this product.

To do this there are important factors to be taken into account, probably the most important being seasonal factors. The summer season to Mallorca, for example, starts as early as May and ends in October. But the demand for holidays is less in May and October than July and August, so prices must reflect the seasons, often three:

- *Low season* — April/May and October

- *Mid season* — June and September

- *High season* — July/August.

In pricing, obviously, low season is offered at the lowest price to attract more customers than would otherwise travel and high season at the highest to maximise income when demand is buoyant. The costing also takes into account other variables such as the number of children's fares on an aircraft. Having worked out the costs, the tour operator must then arm the retail trade — travel agents — with the means of selling this and other products.

Brochures

Brochures will be prepared containing details such as days and times of departure of flights, and prices. Along with this there will be a concise description of the resort, the accommodation, including its location and size, and a list of facilities available with the accommodation. To comply with the Trade Descriptions Act the tour operator's description must be accurate; for example a hotel situated ten miles from the nearest beach cannot be described as a ten-minute stroll from the beach. Unlike most other purchases, a package holiday is sold sight unseen and it is paid for in advance; the customer must rely on the brochure description.

This process takes some considerable time. Prices for seats and accommodation for a summer holiday brochure will probably have been negotiated between March and June the year before. The brochure itself was, typically, prepared from June to August and ready to go for editing and the printers at the end of September. It is usual to aim at having the new brochure ready for late December or early January, but some operators now try to be ready early in December. When supplied with the brochure the travel agent can retail the product.

Discounts and Special Offers

The tour operator's ground work in advance was not confined to preparation of the brochure; in many cases, deposits have been made to airlines and hotels to secure the flights and rooms for the coming season. For that reason the tour operator needs to start the cash flow from passengers as early as possible; to encourage this, early booking reductions and discounts may be offered. It is common to require the balance of the customer's money some six or eight weeks before departure.

Around the weekend before departure, if the tour operator has still to sell seats and accommodation which the company has paid for, it will sell them off at reduced rates hoping to cover costs; their sale at marginal rates ensures some contribution towards costs which cannot otherwise be recovered. Some people wait with interest for these special offers usually made in the week before departure, but it has to be emphasised that the customer may have little or no choice and there may be no such offers available, particularly at peak times.

Tour operators cater for the home market and therefore do not need the sophisticated retail networks of airlines. They usually have reservations departments and travel agencies can make bookings by telephone. Operators work on a first come first served basis; the deposit must be paid at the time of booking. Some tour operators sell their products through the travel trade computer systems as well.

Student Questions and Assignments

1. List what you think are the most popular foreign destinations from Ireland and give reasons for their popularity.

2. On a scheduled flight, to the UK for example, there are different fare structures. Suggest reasons for this.

3. Airlines can only operate from the country of origin. Give reasons why.

4. Discuss how and why Irish airlines combine the scheduled and charter areas of business.

5. What are the basic factors that influence a passenger to travel by sea rather than by air?

6. For what reasons would the business traveller require car hire on arrival at his or her destination? What kind of accommodation would best suit the needs of the business traveller? Why might he/she require car hire on arrival at his or her destination?

7. Explain why there are reduced fares and late special offers on charter flights. Why are charter flights most likely to depart at unsociable hours?

8. List the accommodation types and resort facilities the following holidaymakers might require:

   — honeymoon couple

   — group of passengers in their twenties

   — family of two adults with three children

   — individuals interested in sporting activities and touring.

9. Give an explanation of the difference in cost between high season and low season.

10. Why are discounts and early booking incentives offered to passengers on package tours?

11. Comparing a destination such as Kerry to a Continental sun destination, discuss the differences in accommodation and facilities.

12. Give examples of the different types of accommodation that a tour operator would have to contract to meet the needs of all various sectors of the market.

13. Give examples of extras that can be included in a package tour to make it more attractive. What extra costs are added to the price of a travel ticket or package holiday?

14. Discuss the implications of airline deregulation and its effect on the market when it is introduced.

15. Name some well-known Irish tour operators, not including travel agents.

12 The Travel Trade

Objectives

At the end of this chapter the reader will be able to:

- describe how the retail travel trade operates and distinguish between travel agencies and tour operators

- understand ticketing and booking procedures generally

- identify key government regulations in relation to bonding and licensing

- appreciate the role of the travel agent in assessing clients' requirements and the importance of product knowledge

- demonstrate an awareness of the governing bodies associated with the travel industry.

In this age of high technology and sophisticated air travel a trip to the local travel agent can supply the prospective traveller with brochures, timetables and fare structures to almost every destination in the world and covering most kinds of travel, whether Caribbean cruise, two-week holiday in the sun or business trip to Hong Kong. There are over 360 travel agents in the Republic of Ireland alone and, as the title implies, they are agents or retail outlets for travel trade products.

In the last chapter, many of the product areas available to business and holiday travellers abroad were discussed. These included:

- air carriers: scheduled services to destinations around the world

- sea carriers: ferry services to Britain and the Continent and cruises abroad

- coach companies: transport to all UK destinations and tours to Europe

- car hire: car rental at worldwide destinations

- accommodation: hotels or self-catering around the world

- tour operators: package holidays to tourist destinations.

Each of these product areas offers products for sale by the travel trade in Ireland and within the travel trade most retail outlets are travel agents. This chapter looks at the work of the travel agent and its place in the travel trade.

Travel agents retail travel products; because they are acting as agents for the products they earn commission on what they sell. There are various commission arrangements depending on the type and cost of the products, but 10% could be considered an average commission.

As with all retail outlets, there are many factors that combine to contribute to the success of a travel agency and most important of these are:

- location: a good position in a commercial area can guarantee a certain volume of passing trade. So the better or worse the location, the better or worse their chances of taking a share of the business available

- experienced staff: the quality of staff with the agency is vital as it is selling a non-tangible product; the better the staff are at handling prospective clients' enquiries, the better the chance of turning enquiries into bookings with that agency.

The Work of the Travel Agency

There are many kinds of enquiry handled every day by a travel agency. Here are three of them and the information that has to be produced:

Q   A person looking for the cheapest possible way to get to London

A   Timetables and fares for coach and sea travel to the UK, with the alternative of low-price APEX or PEX fares by air

Q   Another person wants a flight to Amsterdam with accommodation and car hire

A   Timetables and the various fares to Amsterdam, details on a selection of hotels of different grades and the rates for car hire with some operators in the Netherlands

Q   A young couple is interested in a two-week holiday at a lively resort on a self-catering basis

A   Brochures of selected tour operators with inclusive holidays at suitable resorts and apartments within their price bracket.

In each case the travel agent must be aware of all the possibilities available to the client, know in what brochures to find them and how to access other necessary information on the computer system. It is important to know how to make a booking for every product which is handled, to be able to calculate its cost and, for scheduled airline and coach products, issue tickets for it: it will be seen that this can be complex. As has been said, the more efficient and knowledgeable the agent appears to be, the greater the chances of getting the client's booking.

Assessing the Holiday Client's Requirements

The travel agent ascertains the requirements of the client in the initial discussion. When selling travel by sea or air this is not difficult as the kind of transport often depends on the client's budget; the agency has only to produce the fare structures and timetables for the client. The decision can be left to the client.

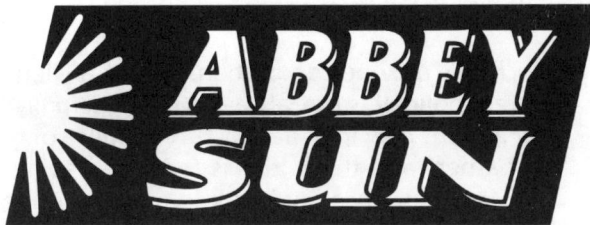

However, this is not so for clients who are interested in booking holidays. Clients who wish to travel abroad on holiday often rely on the advice of their travel agent in regard to the package they purchase. Apart from its cost, other factors to be taken into account are choice of destination, weather conditions, location of accommodation, local customs and facilities available. A travel agency can use the brochure to help sell a package but it is important to be able to steer the client in the right direction. Here are some examples of how it would do this:

- For young single passengers travelling abroad, factors to be taken into account may include location and destination. There would be no point to advising passengers in their early twenties to book a holiday in a resort that was predominantly family oriented. Even though the accommodation and other details might be of excellent standard, most people in this age group are particularly interested in sharing in night life with others of their own age; the absence of facilities to cater for their needs could make or break their holiday. So apart from accommodation the travel agent would have to consider the kind of destination that would suit this age group.

- Weather conditions are another important factor. If the client wants to sunbathe, two weeks abroad with no sun would probably spoil the holiday. In high season almost every sunny destination is sure to oblige, but in the low season a travel agent must take weather conditions into account and from experience advise on the best possibilities.

- Family bookings require careful attention as well, with particular reference to facilities for children, in-house entertainment for parents and so on. Weather conditions can be important too: countries with extremely hot temperatures in summer are generally not suitable for young children.

- Each client who goes into a travel agency has different require-ments; one may require a resort with a selection of golf courses and the next may prefer to spend the duration on the beach and want to be located close to it, and yet another may want a destination with plenty of interesting sights to visit. The range of requirements seems endless but the travel agent must find the package most suited to the client's needs.

- Brochures may be comprehensive but a client's perception of the perfect holiday is not always what is actually required. For exam-ple, a client may look at a picture of miles of golden sands without sunbathers and think 'this is for me — somewhere away from it all'. However, once booked into a hotel beside these golden sands the party may find that it is in fact a sparsely populated area and social life is restricted to their own company; in many cases they will not enjoy this kind of holiday. So the travel agent must carefully assess the client so as to advise on the most suitable holiday: for most people the cost of a two-week summer holiday is one of the greatest annual expenditure decisions.

Great Expectations

An important factor that a travel agent has to take into account is that holidays are normally booked some months in advance; naturally clients look forward to their holidays. Because of the lapse of time involved between booking a holiday and actually going abroad, expectations increase. The travel agent must take this into account when recom-mending a particular destination.

While the information in the brochure is carefully checked to ensure it is as accurate as possible, naturally it is the positive points that are emphasised, so a travel agent must be careful not to oversell the product; in the context of the expectations of the client, it could be a recipe for disappointment. As in any field, retailer (the travel agent) and producer (tour operator) aim to sell their product profitably while ensuring that the customer is so satisfied with the product that he or she will want to buy the same brand from the same retail outlet another time.

The treatment of complaints when they do arise is discussed later in this chapter.

Computer Systems

Although major airlines generally have their own outlets in large cities, the retailing of their products is largely done by travel agencies. All major airlines offer their services through computer systems; their timetables, ticket prices and so on are included by arrangement on central systems. The systems are now so sophisticated that they can supply up-to-date timetables for every destination in the world, all the

possible fares and their conditions, the local time and other information such as how far the airport is from the city and then accept reservations and issue tickets. Some tour operators arrange to include their reservation systems on these computer networks too.

Travel agents take these services, which are essential to their operations, paying a rental for them unless they have a substantial turnover. They access the information through their office computers. There are many of these systems in use throughout the world including *Sabre*, *Pars*, *Worldspan* and *Gallileo*; the last of these is most commonly in use in Ireland through the national distribution system TIMAS.

Airline Ticket Sales

Using the computer system, a travel agency can sell any flight to any destination in the world; however, for obvious reasons it would be totally impracticable to hold ticket stocks for every airline in the world. For example, if a passenger wanted to go from Dublin to London on an Aer Lingus flight, then on to Hong Kong with British Airways and from there to Singapore with Singapore Airlines, it would not be practicable to issue three different tickets to the passenger and then pay the three fares over to the three airlines.

So instead the client is issued with one ticket which has a page or coupon for each stage of the journey. Taking the example mentioned above, these would be:

- Coupon 1 Dublin to London

- Coupon 2 London to Hong Kong

- Coupon 3 Hong Kong to Singapore

and so on.

The total price of the ticket is then paid to a central clearing house; this is known as the *Bank Settlement Plan* or BSP; BSP in turn pays each of the participating airlines the total sums due to them. Many countries have BSP centres and the world headquarters are in Geneva. Travel agents must remit all money they receive for airline tickets to BSP on a weekly basis; the cash they receive and blank ticket stocks are very rigorously supervised.

The airline business has evolved a language of its own, or rather a directory with abbreviations of the most common words, coded so that they may be understood in all countries of the world and by the people of many cultures who work in the industry. To the ordinary person in the street reading a scheduled airline ticket can be difficult, so it may be useful to consider a few of the headings concerned.

Airports

The abbreviation for an airport in any city in the world is normally a three-letter one: Dublin = DUB.

Where there is more than one airport for a city, London has Heathrow, Gatwick, Luton and Stansted airports, the three-letter code identifies the airport as well as the city: Heathrow airport, London = LHR.

Flights

In general, scheduled flights have three digits following the airline's code: flight EI 123 to London.

However it should be emphasised that this is not invariable: charter flights and duplicate or extra flights, for instance, may be given four digits.

Fares

The amount of the fare is entered on the ticket, but as well as this, the class of travel is also shown in code, for example: Y = Economy or Coach class. This enables the airlines concerned and other travel agents to know the particular conditions under which the ticket holder is travelling.

Times

The twenty-four-hour clock is used on all airline tickets, for example: 17.35 is 5.35 p.m. All times are expressed in local time; so if the traveller is booked on a flight from Hong Kong to Singapore at 10.00 hrs, the flight leaves at 10.00 Hong Kong time, not Irish time.

Booking with Sea Carriers

Because the market for a sea carrier is predominantly at either end of each route, ferries do not need the sophisticated international booking network used by airlines. So ferry bookings are handled mainly by the companies' local offices and by travel agents. Brochures and flyers with timetables and fares are used in the promotion of their products.

Ferry fares may be low compared to air travel, so the margin or commission is in turn low; for this reason many travel agencies do not consider it worthwhile to retail low cost tickets such as Dublin to London. However some agencies do offer this service.

Sea cruises are available from all travel agents. Cruises represent a small segment of the market in Ireland and the perception of their cost limits the volume of bookings.

Coach Touring

This kind of tour is normally retailed through travel agents. Brochures on the various destinations are available with descriptions to attract the passengers.

Coach companies have created their own niche and cater to the requirements of certain sectors of the market.

Car Hire

Passengers who wish to include car rental in their travel arrangements will find this can be handled by their local travel agency. The travel agency makes its bookings to the local office of the car hire company; then, through the company's international network, the booking is passed to the pick-up point by the car hire company. This system of advance bookings is necessarily provided only by the large and international companies.

Accommodation

The travel agency usually makes accommodation bookings either with large hotel chains or groups or through a company such as *Utell*; in either case the booking is passed by the group through its network to the hotels in question.

Long Haul Holidays

There is growing demand for package holidays to destinations as far flung as Africa, the Far East and the United States of America. If the demand were great enough a tour operator could meet it by setting up packages to these destinations as described in the last chapter. However apart from those to the Holy Land and Florida and, perhaps one or two other parts of the US, there are few, if any, holidays available from Ireland to continents other than Europe; there is not sufficient demand. This does not mean that inclusive holidays to them are denied to the Irish public; they are available as products of UK tour operators through the travel trade in Ireland, and the flights to the UK airport of departure are added to the cost and itinerary. So destinations such as Kenya, Bangkok and even further afield are available. In fact long haul holidays are becoming more popular and although they do not yet generate enough business to set up inclusive tours from Ireland, it may be only a matter of time.

Activity Holidays

This is another steadily rising segment of the market. People are not as content to just laze about on holiday as they were and there is a growing demand for a combination holiday with some form of activity included in the package, for example, skiing. Indeed, other sport oriented holidays such as wind-surfing, golfing, sailing or tennis holidays can be organised on request by tour operators. Operators can tailor this kind of package for the individual or for groups.

Group Bookings

There are many kinds of holiday that attract group bookings and they are often sport oriented, like golfing groups, though they can be arranged for any group or society of which a group bridge holiday in the Canaries would be an example. Another growing sector of the market is *conference groups* and *incentive sales groups*.

Conference bookings are required by large companies for their staff and professional associations which like to run their annual conferences at foreign destinations. Their requirements are similar to those for package holidays except that they need hotels with conference and other specific facilities. Incentive holidays are normally sought by large companies which offer the incentive of a fully paid conference/holiday to their top sales staff to reward achievement. Packages of this sort usually include organised meals, excursions and entertainment for the group; these are easily organised by the tour operator and travel agent. This is a relatively new area of the trade but obviously it is very welcome to travel agents as they are dealing with large numbers.

Corporate Accounts and Business Travel

One of the most profitable areas for a travel agent is the business traveller. In the last chapter it was noted that the business traveller often requires tickets that are more flexible and therefore more expensive; furthermore the business traveller has a high loyalty to a reliable travel agent and therefore represents business that is less volatile than the annual holiday customer.

For these reasons travel agents aim to attract companies which do a lot of business travel. They encourage business travellers to deal regularly with them by offering credit facilities, taking care to find the best possible fares and routing, and providing additional services such as delivery of tickets — anything to encourage companies to deal with the agency. This is a distinct part of the travel agency business and there is normally a section set up within an agency to deal solely with it. In fact some travel agents specialise in this business and forego counter sales altogether.

Tour Operating

Some travel agents are involved in tour operating in a small way, arranging specialised packages to increase business. One example of this would be weekend breaks to London with dinner and a show included in the package cost. Another would be a travel agent organising group bookings to events outside the country, such as important football fixtures. Thus although travel agencies all retail the various products of the trade, some seek niche markets to increase total business or to provide remunerative trade off season.

Travel Insurance

People who travel abroad should have insurance cover against unexpected eventualities. Examples of the unexpected include: accident, illness involving hospital and medical fees, loss or theft of possessions, and serious travel delay causing extra expenditure. There are many insurance packages available and as a general rule the more it costs, the more it covers.

Medical insurance is possibly the important element of travel insurance; EC residents travelling within the Community are entitled to an *E111 form* free from their local Health Boards; this will provide basic medical treatment at no or low cost in most EC countries. But proper medical insurance is regarded as essential for travellers heading for destinations further afield where the high cost of medicine or of returning a patient home could mean financial ruin; the recommended cover against potential medical expenses in the United States was IR£2m in 1992.

Travel insurance usually meets the needs of the average person but may not cover high risks such as pre-existing illness, like terminal cancer, or the loss of valuables such as jewellery or special photographic equipment. Some valuables may be covered worldwide by the traveller's household insurance or a suitable extension readily arranged; if there is no household cover, additional insurance can be bought through a travel agency. Extended cover for many special needs may be available through an insurance broker.

The independent traveller on a business or personal journey can purchase travel insurance from the travel agent. The person who pays by credit or charge card often has automatic, but limited, free travel accident insurance, but this usually does not cover the other important risks.

Tour operators require those for whom they arrange holidays to take the travel insurance they have arranged with an insurance company. In this way the tour operator can be certain that their clients are properly insured against any serious incident while they are being served by the company abroad. Commission on the travel insurance they sell is a valuable source of income to tour operators, travel agents and insurance brokers.

Complaints

It is inevitable in every business that there be a proportion of people who have to make complaints about their purchases. These may arise from faults in the customer's selection of the product, the retailer's delivery of it, the product itself or the people who make up the product. This is the same whether the customer is buying a car, a carpet, a car wash, a meal or a holiday.

When someone has bought something and later, for one reason or another is not satisfied with it, the general rule is to return to the retailer with the complaint. In the case of an electrical appliance, for example, the customer can see it, take it home and examine it and if it does not meet his or her requirements it can be returned to the retailer.

This rule applies to the travel trade too; but it is a particular problem in this trade because the product is intangible. If a holiday property did not have the exact facilities expected, whose fault was it? Was it clearly featured in the brochure or did the travel agent oversell it to obtain a booking? The customer cannot see the product so he cannot know exactly what he is buying; something wrong with it can be the fault of the producer or the retailer.

In the travel trade, the *Trade Descriptions Act* is very important and care is taken to ensure that the description in the brochure accurately reflects the facilities and standards of the product. However in the time between booking a holiday and travelling, passengers can subconsciously enhance the products chosen and later feel that the products actually bought were not the ones they believed they were buying.

In the past a traveller who felt totally dissatisfied with the handling of a complaint by the tour operator could only resort to the law for a remedy, such as recovering the cost of a holiday; if the court did not agree, this was costly for the client, and any case could be expensive and troublesome for the tour operator. All tour operators in Ireland now include on the booking form a clause of agreement which binds the client to arbitration, in the first instance, in the event of the need for settlement of the sometimes contradictory positions of producer, retailer and customer, and this should help to avoid unnecessary legal costs.

Government and Other Taxes

A tax is levied by the Irish government on every sea and air passenger leaving Ireland; it must be paid at the time the ticket is purchased. In 1992 the tax was five pounds.

The traveller may encounter taxes abroad too. Many countries levy departure taxes on outgoing travellers and these affect return journeys to Ireland. Sometimes they are settled by the operator but in other cases, as they are payable in cash at the time of return, the passenger should retain enough change to meet them.

Those on inclusive holidays may not have to provide for local hotel and sales taxes as they will have been costed into the price of the holiday. However the independent traveller may be used to the tax-inclusive prices usual in Europe, but this is not the practice in the US; a hotel room, for example, may be liable for state and local sales taxes and many destinations levy additional tourist taxes on hotel rooms and car hire.

Government Bonding

As discussed earlier, except when business customers are given credit, most products of the travel trade are booked and paid for in advance of travel, sometimes as much as six or seven months before departure. The full amount or deposit and balance are paid by the customer to the retailer and passed on to BSP, in the case of air tickets, or the tour operator in the case of package holidays.

To ensure that passengers' money remains safe in their hands, the travel agent and the tour operator are obliged by law to enter a *bond* as well as a licence to operate. Thus passengers who have made bookings and paid the travel agent or tour operator for them are protected against possible circumstances such as bankruptcy or misappropriation of funds. The amount of the bond the company enters into is related to its annual turnover. If a person has arranged a holiday and the travel agency or tour operator goes into liquidation, the bond will ensure a refund at a later date; if the tourist is actually abroad on the holiday the bond covers early repatriation or continuation of the holiday.

Government Regulation

The Department of Transport, Energy and Communications governs the travel trade.

The carriage of passengers by air comes under its jurisdiction and licences are granted by the Department to carriers to operate their services. Their supervision ensures that operational and safety standards are within existing rules and statutory requirements. Sea carriers are similarly regulated with the involvement of the Department of the Marine in relation to standards, particularly those concerning safety.

The market has been controlled in the long-term interests of the consumer with reasonable competition in price and service, while ensuring some stability among carriers and operators with fair trading conditions. When an application was received the Department took a view of the market before deciding whether or not to grant a licence. For example, if the Department considered the market was satisfied with the existing five flights a day to a particular destination, there would be no point in granting a licence for a further five flights: a further licence would mean over-capacity and possibly destructive price competition which would lead eventually to one or more of the carriers suffering serious damage or reductions in essential standards.

Where there is no competition or flights serve destinations outside the EC, this detailed control continues to apply, but within the EC it is being modified: operators have the freedom to make their own decisions in relation to routes on which there are competing airlines, subject to the Department's supervision.

Tour operators, too, have to apply for licences for their inclusive holidays. The principle is the same as for carriers, with the Department's supervising available capacity. Travel agents are also regulated by the Department. They must comply with certain requirements and hold adequate bonds before being granted licences to operate.

Governing Agencies

International Air Transport Association

IATA is the worldwide body for all major airlines. It sets operating standards for its members and negotiates on their behalf with legislating bodies. IATA approves individual travel agents intending to distribute airline tickets and is responsible for BSP around the world.

Irish Travel Agents Association

ITAA represents tour operators and travel agents in Ireland. It sets codes of practice for its members, negotiates with government bodies and suppliers such as airlines, ferry companies and other tour operators. ITAA operates a group bond scheme for its members.

Association of British Travel Agents

ABTA's functions in Britain are similar to those of ITAA. Bonding is not a statutory requirement in the UK, but ABTA operates a compulsory group bonding scheme for its members.

European Confederation of Travel Agents Associations

ECTAA is the European body to which national associations such as ITAA and ABTA belong.

Universal Federation of Travel Agents Associations

UFTAA is the worldwide organisation of which associations of travel agents are members.

Statistics

About 800,000 tickets and travel documents are issued for scheduled airline travel on the Irish market every year. In addition to these, around 230,000 package holidays travelling by air are sold to summer sun destinations; this does not include independent travellers' accommodation, those visiting friends and relatives, inclusive winter holidays or pilgrimages. In all, the number of people carried on charter flights from Ireland is about 350,000. Further travel abroad is undertaken by sea carriers and by sea/coach packages. The numbers for these are less than those for air travel.

Student Questions and Assignments

1. Computer systems are the airlines' most important asset in retailing their products worldwide. Discuss why.

2. How is the revenue for scheduled tickets recovered by the airline?

3. List the products that the travel agent retails.

4. Give examples of the methods employed by travel agents to access costs, timetables and fare structures for travel trade products. How important is a travel agent's influence on the products retailed to the public?

5. What methods can be used by tour operators and airlines to ensure that the travel agent has an in-depth knowledge of their products?

6. In order of importance what areas of the travel business are most lucrative for the travel agency?

7. What sectors of the market would you consider to be on the increase and decrease? Give reasons why.

8. Give reasons for the upsurge in demand for long haul holidays.

9. Give examples of the facilities offered by travel agents to business house clients to entice them to deal solely with one agent.

10. When settling a claim for a package holiday suggest factors that should be taken into account by an arbitrator.

11. From an employment point of view suggest the different areas that an employee could specialise in within the trade.

13 Tourism Marketing and Promotion

Objectives

At the end of this chapter, the reader will be able to:

- appreciate the marketing elements of the tourism industry

- understand the basic philosophy of marketing and explain why marketing is described as a system

- differentiate between product and customer orientation in the direction of marketing activities

- recognise the constraints under which marketing is conducted in the small business environment

- explain the planning function and its role within marketing.

What is Marketing?

Marketing is more than just selling though increases in sales are obviously the ultimate aim. Rather, marketing is a collection of activities, including:

— choice of suitable selling products for your products and services

— merchandising

— sales promotions

— advertising and public relations

— market research

— making the best use of sales people.

The following definitions may help to clarify the term 'marketing' as it is used in business.

Definition 1: The Institute of Marketing ▬▬▬▬▬▬▬▬

'The tools or means available to an organisation to improve the match between benefits sought by customers and those offered by the organisation so as to obtain a differential advantage. Amongst these tools are product, price, promotion and distribution services.'

Definition 2: Inc. Magazine (US) ▬▬▬▬▬▬▬▬▬▬▬▬▬▬▬

'Identifying your customer prospects and determining how best to reach them.'

Definition 3: British Airways ▬▬▬▬▬▬▬▬▬▬▬▬▬▬▬▬▬

'Ascertaining customer needs, tailoring the product as closely as possible to meet those needs, persuading the customer to satisfy their needs and finally, ensuring that the product is easily accessible when the customer wishes to purchase it.'

According to these definitions an organisation should try to satisfy the needs of customers or clients through a co-ordinated set of activities that allow the organisation to achieve its goals. Customer satisfaction is the main aim of the marketing driven organisation. A tourism business must continue to alter, adapt and develop products and services to keep pace with the changing needs, desires and preferences of the customer. The marketing concept stresses the importance of customers and emphasises that marketing activities begin and end with them.

Marketing is not just advertising. Advertising is the communication of ideas, the end result of a strategy or series of strategies. Marketing is far more than communicating the message to the consumer; it finds that customer in the first place and also finds a profitable way of servicing the needs of that customer.

The Three Stages of Tourism Marketing

At its simplest we can say that there are three stages in tourism marketing. Any business in the tourism sector, if it were drawing up a marketing plan might follow these three stages :

- Stage 1   Where is the business now?

- Stage 2   Where does the business want to be?

- Stage 3   What steps must be taken to get there?

Looking back on the development of tourism in Ireland one may see that often the typical Irish tourism business did not, at first, have to forage for business. The consumer tended to find Ireland and its tourism product through informative advertising and years of preconceptions and expectations. Many tourism companies had what they then termed marketing departments. With hindsight many of these were simply order takers, or sales departments, dealing with enquiries that made their way to the hotel or product provider. As recession and competition hit, managements began to place pressure on these departments to deliver new markets.

It took so long for many of these sales departments to convert to marketing departments that many managers became disillusioned by the term marketing; they thought it just a fancy term for selling or advertising. Marketing is more precise in what it promises to deliver. A company that can be described as market-led will, by its marketing activities, not operate in a vacuum or be caught trading in markets that have decayed or died.

Where is the business now?

Market Research

The best way to stay trading and make a profit is to define correctly what consumers need and then to meet those expectations effectively and efficiently; that is the modern marketing concept in tourism. And when the concept of marketing has been grasped, one can appreciate that successful tourism marketing demands market research. Marketing managers constantly have to make decisions about their marketing programmes. Market research provides information that helps managers to make better decisions and allows them to select more wisely from among alternative marketing strategies.

Many businesses in the tourism industry are small firms such as hotels, restaurants, and attractions; they often consider market research to be only for large firms and not for them. This is a misconception. If anything, market research is more important for a small business because it does not have the resources to fall back on if major mistakes are made. Also, without this research, expenditure on promotion may not be properly focused and therefore wasteful.

Marketing is an approach to business that connects a number of separate activities and links them in the search for business success. This success is often measured in terms of profit. Research is a fundamental aspect of the marketing approach. Restrictions faced by many small tourism businesses can include insufficient resources to carry out detailed research. This should not, however, be a barrier to a business taking the marketing approach. Each year Bord Fáilte and the Northern Ireland Tourist Board collect data from visitors and provide that information to the industry to allow the various sectors to evaluate their performance in relation to their competitors and the rest of the industry.

In addition to a knowledge of the market outside an organisation, it is also important that a business have a grasp of its internal strengths and weaknesses as well as the threats and opportunities that are outside the control of the tourism operator.

SWOT Analysis

The guiding principle of an audit of resources should be the SWOT sequence:

- strengths

- weaknesses

- opportunities

- threats.

The order is important. A tourism business should proceed from strength before eliminating weaknesses; maximise opportunities before tackling threats. The time to tackle weaknesses is when they reduce the strength of the enterprise in the marketplace; threats become problems when they limit or reduce opportunities. The basis of all resource planning is identifying profitable opportunities. In a sense, real resources exist outside the business; until a tourism business has visitors, all it has are costs.

Where does the business want to be?

Marketing Strategy and Objectives

Marketing strategy focuses on defining a target market and developing a *marketing mix* to gain and maintain a competitive edge. In Ireland there are two factors involved in the development of strategies: the government sets objectives for the country and for tourism in general; the tourism industry takes some of these general objectives and applies them to the assets it has.

General government objectives might be to increase visitor numbers to particular levels within certain periods; achievement of these objectives is outside the control of the average tourism product provider. The tourism product provider can however respond to the general objectives with a set of local marketing objectives, pertinent to that particular business.

A marketing programme cannot be run without an understanding of the communication process. The 'why' of communication is often forgotten; it relates to the need to have objectives for communication. These objectives come from having a marketing strategy.

There is little or no point in communicating with the consumer just for the sake of it. As we have discussed, tourism operations often find themselves marketing with few resources. An organisation has to be selective and communicate with those markets most relevant to the project in question. Careful identification of markets can assist in the development of messages. These messages are linked to objectives set by the tourism business operator.

Objectives define the expected level of performance that a business will attempt to achieve. Performance is measured in figures, such as visitors or financial turnover, or in the ratios such as occupancy of seats or rooms or the number of visitors or bedrooms per member of staff. However, some measurements represent more meaningful objectives than others: for example to achieve a 50% increase in turnover to IR£750,000 would mean little without reference to costs or profitability. Sometimes an organisation will have several objectives, some related to the business as a whole, some related to the individuals in it.

Objectives may be handed down by a board of directors or an owner or manager. In a technique called *Management by Objectives* this process is formalised: managers and supervisors are involved in setting objectives for their responsibility areas and they thus have a commitment to achieving the objectives.

Objectives must be expressed in relation to a set of desired results to be achieved within a specific period of time. If, for example, an accommodation provider defined his or her objective to increase business in a particular year, this would be just an intention, not an objective, because the statement does not contain a measure. Again, stating how something will be achieved is not an objective unless results can be measured.

Objectives must be tested before they can be adopted. The business will examine an objective against the capacity of the business to respond to the new level of trading, the capability of the business to deliver on promises made, the infrastructure of the business (its staff, finances and so on) and any time constraints on achieving the objectives. In some cases the objectives will have been set as a result of market research.

How visitors buy

Those involved in tourism marketing need to understand what motivates people to travel. Travel motivators are discussed in Chapter 1.

Classification of visitors by country of origin and by their interest can suggest how they decide to buy. Examples of tourism demand segments include:

- self-catering

- guest house and farmhouse holidays

- golfing holidays

- weekend breaks and short break holidays.

Twenty-five per cent of all visitors from the United States are on package holidays. They tend to be an older and more up-market group. They are generally attracted to Ireland because of ethnic roots and the friendly, green and tranquil image of Ireland.

Most German tourists travel independently. They tend to fall into the categories of:

- general holidaymaker

- special interest (such as cabin cruising or fishing) holidaymaker

- business incentive or conference visitor.

The countryside and friendly people are main attractions.

Most French tourists also travel independently and tend to be up-market. In general they are holidaymakers attracted to Ireland because of the scenery, the pace of life and special interests, such as fishing and golf.

The strategy for marketing in Ireland has been to switch from mass marketing to segmented markets. Mass marketing has become inefficient because it fails to target and attract specific interest groups who constitute the bulk of the holiday market. The 'Only the Best' series of promotional literature issued by Bord Fáilte exemplifies segmented marketing.

Segmentation

Segments should be of a size to provide a tourism provider with an adequate return for effort. The members of each segment should have a high degree of similarity yet be distinct from the rest of the market. Within each segment there are further opportunities to analyse the activities of the tourist. For example, Bord Fáilte segmented the markets as follows in an annual report:

Segmentation by Activity:

'Once again there was a welcome increase in the number of those for whom the sole purpose of their visit was holiday/leisure. One in four British holidaymakers were on their first visit to Ireland.'

Segmentation by geographic location:

'Holidaymakers from the west coast of the United States increased by 35%.'

Whether visitors and home holidaymakers are segmented by demographic or geographic factors or even psychological variables, it is important to remember that there are two aspects to be considered: segmentation of tourists according to their characteristics and segmentation of tourists according to their behaviour. Thus the industry has developed sectors related to transport, accommodation, catering and entertainment. The different products that make up Irish tourism are in turn segmented into groups according to quality, standard and price range. This information is vital at the next stage in the development of strategies to communicate, persuade and inform the visitor.

After (1) evaluating research data and (2) having identified the various segments as they relate to a whole sector or business within a sector, step (3) in marketing planning is to determine future business directions and develop marketing strategies. A business may choose from several strategies. Very often this is represented as a matrix.

The various elements of this matrix can be identified in the many tourism products in Ireland.

Fig. 1 Marketing Strategy Matrix	
Market Penetration (same product — same market)	Market Development (same product — same market)
Product Development (new product — same market)	Diversification (new product — new market)

Marketing Strategies

There are four main strategies available to the marketeer:

— Market Penetration

— Market Development

— Product Development

— Diversification.

Market Penetration

Market Penetration is a strategy of increasing sales in current markets with current products. To implement this strategy, a product provider would probably increase the advertising budget and the size or productivity of its marketing department. An hotel owner pursuing this strategy might define as an objective taking a 50% share of the available business market for a particular city.

In Ireland the industry has taken combinations of these strategies. The first, Market Penetration, is best illustrated by the activities of the Ryan Hotel Group in the development of the Home Holiday market. A combination of strategies, a flexible product and a clear communications plan allowed them to corner a substantial share of the available market. By definition, market penetration implies that the business generates growth through taking a share of the business enjoyed by the competition. It is a fiercely competitive strategy in that the business is usually won on price as the customer generally has a wide range of options to choose from.

Examples of market penetration are evident as a strategy on the Dublin-London air route as the airlines vie for market share. Pricing is used as a promotional tool and the similarity of the services offered means that the customer is often won over with promotional offers and promises of extra services. Market penetration is in itself a weak marketing strategy for growth as the tactics used can undermine the perception of the product.

Market Development

Market development is the strategy of increasing sales of current products in new markets. An example of market development would be the effort to develop a market for Ireland in Australia and New Zealand and even Japan. The challenges to be faced in market development are many and costly. Bord Fáilte and the Northern Ireland Tourist Board hope to develop a new market of visitors to Ireland from among the 600,000 Australians who visit Britain each year. Both organisations need to be fully aware of the images these people have of Ireland and what travel motivators can be appealed to in the effort to attract even a small amount of them to visit Ireland.

Many hotel groups in Ireland have taken a strategy of market development in the development of the *Golden Years* market, filling off-peak and shoulder capacity with holidays for the over-55 segment. This is true market development in that the customers attracted are generally not replacing existing business, but are new customers. Companies operating boat hire on the Shannon have adopted this strategy in the last few years by attracting the domestic market to the river. Following years of catering to a Continental market they have begun to develop new markets at home.

A number of Irish hotels are experimenting with APEX hotel bookings, allowing discounts for early pre-payment for accommodation. The approved accommodation sector, including the farmhouse accommodation providers, have begun to experiment with dealing with tour groups. A number of accommodation providers in a region join together to cater for larger groups that otherwise might have gone to the hotel sector.

Product Development

Product Development is a strategy for increasing sales by improving present products or developing new products for current markets. In Ireland over the last three decades, a series of new products has evolved, and facilities have been developed to hold existing business and to attract new business. For example, country house hotels and castles have increased in number and camping facilities and bed and breakfast accommodation have improved greatly. Crag Cave in Kerry is an example of the development of a product that has in itself helped to develop the Kerry region product.

The addition of leisure centres to hotels around Ireland is a clear example of product development. This strategy is probably the most difficult to manage in that it often takes a considerable amount of time to change or amend the product. The competition is generally reacting in the same way and any competitive advantage can be quickly lost. The Jurys Hotel group has developed a number of properties to cater for the low spend economy market. These Inns will enjoy competitive advantage for the time it takes until a competitor can react either by amending their existing premises or building similar ones. Competition often results in tactics related to price reduction and special offers. Irish camping and caravan site operators are another example of a sector that has developed products to attract new business. The end result is improvements that might have once been an attraction in themselves but are now expected as the standard or norm.

Diversification

There are three major considerations in assessing opportunities and resources. Market opportunity must be evaluated, environmental forces must be monitored and the company's capabilities have to be understood. The marketing strategy of diversification is often quite radical. It implies that the business must change its core operation and diversify into an often unrelated activity.

Business people, and those involved in the marketing of Irish tourism, can think in an imaginative way about the resources and facilities in the country; this has resulted in a variety of new and exciting products. Diversification as a strategy has appeared in the use of post-primary boarding schools as centres, during the summer, to teach English to foreign students.

The Product Life-Cycle

'If it's living, it's dying.' The concept of product life-cycle describes what happens to a market when no steps are taken to change direction.

The Tourist Market Mix

The key to the profitable employment of these technique-related areas of marketing is the *market mix* concept. The mix accounts for differences in marketing tactics employed in different industries as well as those adopted by competitors in the same market. However, varying the mix will only be valuable if it results in significant customer benefits, improves the cost effectiveness of supplying those benefits, or reduces or eliminates expenditure on activities that do not produce rewards.

Small businesses have a high failure rate, principally because of insufficient demand at the price required to make a reasonable profit. They find it difficult to cope with the organisational problems created by growth and fail to maintain quality and standards in the growth period.

When a new product is launched, it meets a need, it has novelty value and it may be accompanied by a great deal of publicity. Left to itself its sales will grow fairly rapidly to a peak and gradually decline as others copy it and new products absorb the consumers' discretionary spending. The product life-cycle can be illustrated by the decline in the popularity of the holiday camp. From growth in the post-war years to a peak in the 1960s, maturity in the early 1970s and eventual decline in the 1980s, the concept of a holiday camp has run through all four phases of the life-cycle (see figure 2).

Fig. 2 Product Life-Cycle

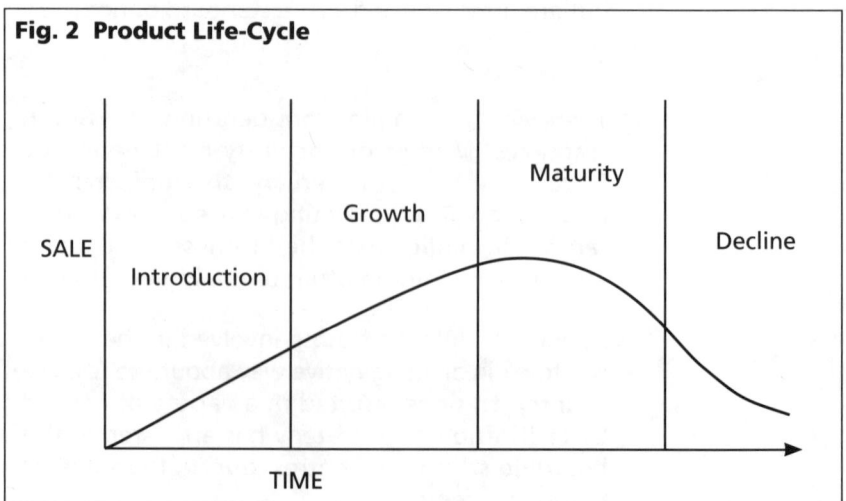

The decline of a product in the tourism sector does not have to imply its disappearance. The re-launch of the Mosney Holiday Centre as a revitalised product is an example. Whilst the notion of a holiday with pre-arranged and regimented activities has come to the end of its life-cycle, the Mosney Holiday Centre has amended the product, removed the holiday camp image and replaced it with services and facilities for a group of customers attracted by value for money holidays.

What steps must be taken to get there?

Marketing Communication

Communication can be viewed as the transmission of information. For the purpose of promotion it is better to view the process as the transfer of feeling or meaning rather than the transmission of information. Marketing communication is the sharing of a perception. When selling an intangible product, such as a weekend break or an adventure holiday, a variety of techniques must be used; these will allow the transfer to potential customers of feelings for what they are about to purchase, as well as confirmation of whatever preconceptions they may have about the products or services on offer.

Promotion Mix

Several types of promotional methods may be used to communicate with individuals, groups and organisations. When a tourism product provider combines various methods to promote a particular product, that makes up the promotion mix. The four possible elements of a promotion mix are: *advertising*, *personal selling*, *publicity* and *sales promotion*. These are in essence the four activities carried out by a tourism organisation in the promotion of a country. They are the same activities as those required to promote a local tourism product or service. For some tourism products all four are used, for others, only two or three are necessary. There are many examples in the tourism industry of companies that do not advertise, but are very involved in PR or direct sales.

Promotion is particularly important to the tourism business for the following reasons:

- product demand is usually seasonal and needs to be stimulated in the off-season

- demand is frequently sensitive to price and subject to general economic conditions both good and bad

- customers usually have to be prompted to buy without first viewing or sampling the product

- brand (customer) loyalty is usually not intense

- most products are subject to severe competition

- most products can be easily substituted.

An existing business that is successful has an established demand for its products. But no matter how strong this demand may be, it will have to be supplemented with continued promotion. The lack of repeat business for many destinations and product providers is one reason. Increased business for an existing tourist supplier, and new business for a new supplier, usually depends on generating demand, or promotion, to attract new customers or introduce old customers to new products. For example, an air carrier opening up a new route must concentrate on new customers.

Promotional material must be informative. Without information it is difficult for the potential visitor to feel satisfied that the product or service will meet perceived needs. Accurate and useful information is needed to attract the reader's attention and enable an informed decision.

Promotion as an investment

Promotion is an investment, rather than an expense. Successful promotion is planned and does not just happen. In many cases it is planned from six months to more than a year ahead and is only finalised when pricing, channels of distribution and budgets have been established.

Personal Selling

One of the most traditional, and most effective, ways of selling is personal selling. Each year Bord Fáilte provides the industry with forums or workshops where industry buyers can meet industry suppliers face to face. Personal selling is the most expensive form of promotion yet in many cases, particularly in dealing with in-coming tour operators, it is the most effective.

Selling to major corporations and selling and promoting conferences and conventions is still for the most part left to face-to-face selling situations. The salesperson will, however, still require promotional materials such as brochures and advertising to support their sales presentations. A major innovation in the Irish tourism industry over the last few years has been the success of sales groups such as Best Western and Quality Hotels in offering a sales representative and a worldwide network of sales offices to independent hotels in the country. This sharing of resources allows the hotels to have widespread representation with minimal overheads.

Publicity

Publicity, the product of public relations (PR) activity, is non-personal communication in news story form, about a destination or a tourism supplier, that is placed in the print or electronic media. It is often considered to be free, however that is inaccurate as there is always a cost, in terms of time, lost capacity or resources. The use of press visits and media information has proved to be one of the more successful strategies adopted by Bord Fáilte and the Northern Ireland Tourist Board.

One concept to consider when looking at the various elements of the promotion mix is the credibility of the various factors. The most credible in the eyes of the consumer are stories written by journalists. Once a piece is written with an element of balance, the reader accepts that the trip was paid for by the tourism supplier and that the journalist was hosted. Yet it is still a more credible source of feeling for the consumer than paid advertising.

Ireland
OF THE WELCOMES

Aer Lingus

CARA

Publicity and image building activities on behalf of the tourism industry forms a major part of Bord Fáilte's activities in North America. *Good Morning America* was persuaded to broadcast live from Kilkenny for three days to an audience of 5 million people across America. Bord Fáilte underwrote an eight-part television series — *Ireland* — on Channel 13, New York's Public Broadcasting Service station. In any one year over 150 media trips are arranged from the United States, 60 from Canada and another 230 from European countries in association with the airlines operating to Ireland.

Television travel programmes such as *Bon Voyage*, *Wish you Were Here* and the BBC *Holiday Programme* command large audiences and have proved to be a powerful influence in the choice of Ireland as a holiday destination among British and home holidaymakers alike.

The cost of communicating is measured in marketing as CPT, cost per thousand (m=mille). Using publicity the CPM can be very low, so low that it is often thought of as free.

Sales Promotion

This is an activity that acts as a direct sell to the customer, offering added value or other direct inducements to buy. There is a tendency for some operators to use price discounting in sales promotion. This can, however, have a detrimental effect on the image and perception of the product. The provision of high quality brochures and information is one of the more effective sales promotion techniques; branding of various tourism products is another sales promotion technique. Many independent hotels and accommodation providers pool their resources in the production of sales promotion material.

In summary, any form of communication made to the market must be planned, appropriate and have a series of objectives for the messages transmitted.

In general these objectives are to inform, persuade and entertain. A knowledge of what is motivating the consumer to buy, combined with a thorough knowledge of the market the business is operating in, will ensure that the cost of promotion is matched with a return on investment.

Student Questions and Assignments

1. Discuss performance objectives, and explain why an objective should be quantified.

2. What are the sources of information available to a tourism operator in preparing a marketing plan?

3. Define geographical segmentation and explain why it may not necessarily be a good method to use.

4. Explain the term 'target market'.

5. Promotion is sometimes referred to as persuasive communication. What does this mean?

6. Define the term 'positioning'.

7. 'Compared to large tourism businesses, small tourism businesses are at a disadvantage when it comes to marketing.' Discuss.

8. List the four elements of the marketing mix.

9. What are the four marketing strategies available to a business? Give examples from Irish tourism.

10. Discuss the concept of the product life-cycle in relation to a tourism product with which you are familiar.

Suggested CERT References

- Tourism Study Pack (Parts 1 & 2)

- A Practical Guide to Customer Relations

- Bon Sejour! French language audio-pack for people working in tourism

- Schöne Tage! German language audio-pack for people working in tourism

- FÁILTE — Customer Care Resource Pack

- A Handbook of Essential Law of the Irish Hotel and Catering Industry

- Heritage Study Pack

- Leisure Tourism Study Park

- CERT Manpower Survey of the Hotel, Catering and Tourism Industry in Ireland

These publications are available from CERT House, Amiens Street, Dublin 1. Telephone 01–8742555.

CERT

THE STATE TOURISM
TRAINING AGENCY

Glossary of Terms

ABTA: Association of British Travel Agents.

Access transport: Modes of transport between countries.

À la carte menu: Each item is individually priced with a wide selection of choice generally available.

APEX: Advance purchase excursion ticket.

Bed night: Method of calculating turnover in accommodation units based on the number of beds occupied each night e.g. an occupied twin room = 2 bed nights.

Bonding: A form of indemnity for clients and customers against the risk of failure of travel companies.

BSP: Bank Settlement Plan.

Carrier: Public transport company such as air, rail, bus and ferry.

CERT: State Tourism Training Agency responsible for recruitment, education and training for hotels, catering and tourism.

Charter: Hire of transport e.g. aircraft, ship, bus for one or more journeys.

Charter flight: Flight booked exclusively for the use of a specific group of people.

CRS: Central Reservation System e.g. Galileo, Sabre, Pars, World Span, Amadeus.

DART: Dublin Area Rapid Transport.

Deregulation: Policy to reduce state control over airline operations and to allow market forces to shape the airline industry.

Direct income: Income which businesses receive directly from tourist expenditure on goods and services.

Domestic tourism: Tourist trips which take place in the tourist's own country.

ECTAA: European Confederation of Travel Agents Associations.

EIS: Environmental Impact Study — detailed study carried out prior to any major construction development to assess its potential environmental impact.

ENFO: Environment Information Service.

EPA: Environmental Protection Agency.

Excursionist: A visitor who stays for less than 24 hours or a day visitor.

Fifth Freedom of the air: The privilege of loading passengers, mail or freight on an aircraft not belonging to the country to which those passengers, mail or freight are destined, and off-loading passengers, mail or freight from an aircraft not of the country from which these originated.

Foreign Exchange earnings: Total income received from out-of-state visitors — in the Republic of Ireland this includes visitors from Northern Ireland and excursionists from all markets — and including all income received from them by carriers.

Full-board: Accommodation with all meals.

Gross National Product (GNP): A measure of the total annual production of goods and services of a country.

Ground handling agent: Person or organisation who looks after the tour operator's interests at a destination for a handling fee.

Gulliver: Tourism industry computerised information and reservation system for Ireland.

Half-board: Accommodation with breakfast and one main meal.

IATA: International Air Transport Association.

IHF: Irish Hotel Federation.

Incentive tour: Tour arranged especially for employees or agents of a company as a reward for achievement.

Indirect income: Income which businesses receive from tourist-related goods and services supplied to other business.

Induced income: Income which businesses receive from all goods and services supplied to other businesses and which arise from either direct or indirect tourist income.

Internal transport: Transport networks within a country.

International tourism: Tourist trips which take place outside the tourist's country of residence.

ITAA: Irish Travel Agents Association.

ITIC: Irish Tourist Industry Confederation.

Job equivalents: The number of full-time jobs that would provide the equivalent level of employment as that provided by all jobs in the industry — full-time, part-time, permanent or seasonal.

Leakage: Anything which causes the profits from tourism to drain away from the place where tourism occurs e.g. imported materials and goods, wages paid to non-residents.

Load factor: Percentage of seats on aircraft occupied by fare-paying passengers.

Market segmentation: Group of actual or potential visitors or customers who can be expected to respond in the same way to a given offer. It is a finer, more detailed breakdown of a market.

Market share: Organisation's share of the market relative to its largest competitor.

Marketing mix: Means or tools available to an organisation to improve the process of matching the benefits sought by the customers to those offered by an organisation so as to obtain a profit. Amongst these tools or processes are price, product, promotion and distribution services.

Multiplier effect: Situation whereby each new person employed in tourism can help to create employment and generate income elsewhere in the country.

OECD: Organisation for Economic Co-operation and Development.

OPW: Office of Public Works.

Overseas visitor revenue: Total income received from overseas visitors; in the Republic of Ireland this includes foreign exchange earnings excluding carrier receipts and expenditure by Northern Ireland visitors and all excursionists.

Package tour: A holiday including most of the following elements: transport to the destination, food and accommodation, transfers, services of a holiday representative and excursions (also known as inclusive tour).

PEX: Pre-purchase excursion ticket.

Product: Term used in marketing to identify not only the product but its characteristics and properties, services, availability and price factors that differentiate the product from those offered by the competition.

Product life-cycle: Term used in marketing to refer to the stages through which a product will pass in the course of its life. The pattern is divided into four stages — birth, growth, maturity and decline. A marketeer can adopt a series of strategies to exploit the profit opportunities of a product or service by identifying the stages in its life-cycle.

RTO: Regional Tourism Organisation.

Rural tourism: A range of activities, services and amenities provided by farmers and rural people to attract tourists to their areas and so generate extra income.

Scheduled flights: Airline services operating on defined routes, whether domestic or international, which must adhere to published timetables regardless of load factors.

Self-catering accommodation: Guest accommodation without meals and housekeeping. Guests are responsible for making their own catering arrangements (also known as non-serviced accommodation).

Serviced accommodation: Guest accommodation with house-keeping and catering services.

Sustainable tourism: Planned, locally controlled tourism development in harmony with nature, the community and its culture.

SWOT analysis: Analysis of the strengths, weaknesses, opportunities and threats facing an organisation used as a basis for developing a business plan.

Table d'hôte menu: Entire meal comes at a fixed price with a limited selection of choices for each course.

TIC: Tourist Information Centre (Northern Ireland).

TIMAS: Travel Industry Multi Access System.

TIO: Tourist Information Office.

Tour operator: A company which buys travel products in bulk, such as airline seats and accommodation, and which combines other elements into holiday packages for sale through travel agents or direct to the public.

Tourism: Movement away from place of residence, for a particular length of stay and for a particular purpose.

Tourism revenue: Total income received through foreign exchange earnings and domestic tourism revenue.

Tourist: Any visitor staying more than 24 hours in a country and making an overnight stay.

Tourist destination: An area with natural attributes, features or attractions that appeals to non-local visitors, excursionists and tourists.

Tourist multipliers: Percentages applied to direct, indirect and induced incomes in order to estimate the full impact on employment and incomes throughout the economy of the initial injection of tourism expenditure.

Travel agent: Person or organisation who retails travel services, such as carriers' and tour operators' products, to the general public on a commission basis.

UFTAA: Universal Federation of Travel Agents Associations.

Utell International: Hotel representative agency which markets, sells and handles reservations for hotels on a commission basis.

VAT: Value Added Tax.

VFR: Visiting friends and relatives.

Visitor: Any person travelling to a country or region outside normal place of residence for any reason other than following an occupation remunerated from within the country or region visited.

WTO: World Tourism Organisation.